CIMA

Management

P2

Advanced Management Accounting

Course Book

For exams from
4 November 2019
to January 2021

BPP
LEARNING
MEDIA

First edition 2019

ISBN 9781 5097 2751 3

e-ISBN 9781 5097 2752 0

ISBN (for internal use only) 9781 5097 2776 6

British Library Cataloguing-in-Publication Data

A catalogue record for this book is available from the British Library

Published by

BPP Learning Media Ltd

BPP House, Aldine Place

London W12 8AA

learningmedia.bpp.com

Printed in the United Kingdom

Your learning materials, published by BPP Learning Media Ltd, are printed on paper sourced from sustainable, managed forests.

We are grateful to the Chartered Institute of Management Accountants for allowing us to reproduce extracts from the CIMA exam blueprint. An up-to-date version of the full blueprint is available at www.cimaglobal.com/examblueprints.

A note about copyright

Dear Customer

Contents

Introduction

Description of the paper   iv

Syllabus   v

Examination structure   xiii

How to pass   xvi

The Case Study exam and links with P2   xviii

Features in this Course Book   xix

1   Analysing and managing costs   1

2   Quality management   21

3   Value management   41

4   Data for decision making   57

5   Project appraisal   71

6   Further aspects of project appraisal   101

7   Pricing strategies   121

8   Decision making in responsibility centres   145

9   Performance measurement   165

10   Transfer pricing   187

11   Risk and uncertainty   205

12   Analysis and management of risk   235

Test your learning answers   249

Appendix 1: Mathematical tables & exam formulae   261

Index   269

Bibliography   273

Description of the paper

P2 is concerned with how to create value for the organisation through the effective management of costs, quality and capital investment. P2 also considers how to measure and manage the performance of the organisation and of divisions within the organisation. Finally, P2 considers the importance of risk management.

In all of these areas the focus of P2 is on managing performance over the medium-term in order to create value.

Syllabus

P2 examination blueprint

The syllabus outcomes each detail what you need to **know**, and each syllabus outcome has a number of associated representative task statements which make clear what you need to be able to **do** with that knowledge, eg do you need to simply be able to identify and understand a theory or do you need to use that theory to perform calculations? You will also see these critical representative task statements clearly referenced at the beginning of each chapter as well as throughout the chapters, giving you confidence that you are learning exactly what you need for success in your CIMA exam.

BPP worked closely with CIMA to help create these vital exam blueprints, so you can trust our learning materials to give you all the information you need to pass your exam.

Areas and weightings

Content area	Weighting
A. Managing the Costs of Creating Value	20%
B. Capital Investment Decision Making	35%
C. Managing and Controlling the Performance of Organisational Units	30%
D. Risk and Control	5%
	100%

(CIMA exam blueprint, 2019)

Blueprint

*Key: RU = Remembering and understanding; AP = Application; AN = Analysis; EV = Evaluation

P2A: Managing the Costs of Creating Value		Skill level				
Lead outcome	Component outcome	RU	AP	AN	EV	Representative task statement
1. Cost management and cost transformation methodology to manage costs and improve profitability	a. Activity-based management (ABM) methodology	✔				Understand how activity-based management uses activity based costing to drive profitability and customer satisfaction.
	b. Cost transformation techniques	✔				Understand the rationale for the use of ABC as the foundation for managing costs.
			✔			Use activity-based management to improve efficiency of repetitive overhead activities.

P2A: Managing the Costs of Creating Value			Skill level			
Lead outcome	Component outcome	RU	AP	AN	EV	Representative task statement
				✔		Analyse activity-based cost methods in tracing costs to 'cost objects', such as customers or distribution channels, and the comparison of such costs with appropriate revenues to establish 'tiered' contribution levels, as in the activity-based cost hierarchy.
				✔		Analyse customer profitability and channel performance using activity-based management to identify areas for improvement.
2. Quality management methodologies	a. JIT		✔			Determine the impacts of just-in-time (JIT) production, the theory of constraints and total quality management on efficiency, inventory and cost.
	b. Quality management		✔			Determine the benefits of JIT production, total quality management and theory of constraints and the implications of these methods for decision-making.
	c. Kaizen		✔			Demonstrate the concepts of JIT, TQM, and Kaizen and how they drive the continuous improvement of products and processes in an organisation.
	d. Process re-engineering		✔			Determine how business process re-engineering can identify non-value adding activities and reduce costs.
3. Value management techniques to manage costs and improve value creation	a. Target costing		✔			Calculate target costs and target prices and identify methods to reduce any cost gaps.

BPP LEARNING MEDIA

P2A: Managing the Costs of Creating Value		Skill level				
Lead outcome	Component outcome	RU	AP	AN	EV	Representative task statement
	b. Value chain analysis		✔			Determine how research and development, product design, process environment, production, distribution, marketing and customer service together to improve products and services for customers.
	c. Life cycle costing			✔		Analyse the value chain and management of contribution/profit generated throughout the chain.
		✔				Understand life cycle costing and its implications for marketing strategies.
			✔			Use life cycle costing and budgeting in costing decisions.

P2B: Capital Investment Decision Making		Skill level				
Lead outcome	Component outcome	RU	AP	AN	EV	Representative task statement
1. Data required for decision-making	a. Relevant cash flows		✔			Determine relevant cash flows and their timings for the entire project lifecycle including consideration of tax, inflation and working capital.
			✔			Calculate relevant cash flows taking account of tax, inflation, and working capital, and the use of perpetuities to derive final project value.
			✔			Determine non-financial factors in medium-term decision making.
	b. Non-financial information		✔			Determine the benefits, costs, and common problems with collecting, analysing and presenting high-quality data.

P2B: Capital Investment Decision Making		Skill level				
Lead outcome	Component outcome	RU	AP	AN	EV	Representative task statement
			✔			Determine the role of business intelligence systems in identifying new business opportunities and reducing costs.
2. The steps and pertinent issues in the decision-making process	a. Investment decision-making process	✔				Understand the process of investment decision-making, including origination of proposals, creation of capital budgets, go/no-go decisions on individual projects (where judgements on qualitative issues interact with financial analysis).
	b. Discounting		✔			Determine the financial consequences of dealing with medium-term projects, in particular the importance of accounting for time value of money.
			✔			Use discounting, including the use of annuities in comparing projects with unequal lives.
	c. Capital investments as real options		✔			Use profitability index in capital rationing situations.
			✔			Determine capital investment real options (ie to make follow-on investment, abandon or wait decisions).
3. Investment appraisal techniques	a. Payback		✔			Calculate ARR, payback, NPV, IRR, modified IRR (based on a project's terminal value).
	b. ARR			✔		Analyse the relative strengths and weaknesses of ARR, payback, NPV, IRR, modified IRR (based on a project's terminal value).
	c. IRR			✔		Use NPV, IRR, and payback to analyse financial aspects of projects and prioritise accordingly.

P2B: Capital Investment Decision Making		RU	AP	AN	EV	Representative task statement
Lead outcome	Component outcome					
	d. NPV			✔		Use investment appraisal techniques for prioritisation of projects that are mutually exclusive.
				✔		Use investment appraisal techniques for comparison of projects that have unequal lives.
4. Pricing strategies	a. Pricing decisions	✔				Understand pricing decision.
	b. Pricing strategies			✔		Analyse pricing strategies and the financial consequences of market skimming, premium pricing, penetration pricing, loss leaders product bundling/operational extras and product differentiation to appeal to different market segments.

P2C: Managing and Controlling the Performance of Organisational Units		RU	AP	AN	EV	Representative task statement
Lead outcome	Component outcome					
1. Responsibility centres reporting	a. Cost centres, revenue centres, profit centres, and investment centres			✔		Analyse responsibility centres and responsibility accounting and the relationship to an organisation's strategy (eg cost, revenue, profit, and investment centres).
				✔		Analyse how controllable and uncontrollable costs and revenues impact a manager's performance related to responsibility centres.
				✔		Analyse appropriate costs and measures of performance for responsibility centres.

P2C: Managing and Controlling the Performance of Organisational Units			Skill level			
Lead outcome	**Component outcome**	**RU**	**AP**	**AN**	**EV**	**Representative task statement**
			✔			Use data analytics and visualisations to analyse responsibility centres to enhance management performance and accountability.
	b. Reports for decision-making		✔			Prepare the reports used for each type of responsibility centre to assist management assess performance.
2. Approaches to the performance and control of organisations	a. Budgets and performance review		✔			Identify and calculate key KPIs for each type of responsibility centre (eg profitability, liquidity, asset turnover, return on investment, residual income, and economic value added).
				✔		Analyse key KPIs for each type of responsibility centre.
	b. Other approaches to performance review		✔			Use internal and external benchmarking as a key input in performance evaluation.
	.		✔			Use non-financial measures as a key input in performance evaluation.
			✔			Use a balanced scorecard approach to measure an organisation's performance from the four key perspectives.

P2C: Managing and Controlling the Performance of Organisational Units		Skill level				
Lead outcome	Component outcome	RU	AP	AN	EV	Representative task statement
3. Behavioural and transfer pricing issues related to the management of responsibility centres	a. Behavioural issues	✔				Understand the likely behavioural consequences of performance measurement within an organisation including the behavioural consequences of performance management and control in responsibility centres and the behavioural consequences arising from divisional structures including internal competition and internal trading.
	b. Use and ethics of transfer pricing	✔				Understand the theory of transfer pricing, including perfect, imperfect and no market for the intermediate good.
			✔			Calculate negotiated, market, cost-plus and variable cost-based transfer prices.
			✔			Determine dual transfer prices and lump sum payments as means of addressing some of the issues that arise in transfer pricing decisions.
			✔			Determine how the different methods of calculating transfer prices affect manager autonomy, motivation, goal congruence and unit performance.
				✔		Analyse the effects of transfer pricing on divisional and group profitability.

P2D: Risk and Control		Skill level				Representative task statement
Lead outcome	Component outcome	RU	AP	AN	EV	
1. Risk and uncertainty associated with medium-term decision-making	a. Sensitivity analysis			✔		Use sensitivity analysis, expected values, standard deviations and probability tables to quantify and analyse risk.
	b. Analysis of risk		✔			Use probabilistic models and interpretations of distribution of project outcomes for risk quantification.
			✔			Use the results of digital analyses to test the impact of varying inputs on project viability.
			✔			Use decision trees for multi-stage medium-term decision problems.
		✔				Understand decision-making in conditions of uncertainty.
2. Types of risk in the medium-term	a. Types of risk		✔			Determine upside and downside risks.
	b. Managing risk		✔			Use the TARA framework – transfer, avoid, reduce, and accept.
			✔			Determine business risks and the ethical implications and risk to the public interest.
			✔			Determine the costs and benefits associated with investing in information systems and big data.

(CIMA exam blueprint, 2019)

Examination structure

The Objective Test exam

Pass mark	70%
Format	Computer-based assessment
Duration	90 minutes
Number of questions	60
Marking	No partial marking – each question marked correct or incorrect All questions carry the same weighting (ie same marks)
Weighting	As per syllabus areas All representative task statements from the examination blueprint will be covered
Question Types	Multiple choice Multiple response Drag and drop Gap fill Hot spot
Booking availability	On demand
Results	Immediate

What the examiner means

The table below has been prepared by CIMA to further help you interpret the syllabus and learning outcomes and the meaning of questions.

You will see that there are five skills levels you may be expected to demonstrate, ranging from Remembering and Understanding to Evaluation. CIMA Certificate subjects only use levels 1 to 3, but in CIMA's Professional qualification the entire hierarchy will be used.

Skills		Verbs used	Definition
Level 5	Evaluation *The examination or assessment of problems, and use of judgment to draw conclusions*	Advise	Counsel, inform or notify
		Assess	Evaluate or estimate the nature, ability or quality of
		Evaluate	Appraise or assess the value of
		Recommend	Propose a course of action
		Review	Assess and evaluate in order, to change if necessary
		Select	Choose an option or course of action after consideration of the alternatives

Skills		Verbs used	Definition
Level 4	**Analysis** *The examination and study of the interrelationship of separate areas in order to identify causes and find evidence to support inferences*	Align	Arrange in an orderly way
		Analyse	Examine in detail the structure of
		Communicate	Share or exchange information
		Compare and contrast	Show the similarities and/or differences between
		Develop	Grow and expand a concept
		Discuss	Examine in detail by argument
		Examine	Inspect thoroughly
		Monitor	Observe and check the progress of
		Prioritise	Place in order of priority or sequence for action
		Produce	Create or bring into existence

Skills		Verbs used	Definition
Level 3	**Application** *The use or demonstration of knowledge, concepts or techniques*	Apply	Put to practical use
		Calculate	Ascertain or reckon mathematically
		Conduct	Organise and carry out
		Demonstrate	Prove with certainty or exhibit by practical means
		Determine	Ascertain or establish exactly by research or calculation
		Perform	Carry out, accomplish, or fulfil
		Prepare	Make or get ready for use
		Reconcile	Make or prove consistent/compatible
		Record	Keep a permanent account of facts, events or transactions
		Use	Apply a technique or concept

Skills		Verbs used	Definition
Level 1/2	**Remembering and understanding** *The perception and comprehension of the significance of an area utilising knowledge gained*	Define	Give the exact meaning of
		Describe	Communicate the key features of
		Distinguish	Highlight the differences between
		Explain	Make clear or intelligible/state the meaning or purpose of
		Identify	Recognise, establish or select after consideration
		Illustrate	Use an example to describe or explain something
		List	Make a list of
		Recognise	Identify/recall
		State	Express, fully or clearly, the details/facts of
		Outline	Give a summary of
		Understand	Comprehend ideas, concepts and techniques

(CIMA exam blueprint, 2019)

How to pass

Effective study

Study the whole syllabus

You need to be comfortable with all areas of the syllabus, as questions in the Objective Test exam will cover all syllabus areas. Wider reading will help you understand the main risks businesses face, which will be particularly useful in the integrated case study exam.

Lots of question practice

You can develop application skills by attempting the Test Your Learning questions at the end of each chapter. While these might not be in the format that you will experience in your exam, doing the full question will enable you to answer the exam questions. These have been designed to test as much breadth and depth of your knowledge as possible – they don't follow the exam format but will leave you well prepared to tackle any exam question on the topic. For example, you will only be able to answer a question on an element of an interest rate swap calculation if you know how to do the full calculation. When preparing for your exam you should practice exam standard questions, which you will find in the BPP Exam Practice Kit, your recommended accompanying study support to this Course Book.

Good exam technique

The best approach to the computer-based assessment (CBA)

You're not likely to have a great deal of spare time during the CBA itself, so you must make sure you don't waste a single minute.

You should:

(a) Click 'Next' for any that have long scenarios or are very complex and return to these later

(b) When you reach the 60th question, use the Review Screen to return to any questions you skipped past or any you flagged for review

Here's how the tools in the exam will help you to do this in a controlled and efficient way.

The 'Next' button

What does it do? This will move you on to the next question whether or not you have completed the one you are on.

When should I use it? Use this to move through the exam on your first pass through if you encounter a question that you suspect is going to take you a long time to answer. The Review Screen (see below) will help you to return to these questions later in the exam.

The 'Flag for Review' button

What does it do? This button will turn the icon yellow and when you reach the end of the exam questions you will be told that you have flagged specific questions for review. If the exam time runs out before you have reviewed any flagged questions, they will be submitted as they are.

When should I use it? Use this when you've answered a question but you're not completely comfortable with your answer. If there is time left at the end, you can quickly come back via the Review Screen (see below), but if time runs out at least it will submit your current answer. Do not use the Flag for Review button too often or you will end up with too long a list to review at the end. Important note –studies have shown that you are usually best to stick with your first instincts!

The Review Screen

What does it do? This screen appears after you click 'Next' on the 60th question. It shows you any incomplete questions and any you have flagged for review. It allows you to jump back to specific questions or work through all your incomplete questions or work through all your flagged for review questions.

When should I use it? As soon as you've completed your first run through the exam and reached the 60th question. The very first thing to do is to work through all your incomplete questions as they will all be marked as incorrect if you don't submit an answer for these in the remaining time. Importantly, this will also help to pick up any questions you thought you'd completed but didn't answer properly (eg you only picked two answer options in a multi-response question that required three answers to be selected). After you've submitted answers for all your incomplete questions you should use the Review Screen to work through all the questions you flagged for review.

The different Objective Test question types

Passing your CBA is all about demonstrating your understanding of the technical syllabus content. You will find this easier to do if you are comfortable with the different types of Objective Test questions that you will encounter in the CBA, especially if you have a practised approach to each one.

You will find yourself continuously practising these styles of questions throughout your Objective Test programme. This way you will check and reinforce your technical knowledge at the same time as becoming more and more comfortable with your approach to each style of question.

Multiple choice

Standard multiple choice items provide four options. One option is correct and the other three are incorrect. Incorrect options will be plausible, so you should expect to have to use detailed, syllabus-specific knowledge to identify the correct answer rather than relying on common sense.

Multiple response

A multiple response item is the same as a multiple choice question, except **more than one** response is required. You will normally (but not always) be told how many options you need to select.

Drag and drop

Drag and drop questions require you to drag a 'token' onto a pre-defined area. These tokens can be images or text. This type of question is effective at testing the order of events, labelling a diagram or linking events to outcomes.

Gap fill

Gap fill (or 'fill in the blank') questions require you to type a short numerical response. You should carefully follow the instructions in the question in terms of how to type your answer – eg the correct number of decimal places.

Hot spot

These questions require you to identify an area or location on an image by clicking on it. This is commonly used to identify a specific point on a graph or diagram.

A final word on time management

Time does funny things in an exam!

Scientific studies have shown that humans have great difficulty in judging how much time has passed if they are concentrating fully on a challenging task (which your CBA should be!).

You can try this for yourself. Have a go at, say, five questions for your paper, and notice what time you start at. As soon as you finish the last question try to estimate how long it took you and then compare to your watch. The majority of us tend to underestimate how quickly time passes and this can cost you dearly in a full exam if you don't take steps to keep track of time.

So, the key thing here is to set yourself sensible milestones, and then get into the habit of regularly checking how you are doing against them:

- You need to develop an internal warning system – 'I've now spent more than three minutes on this one calculation – this is too long and I need to move on!' (less for a narrative question!)
- Keep your milestones in mind (eg approximately 30 questions done after 45 mins). If you are a distance from where you should be then adjust your pace accordingly. This usually means speeding up but can mean slowing down a bit if needs be, as you may be rushing when you don't need to and increasing the risk of making silly mistakes.

A full exam will be a mix of questions you find harder and those you find easier, and in the real CBA the order is randomised, so you could get a string of difficult questions right at the beginning of your exam. Do not be put off by this – they should be balanced later by a series of questions you find easier.

The Case Study exam and links with P2

Upon passing all of the exams at the Management level, you will be eligible to sit the Management Case Study exam. As an example, you will need to have passed E2, F2 and P2 to sit the Management Case Study exam. CIMA will release a pre-seen document, providing comprehensive operational, strategic and financial details about a fictional company that you will be working for in your Management Case Study exam. There are four exam sittings a year (February, May, August and November) and at each sitting there are five exam variants; your exam will be selected from these five at random.

The format of the Management Case Study exam is a three-hour CBE, comprising three or four scenario-based questions, with each scenario having three or four associated requirements. These requirements will feature a mix of narrative and calculation questions, and the provision of the pre-seen and exam scenarios will necessitate a high degree of application. Therefore, what you study in this Course Book will provide you with part of the core knowledge required to answer the technical content of the Management Case Study exam.

For example, the Management Level Case Study has 30 assessment outcomes, and each of these can be mapped back to knowledge you will have gained studying for the Management Level exams:

- 'I can explain which pricing strategies are appropriate' – this draws on the capital investment decision-making part of the P2 syllabus.
- 'I can apply appropriate project management tools and techniques to effectively manage projects at the appropriate stage in the project life cycle' – this draws on the project management element of E2.
- 'I can explain the relevance of the weighted average cost of capital' – this draws on the F2 syllabus.

When you commence your Management Case Study exam studies, we recommend you attend a BPP course or purchase BPP's Case Study Workbook, which will provide you with essential question practice and exam guidance on how to use the knowledge gained from this Course Book and apply it to the format of the Case Study exam.

Features in this Course Book

Key term

A key definition which is important to be aware of for the assessment

Formula to learn

A formula you will need to learn as it will not be provided in the assessment

Formula provided

A formula which is provided within the assessment and generally available as a pop-up on screen

Activity

An example which allows you to apply your knowledge to the technique covered in the Course Book. The solution is provided at the end of the chapter.

Illustration

A worked example which can be used to review and see how an assessment question could be answered

Assessment focus point

A high priority point for the assessment

Real life examples

A practical real life scenario

1   Analysing and managing costs

Syllabus learning outcomes

Having studied this chapter, you will be able to work through the following syllabus outcomes:

Syllabus area A: Managing the costs of creating value	
1	Cost management and cost transformation methodology to manage costs and improve profitability
a	Activity-based management (ABM) methodology
b	Cost transformation techniques

Exam context

In the exam, you will be expected to demonstrate competence in the following representative task statements:

- Understand how activity-based management uses activity-based costing (ABC) to drive profitability and customer satisfaction
- Understand the rationale for the use of ABC as the foundation for managing costs
- Use activity-based management to improve efficiency of repetitive overhead activities
- Analyse activity-based cost methods in tracing costs to 'cost objects', such as customers or distribution channels, and the comparison of such costs with appropriate revenues to establish 'tiered' contribution levels, as in the activity-based cost hierarchy
- Analyse customer profitability and channel performance using activity-based management to identify areas for improvement

Chapter overview

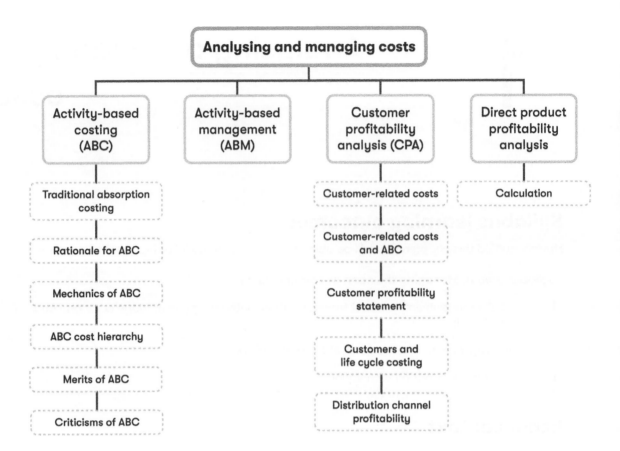

BPP
LEARNING
MEDIA

1 Introduction

In modern, highly competitive business environments, there is continual pressure to keep costs down while having due regard for value generation. This approach to cost management is referred to by the CGMA as cost transformation.

Cost transformation tools aim to build an understanding of costs and value, and often use activity-based techniques. Cost transformation requires a cost-conscious culture to be created and embedded within an organisation; this chapter examines how activity-based techniques can help an organisation create this.

Activity-based management (ABM) can transform a company's cost base by building an understanding of the link between resource consumption and levels of activity, and between costs incurred and value creation.

This chapter starts with a recap of activity-based costing (ABC) but mainly focuses on how activity-based techniques can be used to build an understanding of the profitability of product categories, key customers and distribution channels.

2 Activity-based costing (ABC)

From your earlier studies you will have applied the concept of activity-based costing (ABC).

> **Activity-based costing:** 'An approach to the costing and monitoring of activities which involves tracing resource consumption and costing final outputs. Resources are assigned to activities and activities to cost objects based on consumption estimates. The latter use **cost drivers** to attach activity costs to outputs'. (*CIMA Official Terminology*)

2.1 Traditional absorption costing

Traditional **absorption costing** uses a **single basis** for absorbing all overheads into cost units for a particular cost centre; for example, **labour hours or machine hours.**

Until recently, **overheads** (or indirect costs) often accounted for a **very small proportion of total cost,** so the simplistic assumption that all costs within a cost centre related to a single variable (eg labour hours or machine hours) could be made.

Activity 1: Absorption costing

N Co bills its customers on the basis of total cost + 10%.

N Co currently uses a system of absorption costing. Production overhead costs are absorbed using machine hours, and purchasing overhead costs are absorbed on the basis of material cost.

N Co's budget production for the year is 100,000 units and machine time is expected to be 0.5 hours per unit. The budget costs are shown below.

Cost type	$'000
Materials	2,500
Labour	1,250
Production overheads	4,500
Purchasing department overheads	750
Total	**9,000**

An order for 1,000 units is currently being costed for a new customer. This order is expected to incur total material costs of $40,000, total labour costs of $20,000 and will take 400 machine hours and will be produced in a single batch using one supplier.

Required

Which of the following total prices should N Co quote for this order, based on its current policies?

A $99,000

B $66,000

C $118,800

D $128,700

Solution

2.2 Rationale for ABC

Over recent decades, overhead costs have become a **greater proportion of total production costs.** This means that it has become more important to understand what is driving overhead costs and to apportion overhead costs to products more accurately.

Control of overheads has also become more important. It has been suggested that overheads are not simply fixed costs but that they can be seen as **long-term variable costs** which are **related** to the **complexity** and **diversity of production**.

Overheads such as machine set-ups, inventory handling, and scheduling **do not increase with the volume of output.** They are fixed in the shorter term but they vary in the longer term according to the range and complexity of output. If a **single product** is made, **some support activities**, such as production scheduling, will **not exist**.

ABC aims to control overhead costs by **identifying their causal factors** (cost drivers).

Exam focus

An assessment question could ask you to identify the factors that make the use of ABC more or less valuable to an organisation.

2.3 Mechanics of ABC

KEY
TERM

Cost driver: A cost driver is a 'factor influencing the level of cost. Often used in the context of ABC to denote the factor which links activity resource consumption to product outputs; for example, the number of purchase orders would be a cost driver for procurement cost' (*CIMA Official Terminology*).

In ABC, overheads are first grouped into cost pools (ie costs caused by the **same activity**) and then related to the cost objects according to the cost driver activity created by the cost object (eg a product unit). Each type of overhead is absorbed using a different **basis** depending on the cost driver.

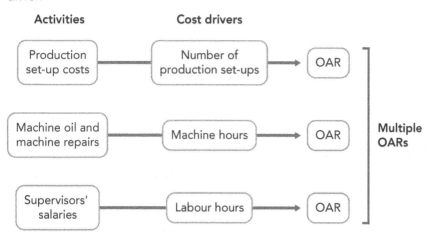

2.3.1 Stages in ABC calculations

Stage	
1	Overheads are collected into cost pools (or activities). Identify the cost drivers for each activity (ie what causes the activity to be incurred).
2	Identify the cost drivers for each activity (ie what causes the activity to be incurred).
3	Calculate the cost per unit of cost driver. Cost driver rate = $\dfrac{\text{Total cost of activity}}{\text{Cost driver}}$
4	Absorb activity costs into production based on the usage of cost drivers. The cost driver rate can be used to cost products, or other cost objects such as customers or groups of customers (see section 4).

 Illustration 1: ABC

Using the same information as for Activity 1, N Co is now considering moving to an ABC system where overhead costs are absorbed using the following cost drivers:

Cost pool	Cost driver	Budgeted activity
Production overheads	Production runs	2,000 production runs
Purchasing overheads	Number of suppliers	75 suppliers

Required

What is the change in the total price of the order as a result in the move to an ABC system?

$ [   ]

Solution

The correct answer is:

$ 39,325

Production overhead = $4.5m/2,000 production runs = $2,250 per production run

Purchasing overhead = $750,000/75 = $10,000 per supplier

Cost type	$'000
Materials	40
Purchasing overheads (1 × $10,000)	10
Labour	20
Production overheads (1 × $2,250)	2.25
Total	**72.25**
Mark-up 10%	7.225
Price	**79.475**

This is a fall of $118,800 − $79,475 = $39,325

This illustrates the potential importance of ABC on decision making.

Exam focus

An assessment question could ask you to calculate the cost per unit of cost driver or the cost per unit of finished product or service using an ABC system.

2.4 Activity-based cost hierarchy

Cooper and Kaplan (1991) suggest that cost drivers operate at different levels in organisations:

Classification level	Cause of cost	Example	Cost driver
Unit level	Production of a single unit of product or delivery of single unit of service ie volume-related	Direct materials Direct labour Machine maintenance	Units produced
Batch level	A group of things being made in a single production run	Purchase orders, set-ups, inspection	Batches produced
Product (or service) sustaining level	Development, production and sale of individual product or service type	Production scheduling Product-specific R&D and marketing	No. of different products or services produced
Facility sustaining	Existence of facility	Building depreciation and maintenance Organisational-level administration, advertising and IT	None

Cost per unit will be **different** under absorption costing and ABC if most overheads are batch or product sustaining costs because absorption costing does not account for non-volume-related overheads with the same precision as ABC.

Cost per unit will be **similar** under absorption costing and ABC if most overheads are unit level or facility sustaining because:

- Absorption costing deals with volume-related (unit level) overheads
- Facility-sustaining overheads are apportioned to cost units in the same way under both ABC and absorption costing (since there are no cost drivers for this type of overhead)

Activity 2: ABC hierarchy

WTL manufactures and sells four products – W, X, Y and Z – from a single factory. The sales of each product are independent of each other.

WTL has a significant number of competitors and is forced to accept the market price for each of its products. It is currently reviewing the profit it makes from each product. This is shown below for the latest period:

Product	W	X	Y	Z	Total
Profit/Loss ($)	150,000	(80,000)	330,000	(200,000)	200,000

(a) Machine hour-related overheads: these have been apportioned at $310/hour

Profits have been calculated after allowing for overhead costs which have been absorbed using a single absorption rate based on labour hours.

WTL is concerned that two of its products are loss-making and has carried out an ABC analysis of its overhead costs. This has identified four types of overheads:

(b) Batch-related overheads: these have been apportioned at $230 per production run
(c) Product-specific fixed overheads (which would only be avoided if the product were discontinued): these have been identified for each product
(d) General overheads (which would only be avoided by the closure of the factory): these have been apportioned using sales revenue

The result of the ABC analysis is as follows:

Product	W	X	Y	Z	Total
	$'000	$'000	$'000	$'000	$'000
Sales	1,250	2,250	2,000	1,750	7,250
Contribution	600	210	540	500	1,850
Overhead					
Machine-related	(80)	(78)	(32)	(120)	(310)
Batch-related	(50)	(165)	(40)	(75)	(330)
Product-specific	(450)	(50)	(100)	(100)	(700)
General	(53)	(96)	(86)	(75)	(310)
Profit	(33)	(179)	282	130	200

Required

Which product should be discontinued in order to maximise company profits?

A W

B X

C Y

D Z

Solution

2.5 Merits of ABC (compared to absorption costing)

ABC can bring a number of **benefits**:

- A meaningful analysis of costs which should provide a more **suitable basis for decisions** about pricing, product mix, design and production
- Help with **cost reduction** – identifying cost drivers provides an insight into what causes overhead costs
- Oversight of **all overhead costs,** including such 'non-factory floor' costs as quality control and customer service, extending cost accounting beyond its 'traditional' factory floor boundaries

ABC is **more useful if**:

(a) Overheads are a **significant** proportion of total costs and are mainly caused by **non-volume related factors** (batch or product sustaining)

(b) A business is **diverse** (eg many products)

This means that ABC is especially suitable for use in **services** (as well as in some manufacturing businesses) because many services are diverse and are characterised by having a high proportion of costs as overheads (eg banks, hospitals).

2.6 Criticisms of ABC

ABC is not a perfect costing system and **product costs** could still be **inaccurate**. Its suitability for all environments remains unproven.

(a) The **cost** of obtaining and interpreting the new information may be considerable.

(b) Some arbitrary **cost apportionment** may still be required at the cost pooling stage for **facility-sustaining overheads**.

(c) ABC tends to **burden low volume (new) products** with a punitive level of overhead costs and hence threatens opportunities for successful innovation if it is used without due care.

(d) The ability of a **single costdriver** to fully explain the cost behaviour of all items in its associated pool is **questionable**.

Exam focus

An assessment question could ask you to show understanding of the situations in which activity-based costing is more or less suitable; this will require knowledge of the ABC cost hierarchy.

3 Activity-based management

KEY TERM

> **Activity-based management:** Operational ABM: 'Actions based on activity driver analysis that increase **efficiency, lower costs,** and improve asset utilisation'.
>
> Strategic ABM: 'Actions based on activity based cost analysis that aim to change the **demand** for activities so as to improve profitability'. (*CIMA Official Terminology*)

ABC is a technique used to cost a product. ABM involves a number of different techniques that use the information generated by ABC to **control cost drivers** and also to **reduce overheads.**

ABM aims to focus management attention on key customers and products and value-adding activities in order to improve efficiency and to generate **competitive advantage.**

Any application of ABM is likely to involve comparing actual performance to expected performance (sometimes referred to as 'activity-based budgeting').

4 Customer profitability analysis (CPA)

CPA uses ABC principles to identify the most profitable customers or groups of customers. This allows an organisation to determine which **classes of customers** it should concentrate on and the **prices** it should charge for customer services.

When analysing customers, it is not uncommon to find that a high percentage of profits come from a small percentage of customers (often referred to as a Pareto effect).

Profitability can vary widely between different customers because **costs** (including overhead costs) are, to some extent, **customer driven.** Not all customers cost the same to serve, even if they require the same products.

4.1 Customer-related costs

Different customer groups may incur different marketing and distribution costs.

(a) Some types of customers **store and distribute goods** (eg wholesalers) but others don't.

(b) Some retailers require **payment, a discount or specific promotional campaigns (eg special offers)** in order to stock a manufacturer's product(s).

(c) Some customers may take a large amount of salesforce time with **queries, complaints and returns.**

(d) Some customers will demand generous **credit periods** and even then may not pay on time, which creates financing costs for the supplier (eg higher overdraft costs).

4.2 Customer-related costs and ABC

Because different customers use different amounts of activities, it is possible to **build up costs for individual customers or groups of customers** on an activity basis so that their **relative profitability** can be assessed.

Examples of the build-up of customer costs using an activity-based system are shown in the following table.

Activity	Cost driver
Order taking	Number of orders taken
Sales visits	Number of sales visits
Emergency orders	Number of rushed orders
Delivery	Miles travelled

A well-known example of the benefits of applying ABC to customer-related costs is Kanthal (*Kaplan and Cooper, 1998 p.185*), a Swedish company that sells electric heating elements.

Customer-related selling costs represented 34% of total costs. In the past, Kanthal had allocated these costs on the basis of sales value when customer profitability studies were carried out.

The company then introduced an ABC system in order to determine the resources consumed by different customers. An investigation identified two key cost drivers.

(a) **Number of orders placed**

Each order had a large fixed cost, which did not vary with the number of items ordered.

(b) **Non-standard production items**

These cost more to manufacture than standard items.

A CPA analysis, carried out on the basis of the previous year's sales, showed that only 40% of customers were profitable, and that 10% of customers incurred losses equal to 120% of Kanthal's total profits. Two of the most unprofitable customers were actually in the top three in terms of total sales volume but made many small orders of non-standard items.

Activity 3: CPA analysis

BB manufactures components for the heavy goods vehicle industry. The following annual information regarding three of its key customers – P, Q and R – is available.

	P	Q	R
Gross margin	$897,000	$1,070,000	$1,056,000
General administration costs	$35,000	$67,000	$56,000
Units sold	4,600	5,800	3,800
Orders placed	300	320	480
Sales visits	80	50	100
Invoices raised	310	390	1,050

The company uses an activity-based costing system and the analysis of customer-related costs is as follows.

Sales visits: $420 per visit

Order processing: $190 per order placed

Despatch costs: $350 per order placed

Billing and collections: $97 per invoice raised

Required

Using customer profitability analysis, in which order would the customers be ranked?

A   R, Q, P

B   Q, R, P

C   P, Q, R

D   Q, P, R

Solution

Unprofitable customers identified by CPA should be persuaded to alter their buying behaviour so they become profitable customers. In the Kanthal example quoted earlier, unprofitable customers should be discouraged from placing lots of small orders and/or from buying non-standard products.

The activity-based approach also highlights where cost reduction efforts should be focused. Kanthal should concentrate on reducing ordering cost and the cost of handling non-standard items.

4.3 Customer profitability statement

There is no set format, but it would normally be similar to the one below.

Note the inclusion of financing costs.

	$'000	$'000
Revenue at list prices		100
Less discounts given		8
Net revenue		92
Less cost of goods sold		50
Gross margin		42
Less:		
Customer-specific costs	28	
Financing costs (credit period)	2	
Customer-specific inventory	3	33
Net margin from customer		9

 Illustration 2: CPA analysis

Seth supplies shoes to Narayan and Kipling. Each pair of shoes has a list price of $50 and costs Seth $25. As Kipling buys in bulk, it receives a 10% trade discount for every order of 100 pairs of shoes or more.

Narayan receives a 15% discount irrespective of order size, because the company collects the shoes itself, thereby saving Seth any distribution costs.

Required

Complete the following sentence to identify the more profitable customer for Seth.

The cost of administering each order is $50 and the distribution cost is $1,000 per order. Narayan makes 10 orders in the year, totalling 420 pairs of shoes, and Kipling places 5 orders for 100 pairs.

The more profitable customer for Seth is [   ].

Solution

The correct answer is:

The more profitable customer for Seth is Narayan.

It can be shown that Seth earns more from supplying Narayan, despite the larger discount percentage.

	Kipling $	Narayan $
Revenue	25,000	21,000
Less discount	2,500	3,150
Net revenue	22,500	17,850
Less: Cost of shoes	(12,500)	(10,500)
Customer transport cost	(5,000)	–
Customer administration cost	(250)	(500)
Net gain	4,750	6,850

The difference on a unit basis is considerable.

Number of pairs of shoes sold	500	420
Net gain per pair of shoes sold	$9.50	$16.31
Net gain per $1 of sales revenue	$0.19	$0.33

4.4 Customers and life cycle costing

Customers can also be **costed over their expected 'life cycle'** and expected future cash flows relating to the customer may be **discounted back to a present value** (discounting is covered in Chapters 5 and 6).

It is rarely possible to predict accurately the life cycle of a particular customer unless contracts are awarded for a specific time period. Nevertheless, the information is valuable as **the longer the customer remains with the organisation**, the **more profitable** the customer becomes. This helps to show the **importance of creating and retaining loyal customers**.

4.5 Distribution channel profitability

In a similar way, ABC information can also be used to determine the profitability of different **distribution channels**. Distribution channels are the means by which a company transacts with its customers.

Direct channels include shops, sales teams and the internet, whereas **indirect channels** include retailers and wholesalers.

However, different channels will use different activities in exactly the same way that we saw earlier for customers.

Traditionally, channel profitability is analysed based on the product mix sold through each channel. Sales, general and administrative costs are typically allocated to distribution channels on the basis of sales volume or net revenue.

Understanding the specific costs of a channel can enable a company to decide whether the goods and services it is offering may be best offered through a different channel (although decisions should also consider whether customers' needs would be met if the channel was changed).

Exam focus

An assessment question is likely to ask you to apply the concept of CPA to identify the cost or profitability of a customer.

5 Direct product profitability (DPP)

> **Direct product profitability**: Direct product profitability (DPP) is used 'primarily within the retail sector, [and] involves the attribution of both the purchase price and other indirect costs (eg distribution, warehousing, retailing) to each product line. Thus a net profit, as opposed to a gross profit, can be identified for each product. The cost attribution process utilises a variety of measures (eg warehousing space, transport time) to reflect the resource consumption of individual products.' *(CIMA Official Terminology)*

Direct product profitability (DPP) is a costing system used by retail businesses. Traditionally, retailers relied on **gross margins** (sales revenue less purchase cost) to indicate product profitability.

DPP is the profitability a **product category** makes after deducting directly attributable costs such as warehousing, transport and storage (which are identified using ABC principles).

Some examples are given in the following table.

Direct product cost	Examples
Warehouse direct costs	Offloading, unpacking, picking and sorting, space costs, inventory financing costs
Transport direct costs	Fuel, depreciation of vehicle, driver's salary, vehicle servicing
Store/supermarket direct costs	Receiving and inspecting, moving, shelf filling, space costs, inventory financing costs

Normally, warehouse, transport and store costs will be spread across the different goods sold in relation to volume or area occupied, as most costs increase in proportion to the volume of the good or the space it occupies.

5.1 Calculation of DPP

Direct product profit is calculated as follows:

	$	$
Sales		X
Less purchase cost		(X)
Gross margin		X
Less direct product related overheads; eg:		
Warehousing	(X)	
Transport	(X)	
In-store	(X)	(X)
Direct product profit		X

> **Exam focus**
>
> Any costs that are **general** to the organisation (but not specific to any particular product) should be **ignored** when calculating direct product profit.

Activity 4: DPP analysis

F Co, a supermarket group has estimated that its average **store costs** are $5,000 per day and that average store capacity is 10,000 cubic metres.

Its product range includes the following products.

(a)   Six packs of fizzy pop; volume: 0.01 cubic metres; days in store: 5

(b)   Detergent; volume: 0.005 cubic metres; days in store: 4

(c)   Double roll of kitchen paper; volume: 0.185 cubic metres; days in store: 3

Required

Calculate store costs per pack for each product group. (Give your answers to three decimal places.)

Fizzy pop $ ☐

Detergent $ ☐

Kitchen paper $ ☐

Solution

Chapter summary

Analysing and managing costs

Activity-based costing (ABC)

Traditional absorption costing

Single absorption rate (per cost centre)

Rationale for ABC

Overheads are driven by complexity and diversity

Mechanics of ABC

(a) Collect overheads into cost centres
(b) Identify cost drivers
(c) Calculate cost per cost unit of cost driver
(d) Use to cost products

ABC cost hierarchy

- Unit level
- Batch level
- Product sustaining level
- Facility sustaining level

Merits of ABC

Improved decision making and cost control, especially if:
- A diverse and complex business
- High level of overheads
- Overheads are mainly batch level or product sustaining level

Criticisms of ABC

- Cost
- Quality of cost driver
- Penalises new (low volume) products

Activity-based management (ABM)

Focuses management time on key customers and products, in order to generate competitive advantage

Customer profitability analysis (CPA)

Customer-related costs

- Storage
- Distribution
- Salesforce time
- Financing

Customer-related costs and ABC

Cost drivers established for customer related costs

Customer profitability statement

Revenue
less: discounts
    cost of sales
    customer-specific costs

Customers and life cycle costing

Present value of margin from customers over estimated life cycle

Distribution channel profitability

Application of principles of CPA to evaluation profitability of different distribution channels

Direct product profitability analysis

Calculation

Deducts costs attributable to a product category (eg storage, transport)

BPP
LEARNING
MEDIA

Key terms

Activity-based costing: 'An approach to the costing and monitoring of activities which involves tracing resource consumption and costing final outputs. Resources are assigned to activities and activities to cost objects based on consumption estimates. The latter use **cost drivers** to attach activity costs to outputs'. (*CIMA Official Terminology*)

Cost driver: A cost driver is a 'factor influencing the level of cost. Often used in the context of ABC to denote the factor which links activity resource consumption to product outputs; for example, the number of purchase orders would be a cost driver for procurement cost' (*CIMA Official Terminology*).

Activity-based management: Operational ABM: 'Actions based on activity driver analysis that increase **efficiency, lower costs,** and improve asset utilisation'.

Strategic ABM: 'Actions based on activity based cost analysis that aim to change the **demand** for activities so as to improve profitability'. (*CIMA Official Terminology*)

Direct product profitability: Direct product profitability (DPP) is used 'primarily within the retail sector, [and] involves the attribution of both the purchase price and other indirect costs (eg distribution, warehousing, retailing) to each product line. Thus a net profit, as opposed to a gross profit, can be identified for each product. The cost attribution process utilises a variety of measures (eg warehousing space, transport time) to reflect the resource consumption of individual products.' (*CIMA Official Terminology*)

Activity answers

Activity 1: Absorption costing

The correct answer is:

$118,800

Response option	Explanation
$99,000	This is based on average cost of $90 per unit ($9,000,000/100,000) + 10% = $99 per unit and as such is not tailored to reflect the costs and time taken for this order.
$66,000	This is based on total direct costs of $60,000 ($40,000 + $20,000) + 10% = $66,000 and as such does not reflect the overhead costs.
$118,800	
$128,700	This is based on machine time being incorrectly based on 0.5 hours × 1,000 units = 500 hours.

Production overhead/Machine hours = $4.5m/50,000 machine hours (100,000 × 0.5) = $90 per hour. Purchasing overheads are 30% of material costs ($750,000/$2,500,000).

So, the total costs for the order are as follows:

Cost type	$'000
Materials	40
Purchasing overheads (0.3 × $40,000)	12
Labour	20
Production overheads ($90 × 400 hours)	36
Total	**108**
Mark-up 10%	10.8
Price	**118.8**

Activity 2: ABC hierarchy

The correct answer is:

X

Product	W	X	Y	Z
	$'000	$'000	$'000	$'000
Contribution	600	210	540	500
Machine-related	(80)	(78)	(32)	(120)
Batch-related	(50)	(165)	(40)	(75)
Net	470	(33)	468	305
Product-specific	(450)	(50)	(100)	(100)
Net	20	(83)	368	205

Only product X fails to cover all 'relevant' overheads. Faculty-sustaining costs would not be saved if product X was closed down and are therefore not relevant to this decision.

This contrasts with the picture presented by the original profit statement where products X and Z appeared to be loss-making because of the way overheads had been absorbed.

Non-financial factors such as the effect on customers and employees should also be considered before a final decision is made.

Activity 3: CPA analysis

The correct answer is:

Q, P, R

General admin costs are ignored as a non-relevant cost.

	P	Q	R
	$'000	$'000	$'000
Gross margin	897.00	1,070.00	1,056.00
Less: Customer specific costs			
Sales visits (80/50/100 × $420)	(33.60)	(21.00)	(42.00)
Order processing (300/320/480 × $190)	(57.00)	(60.80)	(91.20)
Despatch costs (300/320/480 × $350)	(105.00)	(112.00)	(168.00)
Billing and collections (310/390/1,050 × $97)	(30.07)	(37.83)	(101.85)
	671.33	838.37	652.95
Ranking	2	1	3

Activity 4: DPP analysis

The correct answer is:

Fizzy pop $0.025

Detergent $0.010

Kitchen paper $0.278

Store cost per cubic metre = $5,000/10,000 = $0.50

Store costs would be allocated as follows:

Fizzy pop: $0.50 × 0.01 × 5 days = $0.025 per pack

Detergent: $0.50 × 0.005 × 4 days = $0.01 per pack

Kitchen paper: $0.50 × 0.185 × 3 days = $0.278 per pack

Test your learning

1 **Required**

Is the following statement true or false?

The application of activity-based costing transforms fixed costs into long-term variable costs.

A   True

B   False

2 **Required**

What are the four levels in the Cooper & Kaplan activity-based costing hierarchy?

Level 1: [   ]

Level 2: [   ]

Level 3: [   ]

Level 4: [   ]

3 **Required**

What is a Pareto effect in the context of customer profitability analysis?

4 **Required**

Give two examples of how unprofitable customer accounts could be managed so that they return to profitability.

5 A wholesaler has estimated that its store space cost is $1.00 per cubic metre per day.

Its product range includes the following products.

(a) 'Four packs' of tinned soup; volume: 0.02 cubic metres; days in store: 5

(b) Bleach; volume: 0.01 cubic metres; days in store: 4

(c) Packs of toilet rolls; volume: 0.37 cubic metres; days in store: 3.

Required

State how space costs would be allocated to the products using direct product profitability. (Give your answers to two decimal places.)

Soup $ [   ]

Bleach $ [   ]

Toilet rolls $ [   ]

2

Quality management

Syllabus learning outcomes

Having studied this chapter, you will be able to work through the following syllabus outcomes:

Syllabus area A: Managing the costs of creating value	
2	Compare and contrast different quality management methodologies
a	JIT
b	Quality management
c	Kaizen
d	Process re-engineering

Exam context

In the exam, you will be expected to demonstrate competence in the following representative task statements:

- Determine the impacts of just-in-time (JIT) production, the theory of constraints and total quality management on efficiency, inventory and cost
- Determine the benefits of JIT production, total quality management (TQM) and theory of constraints and the implications of these methods for decision making
- Demonstrate the concepts of JIT, TQM, and Kaizen and how they drive the continuous improvement of products and processes in an organisation
- Determine how business process re-engineering can identify non-value adding activities and reduce costs

Chapter overview

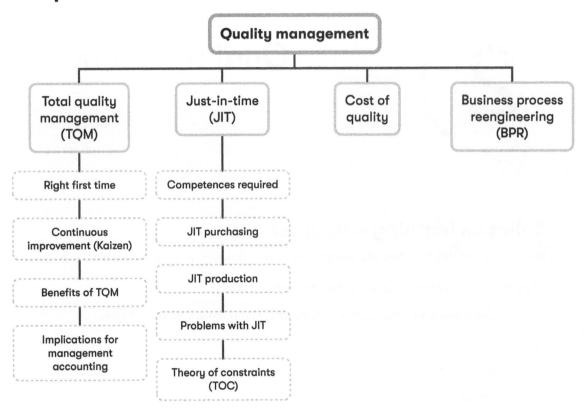

1 Introduction

The modern business environment involves **shorter product life cycles and a greater emphasis on quality** and customer requirements.

This chapter examines the role of **quality management** in managing and transforming costs, including the key methodologies and how they affect the costs of products and services.

The chapter moves on to consider the **closely linked area of just-in-time (JIT) and a number of techniques associated with JIT** including the theory of constraints, throughput accounting and business process reengineering (BPR).

2 Total quality management (TQM)

2.1 Traditional quality management

Traditional views on quality management suggest that in order for an organisation to **consistently** deliver products and services of the level of quality expected by its customers (or other key stakeholders), it must:

(a) Establish acceptable **quality standards** (eg defect rates)

(b) **Design procedures** to delivery this level of quality

(c) **Monitor** actual quality

(d) **Take control action** if quality falls below standard

2.2 Total quality management

In recent decades, increasing demands from customers for high quality and increasingly competitive markets has led to a **change** in manufacturing (and service provision) away from simply minimising production costs.

The **increased emphasis on high quality, highly customised output,** producing exactly what is wanted by the customer when they want it (ie with minimal inventory) is sometimes referred to as 'world class manufacturing'. A key part of this approach is 'total quality management' (TQM).

Quality management becomes **TQM when:**

(a) **Quality standards are set to an extremely high level** (eg zero defects); and

(b) Emphasis is placed on **resolution of problems that cause poor quality** rather than just detecting and correcting problems with quality as they emerge.

> **TQM:** TQM is 'an integrated and comprehensive system of planning and controlling all business functions so that products or services are produced which meet or exceed customer expectations. TQM is a philosophy of business behaviour, embracing principles such as employee involvement, continuous improvement at all levels and customer focus [...]' (*CIMA Official Terminology*).

2.3 Principles of TQM

TQM is built on two fundamental principles:

1. Right first time ⟷ 2. Continuous improvement

2.3.1 Right first time

The **cost of preventing mistakes is less than the cost of correcting them** after they occur, the aim should be **to get things right first time.** Every mistake or delay directly costs an organisation money through **wasted time and effort,** and **lost potential for future sales.**

TQM moves away from relying on inspecting to achieve a predefined level of quality to **preventing the cause** of **any defect** in the first place. To achieve this, TQM requires an awareness by **all personnel** of their role in meeting the customer's quality requirements.

Measures to support 'right first time'	
Control of suppliers	Suppliers are given a rating for their quality levels, with preference given to well-rated suppliers. This method is referred to as 'vendor rating'. It is the **supplier's responsibility to carry out the necessary quality checks,** or face cancellation of the contract.
Internal customers	TQM builds a recognition that the **customer–supplier relationship** extends to **internal customers**: passing substandard material to another division is not acceptable. Some organisations **formalise this** by requiring each internal supplier to make a **service level agreement** (SLA) with its internal customer. An SLA is a statement of the standard of service that will be provided to the internal customer and will cover the range of services supplied, response times and dependability.
Employee empowerment	**Empowerment** has two key aspects: (a) Allowing workers to have the **freedom to decide how to do** the necessary work, using the skills they possess and acquiring new skills as necessary to be an effective team member (b) Making workers **responsible** for achieving production targets and for quality control
Product and process design	This may involve: (a) Reducing the **number of parts** – the fewer the number of parts to be designed, purchased and assembled the lower the chance of errors (b) Using parts or materials that are **already used** by other products; the more common parts used, the less chance there is of a product failing (c) **Production engineering: the process of designing the methods for making a product** (or service) **to the design specification** – it sets out to make production methods as efficient as possible This may involve **computer-aided design (CAD).**

2.3.2 Continuous improvement

It is **always possible to improve** processes, and TQM emphasises the need for employees work together (often in cross-departmental 'quality circles') to make incremental improvements to reduce waste and thereby reduce costs.

TQM aims to foster a consistent, systematic approach to continuous improvement that involves every aspect of the organisation.

2.3.3 Kaizen

Kaizen costing aims to achieve small, incremental cost reductions within existing production processes.

A Kaizen costing process involves the following:

Actual production costs are taken for a given period (for example a year) and used as a base from which cost improvements are expected

An expected rate of **cost reduction during a given period is agreed** based on past experience

Variances are monitored **during the year** against the Kaizen targets

The process then **continues** in subsequent periods

Kaizen relies on **employee empowerment**; workers are given responsibility for proposing changes to achieve the Kaizen targets.

2.4 Implications of TQM for management accounting

Traditional variance analysis provides feedback against a fixed standard, typically at the end of a month. In a TQM environment this is less appropriate because:

- Feedback is too late
- The emphasis on low cost can conflict with quality
- TQM aims for continuous improvement

Non-financial performance measures are especially useful in a TQM environment. They provide more readily available (often real-time) performance measures with a more direct emphasis on quality.

Examples include:

- Number of customer complaints
- Time taken to respond to customer requests
- Number of defective units supplied by suppliers
- Number of defective units produced

3 Cost of quality

Quality management programmes, such as TQM, often involve considerable time and expense.

A cost of quality report helps to assess the success of quality programmes.

The cost of quality can be analysed into the following categories:

Prevention cost	Appraisal cost	Internal failure cost	External failure cost
Costs incurred prior to or during production in order to prevent substandard or defective output from being produced	Costs incurred in order to check that outputs produced meet required quality standards	Costs arising from inadequate quality which are identified **before** the transfer of ownership from supplier to purchaser	Costs arising from inadequate quality discovered **after** the transfer of ownership from supplier to purchaser

Prevention cost	Appraisal cost	Internal failure cost	External failure cost
Examples:	Examples:	Examples:	Examples:
• Preventative repairs and maintenance • Training in quality control • Time spent discussing quality issues (quality circles)	• Acceptance testing • Inspection of goods inwards	• Repair costs • Losses from failure of purchased items	• Administration of customer complaints section • Cost of repairing products returned from customers • Lost sales

The cost of the quality management programme is the total of **prevention and appraisal costs.** These are sometimes called conformance costs.

The **internal and external costs of failure** are sometimes called non-conformance costs; these costs should fall if a quality management programme is succeeding.

It is likely that there will be a **trade-off between expenditure in these two categories;** ie the greater the spend on conformance costs, the lower the resulting non-conformance should be.

The total cost of quality measures whether the investment in conformance costs is paying off in the form of lower non-conformance costs.

The total cost of quality is sometimes measured as a **percentage of sales** to allow for **benchmarking** between organisations of different sizes.

Illustration 1: Cost of quality

Y Co's quality costs for the most recent period are as follows:

Cost type	$
Performing supplier quality ratings	250,000
Sample check of quality of finished products	45,000
Equipment to measure chemical composition of products	75,000
Warranty claims	840,000
Cost of re-inspecting goods that have been re-worked	25,000

Required

What is Y Co's current level of appraisal costs?

A $45,000

B $120,000

C $370,000

D $145,000

Solution

The correct answer is:

$120,000

The answer is calculated as $45,000 + $75,000 = $120,000.

Performing supplier quality ratings	$250,000	Prevention cost – allows best quality suppliers to be used and quality issues to be prevented
Sample check of quality of finished products	$45,000	Appraisal cost
Equipment to measure chemical composition of products	$75,000	Appraisal cost – form of inspection
Warranty claims	$840,000	External failure cost
Cost of re-inspecting goods that have been re-worked	$25,000	Internal failure – only necessary due to non-conformance

Activity 1: Non-conformance costs

	20X6	20X7
	$'000	$'000
Sales revenue	7,900	8,472
Quality control training	40	120
Re-work costs	125	60
Returns	35	15
Customer complaints department	50	23
Inspection of WIP	85	70
Scrap	60	20
Total quality-related costs	395	308

Required

How much has the cost of non-conformance fallen between 20X6 and 20X7 (as a percentage of sales)?

A   1.4%

B   2.0%

C   0.6%

D   0.7%

Solution

Exam focus

Ensure you are able to explain quality conformance costs and quality non-conformance costs and the relationship between them.

4 Just-in-time

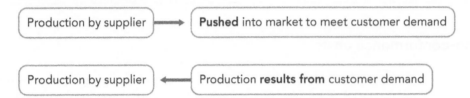

Conventional manufacturing approaches tended to involve **long production of standardised product ranges** to maximise efficiency. The resulting inventory was then used as a buffer to cope with fluctuations in levels of demand. This is sometimes referred to as a **push system**.

JIT aims to reverse this approach and to make a product only in response to a customer order. This is sometimes known as a **pull system**.

KEY TERM

Just-in-time: JIT is a system whose objective is to produce or to procure products or components as they are required by a customer or for use, rather than for inventory (*CIMA, 2005*).

4.1 Competences required for JIT

Competences required in a JIT (zero inventory) environment	
High quality	Without inventory, disruption in production due to errors in quality will directly impact customer orders.
Speed	Purchasing and production lead times need to be reduced because customer orders are being met by production rather than from inventory.
Reliability	Production must be reliable and not subject to hold-ups.
Flexibility	Production must be flexible to respond immediately to customer orders and to produce exactly what the customer needs.
Lower cost	High-quality production, faster throughput and elimination of errors will result in reduced costs.

These competences fit well with TQM and JIT is often used by companies **together with TQM**. Like TQM, JIT requires **close collaboration with suppliers and staff** and shares a philosophy of **continual improvement**.

4.2 JIT purchasing

In a zero-inventory environment an organisation will require a close, long-term relationship with a small number of **trusted high-quality** suppliers. The supplier is required to have a **flexible production system** capable of responding immediately to purchase orders from the organisation. Responsibility for the quality of goods lies with the supplier.

An organisation needs to have confidence that suppliers will deliver material of 100% quality, on time, so that there will be no rejects, returns and hence no production delays.

4.3 JIT production

Without inventory, a **disruption to production at any point in the system becomes a significant problem.** It is argued that this will improve the likelihood of the problem being resolved, because it is critical to deal with the issue. In this sense **inventories** help to **hide problems** within the system.

JIT aims to **restructure** the manufacturing process to bring about more flexible, **high-quality** and cost-effective production.

Characteristics of JIT production	
Low set-up times	If an organisation is to be able to respond quickly to customer orders it needs to be able to reset the machinery quickly to produce for a specific order.
Kanban	This is a signal (originally a card) that signals that a customer order requires specific work. Production only commences when authorised by a Kanban.
Production cells	Grouping machines and workers by product or component (instead of by type of work performed) minimises the **non-value added activity** of materials movement between operations. Products can flow from machine to machine within a production cell without having to wait for the next stage of processing or return to stores. Performance targets based on quality and lead time can be set for each cell. This is sometimes referred to as **cellular manufacturing**.
Minimising non-value adding activities	While a product is being inspected for quality, moving from one part of the factory to another, waiting for further processing and held in store as inventory, value is not being added. In a JIT system, employees work collaboratively to **minimise non-value adding activities.**
Preventive maintenance	Regular maintenance to **prevent machine breakdown**. Staff working on the production line are also brought into the search for improvements in maintenance, and are encouraged to take ownership of their machines and carry out simple repairs on them.

 Illustration 2: Value adding activities

Solo produces one product, the P. Parts for the product are quality inspected on arrival and stored in a warehouse until needed. They are then moved from the warehouse to the machine room where they are machined to the product specification. This work is then inspected and, if satisfactory, the machined parts are moved to the assembly area.

Once this processing is complete, the finished product is inspected and tested. This is then passed to the despatch department, where employees pack it in an attractive box with a printed instruction sheet. Finished goods are stored back in the warehouse until despatched to customers.

Required

Identify non-value adding activities from Solo's current activities listed below.

A   Parts received

B   Assembly and machining costs

C   Inspection costs

D   Storage

E   Time spent moving parts/goods

F   Packaging

G   Despatch

Solution

The correct answers are:

- Inspection costs
- Storage
- Time spent moving parts/goods

In a JIT approach the focus would be on the value adding activities; non-value adding activities would be minimised and, if possible, eliminated.

Receipt of parts, their machining, assembly, packaging and despatch to the customer are essential activities that increase the saleability of the product.

Solo needs to negotiate with its suppliers to guarantee the delivery of high-quality parts to eliminate the need for quality inspection on arrival.

Storage and movement of parts, work in progress and finished goods do not add value; rather they introduce unnecessary delays. The machining, assembly and packaging areas should be in close proximity to avoid excessive movement, and ordering and processing should be scheduled so that there is no need to store parts before they go into production. Similarly, production should be scheduled to finish goods just as they are needed for despatch to avoid storage of finished goods.

Proper maintenance of machinery and good staff training in quality production procedures should ensure finished goods of a consistently high quality, removing the need for inspection and testing.

4.4   Problems with JIT

JIT might not be appropriate in all circumstances.

(a) It is not always easy to predict patterns of demand.

(b) JIT makes the organisation far more vulnerable to disruptions in the supply chain.

4.5   Theory of constraints

In a JIT environment it will be essential to utilise the organisation's resources to turn raw materials into sales as efficiently as possible in order to **maximise throughput.**

> **Throughput:** Throughput (return) is defined as sales revenue less direct material costs. Also referred to as throughput contribution.

The theory of constraints (TOC) focuses on efficient management of **bottlenecks** in the production systems in order to maximise throughput in a cost-effective manner.

> **Theory of constraints:** TOC is a 'procedure based on identifying bottlenecks (constraints), maximising their use, subordinating other facilities to the demands of the bottleneck facilities, alleviating bottlenecks and re-evaluating the whole system' (*CIMA Official Terminology*).

Bottleneck: A bottleneck is a 'facility that has lower capacity than preceding or subsequent activities, and restricts output based on current capacity' (*CIMA Official Terminology*).

The capacity of a simple process is pictured below to illustrate the idea of a bottleneck.

Raw materials → Materials preparation → Component preparation → Final assembly → Sales

100 units per hour — 50 units per hour — 100 units per hour

In this example component preparation is the bottleneck. Due to the capacity of this bottleneck, the maximum level of sales is 50 units per hour. It will be important to identify this bottleneck and maximise efficiency **in this area** in order to maximise throughput.

Output through the bottleneck should never be delayed, otherwise sales will be lost. To avoid this happening **a buffer inventory should be built up immediately prior to the bottleneck. This is the only inventory that the business should hold.**

4.5.1 Throughput measures

There are a number of throughput measures that you need to be aware of. You will need to learn these formulae.

Formula to learn

Return per factory hour =

$$\frac{Sales\ price - material\ cost}{Time\ taken\ to\ produce\ a\ unit\ in\ the\ bottleneck}$$

This encourages managers to focus on managing bottleneck areas of the factory efficiently.

Formula to learn

Cost per factory hour =

$$\frac{Total\ factory\ cost}{Total\ time\ available\ in\ the\ bottleneck}$$

Total factory cost includes conversion costs (labour and overhead) and also inventory costs.

This encourages managers to consider managing all factory costs (including inventory levels) and to switch resources where possible from non-bottleneck areas into the bottleneck area in order to build capacity in the bottleneck.

Formula to learn

Throughput accounting (TA) ratio =

$$\frac{Return\ per\ factory\ hour}{Cost\ per\ factory\ hour}$$

This ratio can be used to rank the order in which different products should be produced.

The **higher** the ratio, the **more profitable** the product and company.

Activity 2: TA ratio

Y Co has 100 machines available in an area that has been identified as a bottleneck.

Each machine has the capacity to be used for 50 hours a week.

Each unit produced incurs 45 minutes of time in the bottleneck area.

The product is sold for $2 and incurs materials costs of $0.5 per unit.

BPP
LEARNING
MEDIA

Total factory costs are $10,000 per week.

Required

What is the TA ratio for Y Co? (Give your answer to one decimal place.)

[   ]

Solution

Exam focus

An assessment question is likely to require a firm grasp of the terminology involved with the theory of constraints.

5 Business process reengineering (BPR)

BPR is about the **fundamental** rethinking and **radical redesign** of **existing** business **processes** to achieve **dramatic** improvements. Information technology is often a factor that enables BPR.

A move from a traditional functional plant layout to a JIT cellular product layout is a simple example of BPR.

BPR can also support TQM because it aims to find innovative ways of meeting customer needs more effectively.

For example, designing new products to better meet customer needs might currently involve a **sequential flow** of ideas from one department to another. BPR would help to co-ordinate the work of different departments so that their design ideas are worked on **in parallel** (ie at the same time) to achieve dramatically quicker and more cost-effective product development. In this case information systems (eg CAD) could enable more effective co-ordination, but BPR **does not always** involve IT.

Based on a problem at a **major car manufacturer**:

A company employs 25 staff to perform the standard accounting task of matching goods received notes with orders and then with invoices. About 80% of their time is spent trying to find out why 20% of the set of three documents do not agree.

One way of improving the situation would have been to computerise the existing process to facilitate matching. This would have helped, but BPR went further: why accept any incorrect orders at all? What if all the orders are entered onto a computerised database? When goods arrive at the goods inwards department they either agree to goods that have been ordered or they don't. Goods that agree to an order are accepted and paid for. Goods that are not agreed are sent back to the supplier. There are no files of unmatched items and time is not wasted trying to sort out these files.

The reengineering of the process resulted in gains for the company: less staff time wasted, quicker payment for suppliers, lower inventory and lower investment in working capital.

Activity 3: BPR

Required
Which of these statements are true?

Select all that apply.

A   Process reengineering is all about incremental changes to how business processes operate.

B   Material handling is an example of a business process.

C   A business process is a series of bottlenecks that need to be managed.

D   Process reengineering requires the redesign of how work is done through activities.

E   Process reengineering focuses on simplification, improved quality, enhanced customer satisfaction and cost reduction.

Solution

Exam focus
Make sure you can link the concept of BPR to TQM and JIT, which are both likely to require process redesign.

Chapter summary

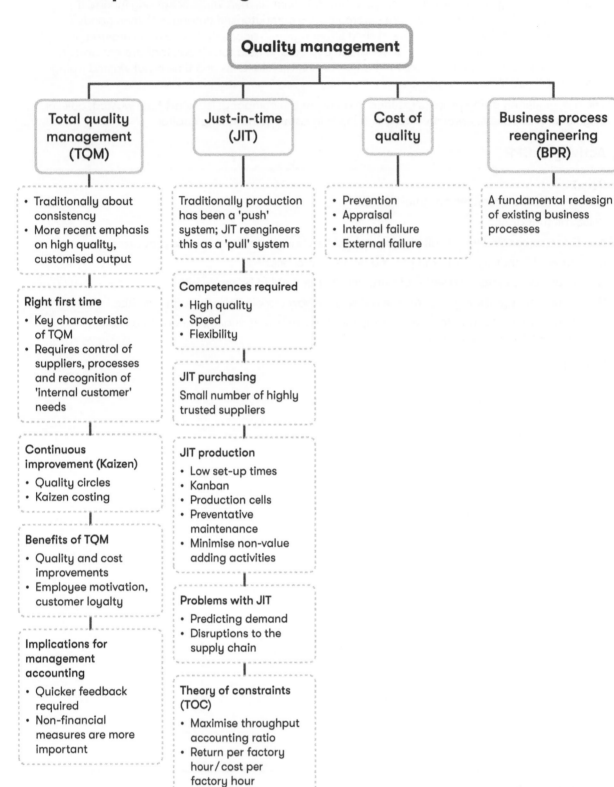

Quality management

Total quality management (TQM)

- Traditionally about consistency
- More recent emphasis on high quality, customised output

Right first time
- Key characteristic of TQM
- Requires control of suppliers, processes and recognition of 'internal customer' needs

Continuous improvement (Kaizen)
- Quality circles
- Kaizen costing

Benefits of TQM
- Quality and cost improvements
- Employee motivation, customer loyalty

Implications for management accounting
- Quicker feedback required
- Non-financial measures are more important

Just-in-time (JIT)

Traditionally production has been a 'push' system; JIT reengineers this as a 'pull' system

Competences required
- High quality
- Speed
- Flexibility

JIT purchasing
Small number of highly trusted suppliers

JIT production
- Low set-up times
- Kanban
- Production cells
- Preventative maintenance
- Minimise non-value adding activities

Problems with JIT
- Predicting demand
- Disruptions to the supply chain

Theory of constraints (TOC)
- Maximise throughput accounting ratio
- Return per factory hour / cost per factory hour
- Inventory only prior to bottleneck

Cost of quality
- Prevention
- Appraisal
- Internal failure
- External failure

Business process reengineering (BPR)
A fundamental redesign of existing business processes

BPP LEARNING MEDIA

Key terms

TQM: TQM is 'an integrated and comprehensive system of planning and controlling all business functions so that products or services are produced which meet or exceed customer expectations. TQM is a philosophy of business behaviour, embracing principles such as employee involvement, continuous improvement at all levels and customer focus [...]' (*CIMA Official Terminology*).

Just-in-time: JIT is a system whose objective is to produce or to procure products or components as they are required by a customer or for use, rather than for inventory (*CIMA, 2005*).

Throughput: Throughput (return) is defined as sales revenue less direct material costs. Also referred to as throughput contribution.

Theory of constraints: TOC is a 'procedure based on identifying bottlenecks (constraints), maximising their use, subordinating other facilities to the demands of the bottleneck facilities, alleviating bottlenecks and re-evaluating the whole system' (*CIMA Official Terminology*).

Bottleneck: A bottleneck is a 'facility that has lower capacity than preceding or subsequent activities, and restricts output based on current capacity' (*CIMA Official Terminology*).

Activity answers

Activity 1: Non-conformance costs
The correct answer is:

2.0%

	20X6		20X7	
	$'000	% sales	$'000	% sales
Prevention costs				
Quality control	40	0.5%	120	1.4%
Appraisal costs				
Inspection of WIP	85	1.1%	70	0.8%
Internal failure costs				
Re-work	125		60	
Scrap	60		23	
	185	2.3%	83	1.0%
External failure costs				
Returns	35		15	
Complaints	50		20	
	85	1.1%	35	0.4%
Total cost of quality $'000	395		308	
Total cost of quality % sales		5% (395/7,900 × 100)		3.6% (308/8,472 × 100)

Total costs of quality are falling demonstrating that as more is being spent on improving conformance failure is falling.

Total costs of quality have fallen by 1.4% as a percentage of sales (5%–3.6%).

Conformance costs (prevention + appraisal) have risen by 0.6% (2.2%–1.6%).

Non-conformance costs (internal + external failure) have fallen by 2% (3.4%–1.4%).

External failure costs have fallen by 0.7% (1.1%–0.4%).

Activity 2: TA ratio
The correct answer is:

1.0

Return per factory hour =

$$\frac{2-0.5}{0.75} = 2$$

Cost per factory hour =

$$\frac{10,000}{5,000} = 2$$

Throughput accounting ratio =

$$\frac{2}{2} = 1$$

Note. This means the factory Y Co is breaking even, as total throughput in units is 5,000 hours/0.75 = 6666.67 units per week. This means that total throughput in $s is 6666.67 × $1.5 per unit = $10,000 per week which just covers total factory costs of $10,000 per week.

Activity 3: BPR

The correct answers are:

- Material handling is an example of a business process.
- Process reengineering requires the redesign of how work is done through activities.
- Process reengineering focuses on simplification, improved quality, enhanced customer satisfaction and cost reduction.

Notes on incorrect answers:

It is Kaizen that is about incremental change.

A business process is a collection of linked tasks.

BPP
LEARNING
MEDIA

Test your learning

1 **Required**

Which of the following is/are correct?

A Cost of conformance = Cost of prevention + Cost of internal failure

B Cost of conformance = Cost of internal failure + Cost of external failure

C Cost of non-conformance = Cost of internal failure + Cost of external failure

D Cost of conformance = Cost of appraisal + Cost of prevention

E Cost of non-conformance = Cost of prevention + Cost of appraisal

F Cost of non-conformance = Cost of appraisal + Cost of external failure

2 **Required**

Which of the categories of quality cost is NOT covered by the following examples?

(a) Administration of quality control

(b) Product liability costs

(c) Acceptance testing

(d) Losses due to lower selling prices for sub-quality goods

A Prevention

B Appraisal

C Internal failure

D External failure

3 JIT purchasing requires [▼] deliveries [▼] the time the raw materials and parts are needed.

In a JIT environment, the responsibility for the quality of goods lies with the [▼].

Required

Complete the preceding statements using the following list:

Picklist:

supplier

well in advance of

large, infrequent

as near as possible to

small, frequent

purchaser

4 The theory of constraints is an approach to production management which aims to maximise sales revenue less [▼] . It focuses on internal processes that are [▼] which act as [▼] .

Required

Complete the preceding statements using the following list:

Picklist:

bottlenecks

material costs

sales revenue

inventory

constraints

conversion costs

5   TA ratio = [▼] per factory hour divided by [▼] per factory hour.

Required

Complete the preceding statement using the following list:

Picklist:

Bottlenecks

Material costs

Sales revenue

Throughput contribution

Total factory cost

Conversion cost

6   **Required**

Which of the following statements relate to Kaizen costing as opposed to standard costing?

A   Employees are often viewed as the cause of problems.

B   Costs are reduced by implementing continuous improvement.

C   The aim is to meet cost performance targets.

D   The aim is to achieve cost reduction targets.

E   It is assumed that current manufacturing conditions remain unchanged

3

Value management

Syllabus learning outcomes

Having studied this chapter, you will be able to work through the following syllabus outcomes:

Syllabus area A: Managing the cost of creating value
3   Value management techniques to manage costs and improve value creation
a   Target costing
b   Value chain analysis
c   Life cycle costing

Exam context

In the exam, you will be expected to demonstrate competence in the following representative task statements:

- Calculate target costs and target prices and identify methods to reduce any cost gaps
- Determine how research and development, product design, process environment, production, distribution, marketing and customer service work together to improve products and services for customers
- Analyse the value chain and management of contribution/profit generated throughout the chain
- Understand life cycle costing and its implications for marketing strategies
- Use life cycle costing and budgeting in costing decisions

Chapter overview

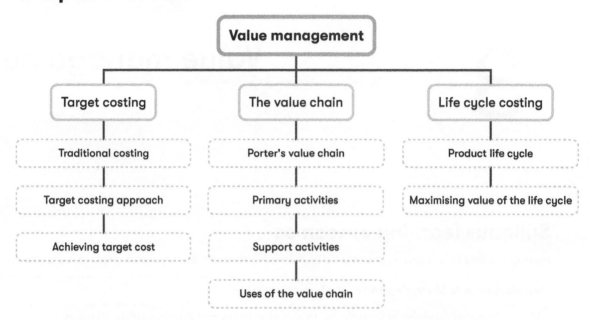

1 Introduction

Cost transformation must always be linked to the value that organisations create.

The modern business environment involves shorter product life cycles and a greater emphasis on delivering value for customers. This chapter looks at how a business can enhance its profits in such environments, focusing on what the customer is prepared to pay and how value is created.

The syllabus specifically mentions target costing (Section 2), life cycle costing (Section 3) and value chain (Section 4); all of these techniques aim to create competitive advantage and to enhance long-term profits.

2 Target costing

In increasingly competitive markets, there is a pressure for organisations to **redesign their products continually,** with the result that **product life cycles** have become much **shorter**. This creates challenges in terms of ensuring that value is created for shareholders during the life cycle.

The **planning, design and development stages of a product's cycle** are **critical to the value creation process**. It has been suggested that in many industries 80% of the cost of manufacturing is determined by the **design** of the product.

2.1 Traditional approach to costing

A commonly used approach to costing involves the following steps:

(a) Develop a product and determine the expected standard production costs

(b) Set a selling price (probably based on cost) with a resulting profit or loss

(c) Control costs through monthly variance analysis

2.2 Target costing approach

KEY TERM

> **Target cost:** A product cost estimate derived by subtracting a desired profit margin from a competitive market price (*CIMA Official Terminology*).

The **target costing approach** is to:

(a) Develop a product concept and the target price customers would be willing to pay

(b) Subtract the desired profit margin from the price to determine target cost

(c) Design the product so that it is capable of being manufactured at target cost

Unlike traditional costing (eg standard costing) target costing is influenced by **external factors** (the price people are willing to pay) and **aims to reduce costs, not simply to control costs** at their expected level.

2.2.1 Setting the target price

Pricing is covered in detail in Chapter 7; a few of the key issues are introduced here.

Target market share	This will be influenced by the firm's **strategy** which might be to dominate the market and aim for high market share (which may require a lower price), or to focus on small market niches and therefore to accept lower market share (which may allow higher prices to be set).
Pricing strategy of rivals	Products that are **varieties of existing products** or **new brands of existing products** enter an already established market and therefore a competitive **price should be fairly easy to set**.
Anticipated demand	**Market research** will be used to estimate demand for new products.

2.2.2 Target cost

A target cost is calculated as:

	$
Target selling price	X
Less target profit	(X)
Target cost	X

A multi-disciplinary team consisting of representatives from a number of different business functions (purchasing, manufacturing, sales, distribution, etc) will then work **collaboratively** to determine the precise product design that will allow the target cost to be **achieved.**

2.3 Achieving target cost

The process of achieving the target cost will involve assessing the **estimated cost** of the product against the target.

If the estimated cost is greater than the target cost, there is a **cost gap.**

There are a number of techniques for addressing the cost gap so that the target cost can be achieved.

2.3.1 Value engineering (or analysis)

Value can be viewed from a number of different perspectives:
- **Cost value** is the cost of producing and selling an item
- **Exchange value** is the market value of the product or service
- **Use value** is what the article does; the purposes it fulfils (performance, reliability)
- **Esteem value** is the prestige the customer attaches to the product

Value engineering (or analysis) seeks to refine the **design** of the product to **reduce** unit cost (so cost value is the one aspect of value to be reduced) and to provide the same (or a better) use value at the lowest cost. Value engineering (or analysis) also attempts to maintain or enhance the **esteem value** of a product at the lowest cost.

The aim is to reduce cost without compromising other aspects of value.

The term 'value analysis' is more commonly used for describing enhancements to existing products, and 'value engineering' for completely new products.

2.3.2 Functional analysis

This involves breaking a product down into its various functions or attributes (eg for a laptop this might be touch screen facility, battery life, weight, processing speed) and estimating (through research/surveys) the amount a customer is prepared to pay for each.

The cost of each function is compared to the value of each function. If appropriate, the functions are modified to reduce cost or, if this is not possible, a function may be eliminated.

2.3.3 Reverse engineering

This involves stripping down a **competitor's** product and analysing their **product design** to provide insights on improving quality or reducing cost.

2.3.4 Other actions to close the cost gap

To implement cost reductions a number of basic actions can be considered:
- Reducing the number of components
- Using cheaper staff or materials
- Using standard components wherever possible
- Acquiring new, more efficient technology
- Training staff in more efficient techniques
- Cutting out non-value adding activities (see value chain in Section 3)

Activity 1: Target costing

A company is about to launch a new product which it believes can be sold for $125 per unit.

It is anticipated that 10,000 units will be sold at this price.

The investment required is estimated to be $1,562,500 and the company requires a return of 20% in the coming year.

Material costs are estimated to be $84.50 per unit.

Estimations for the labour time needed to construct one unit are:

1½ hours – 25% probability

2 hours – 50% probability

2½ hours – 25% probability

Labour costs $7 per hour, and variable overheads will be incurred at a rate of $1.50 per labour hour.

Required
Calculate the cost gap facing the company. (Work to two decimal places.)

$ [   ]

Solution

Exam focus

An assessment question is likely to ask you to calculate target costs or target prices or to identify methods to reduce any cost gaps.

3 Value chain

> **Value chain:** 'The sequence of business activities by which, from the perspective of the end user, value is added to the products and services produced by an entity' (*CIMA Official Terminology*).

Porter's value chain model (*Porter, 1985*) can be used to analyse how the activities of an organisation can work to process inputs, add value to them in some way, and generate outputs for customers.

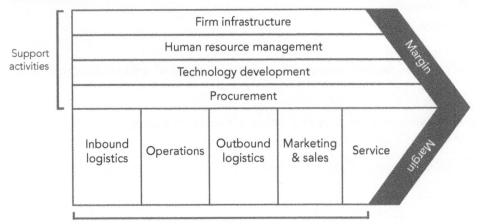

Primary activities

3.1 Primary activities

Primary activities are directly related to production, sales, marketing, delivery and service.

Primary activity	Comment
Inbound logistics	Receiving, handling and storing inputs to the production system (warehousing, transport, inventory control etc)
Operations	Converting resource inputs into a final product
Outbound logistics	Storing the product and its distribution to customers (packaging, warehousing, testing etc)
Marketing and sales	Informing customers about the product, persuading them to buy it (eg advertising, promotion)
After-sales service	Installing products, repairing them, upgrading them etc

3.2 Support activities

Support activities provide purchased inputs, human resources, technology and infrastructural functions to support the primary activities.

Support activity	Comment
Procurement	Acquiring the resource inputs to the primary activities (such as purchase of materials, subcomponents equipment)
Technology development	Designing products, improving processes and/or resource utilisation
Human resource management	Recruiting, training, developing and rewarding people

Support activity	Comment
Firm infrastructure	Planning, finance, quality control

Linkages between these activities or processes (ie competences) allow the firm to turn raw materials, non-current assets, manpower and capital into finished goods and profits.

3.3 Uses of the value chain

An organisation **'creates' value** either by carrying out its activities more efficiently than other organisations, or by linking them together (internally or with external parties such as suppliers) in such a way as to provide a unique product or service.

As **competitive advantage** is gained either from providing **better customer value for equivalent cost** or **equivalent customer value for lower cost**, value chain analysis is essential to determine **where in an organisation's value chain costs can be lowered or value can be enhanced**.

According to Porter (1985), an organisation can develop sustainable competitive advantage by following one of two strategies.

(a) **Low-cost strategy.** Essentially this is a strategy of cost leadership, which involves achieving a lower cost than competitors via, for example, economies of scale and tight cost control. An understanding of the **cost drivers** for each activity will be important here.

(b) **Differentiation strategy.** This involves creating something that customers perceive as being unique via brand loyalty, superior customer service, product design and features, technology etc.

Activity 2: Value chain

Required

To which part of the value chain does the selection of a new supplier belong?

A   Technology development

B   Inbound logistics

C   Firm infrastructure

D   Procurement

Solution

4 Life cycle costing

Traditionally the costs and revenues of a product are assessed on a financial year or period-by-period basis. In contrast, life cycle costing aims to cost a product, service, customer or project over its **entire life cycle.**

Life cycle costing considers all the costs that will be incurred from design to abandonment of a new product and compares these to the revenues that can be generated from selling this product at different target prices throughout the product's life (pricing is covered in Chapter 7).

The **purpose** of **life cycle costing** is to assess the **total costs** of a product over its **entire life** and to assess the **expected profitability** from the product over its full life. Products that are **not expected to be profitable** after allowing for design and development costs or clean-up costs should **not be considered** for commercial development.

Life cycle costing is very useful in the **modern competitive environment,** in which products often have a short life cycle and when a large portion of costs will be committed prior to production commencing.

4.1 Product life cycle

The product life cycle (PLC) can be divided into five stages:

(a) **Development**. The product has a research or design and development stage. Costs are incurred but the product is not yet on the market and there are no sales revenues.

(b) **Introduction**. The product is launched. Capital expenditure costs may be incurred in order to increase the production capacity as sales demand grows.

(c) **Growth**. The product gains a bigger market as demand builds up. Sales revenues increase and the product begins to make a profit.

(d) **Maturity**. Eventually, the growth in demand for the product will slow down and it will enter a period of relative maturity, when sales have reached a peak and are fairly stable. This should be the most profitable phase of the product's life.

(e) **Decline**. At some stage, the market will have bought enough of the product and it will therefore reach 'saturation point'. Demand will start to fall. Eventually it will become a loss-maker and this is the time when the organisation may decide to exit the market.

The level of sales and profits earned over a life cycle can be illustrated diagrammatically as follows.

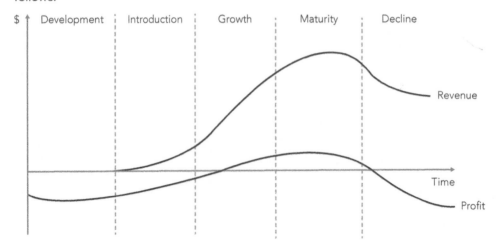

Illustration 1: Life cycle costing

Company X is in a high tech industry and is often first to market with new technological advances. It has recently spent $500,000 designing and developing a new product. The new product is expected to have a life of four years.

The anticipated performance of this product is as follows:

	Year 1	Year 2	Year 3	Year 4
Sales volume (units)	4,000	9,000	30,000	10,000
	$	$	$	$
Marketing costs	1.2 million	0.4 million	0.1 million	0.1 million
Variable production cost per unit	249	249	199	149
Customer service cost per unit	100	100	60	75
Disposal costs				0.2 million

Required

What is the expected life cycle cost per unit? (Give your answer to two decimal places.)

$ _____

Solution

The correct answer is:

$321.64

	Year 1	Year 2	Year 3	Year 4	Total
Sales volume (units)	4,000	9,000	30,000	10,000	53000
Total variable cost per unit ($)	349	349	259	224	
Total variable cost $m	1.396	3.141	7.770	2.240	14.547
Marketing $m	1.2	0.4	0.1	0.1	1.8
Development cost $m	0.5	0	0	0	0.5
Disposal costs $m				0.2	0.2
					17.047
Life cycle cost per unit					$321.64

4.2 Maximising value over the product life cycle

There are a number of ways that value can be increased over the life cycle.

4.2.1 Cost management

Approximately 70%–90% of a product's life cycle costs are determined by decisions made early in the life cycle at the design and development stage. **Target costing** aims to reduce costs incurred due to the product's design and occurs at the **start** of the life cycle.

In the early months of the introduction stage an assessment can be made as to whether the target cost is being achieved. If there is a 'cost gap' then appropriate cost control measures can be implemented (see target costing in Section 2).

Kaizen costing could be applied during the **post-introduction stage** of the life cycle. This focuses on achieving **small, incremental improvements**.

During the post-introduction phase labour time should be expected to get shorter, with experience, in the production of items which are made **largely by labour effort** (rather than by a highly mechanised process); this is sometimes called a learning curve or a **learning effect** (although this learning process does not continue indefinitely.

The learning curve effect can be applied more broadly than just to labour. There are also efficiency gains in other areas:

(a) As methods are standardised **material wastage and spoilage** will decrease.

(b) Machine costs may decrease as **better use is made of the equipment**.

(c) **Process redesign may take place.** As understanding of the process increases, improvements and shortcuts may be developed.

This broader impact of learning is sometimes referred to as an experience curve or as an **experience effect**.

Consideration could also be given to the **value chain model;** ie the **linkages** between different activities and costs. For example, greater investment in getting a product to the marketplace very quickly will give the product as long a span as possible without competitors' rival products in the marketplace. This may increase the value created by the product in the long -run.

4.2.2 Marketing initiatives

(a) **Maximising customer awareness at the start of the introduction phase**

Customers are initially unaware of the product, and the organisation may have to spend heavily on advertising to bring the product to the attention of the market.

(b) **Minimise breakeven time**

Pricing strategies will affect both contribution and volumes generated. A short breakeven time may be very important for liquidity purposes. This is an argument for considering a low price strategy at the start of the product life cycle (pricing strategies are covered in Chapter 7).

(c) **Extend the length of the life cycle itself**

The product may be modified or improved, as a means of sustaining this phase of the life cycle as long as possible.

Exam focus

You need a good understanding of the stages of the product life cycle and the techniques for managing value at different stages.

Chapter summary

Value management

Target costing

A reaction to shorter product life cycles

Traditional costing

Cost + Mark-up = Price

Target costing approach
- Target price – Mark-up = Target cost
- Price depends on rivals, demand and target market share
- Margin depends on strategy and life cycle

Achieving target cost
- Collaborative multi-disciplinary approach to eliminating a cost gap
- Value analysis (or engineering)
- Functional analysis
- Reverse engineering

The value chain

Porter's value chain

Analysis of how to create competitive advantage

Primary activities
- Directly related to production and sales
- Inbound and outbound logistics, operations, marketing and sales, after-sales service

Support activities
- Support primary activities
- Procurement, technology development, human resource management, firm infrastructure

Uses of the value chain

To analyse how to create value either via cost leadership or differentiation

Life cycle costing

Assess expected profits of the whole lifetime of a product, including pre- and post-production costs

Product life cycle
- Development
- Introduction
- Growth
- Maturity
- Decline

Maximising value of the life cycle
- Cost management and product design
- Marketing initiatives
- Kaizen costing

BPP LEARNING MEDIA

Key terms

Target cost: A product cost estimate derived by subtracting a desired profit margin from a competitive market price (*CIMA Official Terminology*).

Value chain: 'The sequence of business activities by which, from the perspective of the end user, value is added to the products and services produced by an entity' (*CIMA Official Terminology*).

Activity answers

Activity 1: Target costing

The correct answer is:

$7.75

		$
Selling price		125.00
Target profit		31.25
Target cost		93.75

		$
Expected cost		$
Material		84.50
Labour (W) (2 × 7)		14.00
Variable overhead (2 × 1.50)		3.00
		101.50

		$
Cost gap		7.75

Workings

Investment $1,562,500 × 0.2 = target profit of $312,500

Profit per unit = $312,500/10,000 = $31.25

Expected time for labour

X	p	px
1½ hours	0.25	0.375
2 hours	0.50	1.000
2½ hours	0.25	0.625
$\sum$px		2.000

Activity 2: Value chain

The correct answer is:

Procurement

Procurement is the process of acquiring resource inputs, and supplier selection is a part of this.

Test your learning

1 **Required**
Put the three terms below in the correct order to represent the traditional costing process.
- Selling price
- Cost
- Profit

(1) [   ]

(2) [   ]

(3) [   ]

2 **Required**
Put the three terms below in the correct order to represent the target costing process.
- Selling price
- Cost
- Profit

(1) [   ]

(2) [   ]

(3) [   ]

3 **Required**
Complete the following statement.

[▼] is cost avoidance or cost prevention before production whereas

[▼] is cost reduction during production.

Picklist:

Value engineering

Kaizen costing

4 **Required**
Match the terms to the correct definitions.

The prestige the customer attaches to the product is [▼]

The market value of the product is [▼]

What the product does is [▼]

The cost of producing and selling the product is [▼]

Picklist:

cost value

exchange value

use value

esteem value

5 **Required**
Is the following statement true or false?

Value chain analysis involves the study of linkages between primary and support activities within a company.

A True

B False

4

Data for decision making

Syllabus learning outcomes

Having studied this chapter, you will be able to work through the following syllabus outcomes:

Syllabus area B: Capital investment decision-making
1   Data required for decision making
a   Relevant cash flows
b   Non-financial information
2   The steps and pertinent issues in the decision-making process
a   Investment decision-making process

Exam context

In the exam, you will be expected to demonstrate competence in the following representative task statements:

- Determine relevant cash flows and their timings for the entire project lifecycle including consideration of tax, inflation and working capital (also partly covered in Chapter 5)
- Determine non-financial factors in medium-term decision making
- Determine the benefits, costs, and common problems with collecting, analysing and presenting high-quality data
- Determine the role of business intelligence systems in identifying new business opportunities and reducing costs
- Understand the process of investment decision making, including origination of proposals, creation of capital budgets, go/no-go decisions on individual projects (where judgements on qualitative issues interact with financial analysis)

Chapter overview

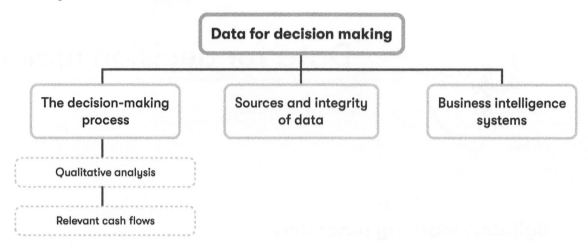

1 Introduction

The quality of decision making depends on the quality and type of data that is available to decision makers. This is especially relevant to capital projects (which is the theme of this section of the syllabus).

Capital projects involve a considerable investment of money in the expectations of future benefits. For such investment decisions to be reliable, they must be based on appropriate data.

This chapter considers the phases of the capital investment decision-making process, **paying particular attention to the aspects of the decision phase itself** (especially to relevant cash flows for financial analysis as this is developed later in the syllabus).

The chapter concludes by exploring different sources of data and the implications of technological advances such as business intelligence (BI) systems.

2 The decision-making process

Capital investment projects involve the outlay of **large sums of money** in the expectation of **benefits that may take several years to accrue**.

The decision whether to proceed with a capital investment project is normally made by a **capital expenditure committee**. As a control mechanism, the committee should follow **a process that covers the following phases:**

1. Creation phase	2. Decision phase Part 1: Qualitative (non-financial) analysis	3. Decision phase Part 2: Financial analysis	4. Implementation phase
Proposals for capital investment projects can come from: • A review of the **environment** to identify opportunities and threats • Proposals from **technical experts** within the organisation • **Incentive schemes** may help to stimulate the creation of new ideas	Qualitative analysis assesses the potential **impact of the proposal on stakeholders** and considers whether the project will support the organisation's overall **strategy** to fulfil its mission. An **initial feasibility study** is conducted to ascertain whether each proposal is broadly viable.	Each proposal is assessed using the organisation's preferred investment appraisal techniques (see Chapter 5). This is likely to be based on **relevant costing.** After financial and non-financial analysis, the **committee decides** whether to proceed with or abandon the project.	This should involve a **post-completion review (or audit)** ie monitoring the performance of the project to identify and address any current or forecast performance issues. This should be an **independent review**, not performed by people involved with the decision to approve the project. It should aim to **learn** from any mistakes that have arisen in the project appraisal process.

Advances in technology allow theses phases to be performed in increasingly sophisticated ways, such as through the use of business intelligence (BI) systems (see later).

Exam focus

Assessment questions will require a sound understanding of the stages of the decision-making process.

3 Qualitative analysis

The viability of a capital investment project is not limited to its financial performance. At the qualitative analysis stage, the committee needs to consider:

(a) Does the investment help the organisation to meet its **mission**?

All organisations should have agreed a set of objectives which seek to deliver the overall mission. It is important that any new projects support rather than undermine its mission.

(b) What **impact** will the investment have on relevant **stakeholders**?

Relevant stakeholders will vary according to the circumstances, but may include staff, customers, suppliers, the government, competitors and the general public.

> ### Exam focus
> Assessment questions will test your understanding of non-financial factors that impact decision making.

Example

East West Railways (EWR), a listed transport company, has invested in cutting-edge technology on all its trains which removes the need for a human driver or on-board guard. Although a substantial financial investment has been made, EWR expects the savings in staff salaries to exceed the costs by a dramatic margin and has therefore undertaken the project without consulting any stakeholders.

Stakeholders who would be impacted by this decision and should have been considered before the project is implemented include:

Employees

Staff are likely to be resistant to the new technology as it will involve large-scale redundancies. They have the power to disrupt services through industrial action and therefore need to be involved in the implementation.

Customers

Customers may be uneasy about having unstaffed trains and therefore use other forms of transport. EWR needs to demonstrate to customers that their safety has been considered and explain how incidents (eg a disruptive passenger on a train) would be managed.

Shareholders

EWR needs to ensure that the project is consistent with the shareholders' attitude to risk and provides an acceptable return. Of particular concern here will be the amount of time shareholders will need to wait to receive a return on their investment and the risks associated with these returns. Ultimately, shareholders can hold directors to account at the AGM or sell their shares.

Suppliers

Given the cutting-edge nature of the technology, EWR needs to be confident that the supplier can deliver what has been promised. This is particularly important given the potential safety implications and the risk of major disruption if the technology fails.

Government/regulators

Rail providers often face state regulation. EWR will need to ensure that it meets whatever standards the regulator or government has set in terms of service. Failure to do so could result in their licence to operate being withdrawn.

Activity 1: Qualitative analysis

The following statements have been made about qualitative analysis in the context of assessing capital investment projects.

(a) Qualitative analysis may cause a financially attractive project to be rejected.

(b) Qualitative analysis should consider internal stakeholders as well as external ones.

(c) Qualitative analysis is only relevant for organisations which do not have profit maximisation as the primary objective.

(d) Qualitative analysis considers how the organisation's objectives may be altered in order to make the project viable.

Required

Which of these statements is/are true?

A (a) only

B (a) and (b) only

C (b) and (c) only

D (a), (b), (c) and (d)

Solution

4 Relevant cash flows for financial analysis

> **Relevant cash flows:** When assessing the financial viability of a capital project, only cash flows that arise as a consequence of the investment should be considered. These are described as **relevant cash flows**.

4.1 Examples of relevant cash flows

Examples of relevant cash flows for a project include the following:

- The purchase of assets for the project as well as any future residual value or disposal cost
- **Additional** contribution generated (sales less variable costs)
- **Additional** fixed costs incurred as a result of undertaking the project
- Any benefit lost as a result of undertaking this project (eg diverting staff from another profit-making part of the business to work on the project); this is referred to as the **opportunity cost**
- Any loss avoided as a result of undertaking the project (eg not having to pay redundancy to staff who would otherwise have lost their jobs)

4.2 Examples of non-relevant cash flows

However, the following costs are not relevant and **should therefore be excluded** from any relevant cash flow calculation:

- Non-cash flows such as depreciation or apportioned fixed overheads
- Costs which have already been incurred, committed to or will be incurred regardless of whether the investment is made. For example, market research may have been undertaken to assess the project. This money will not be refunded if the organisation decides not to undertake the project and therefore is not a relevant cash flow. These are often referred to as **sunk costs**.
- Any costs relating to the **financing** of the project (eg interest or dividend payments); these are normally excluded as they are reflected in the cost of capital (also known as the discount factor).

Exam focus

Relevant cash flows are a very important concept and can be examined numerically or as a discussion OT question.

Activity 2: Relevant costing

The manager of a factory has been asked to build a prototype of a new machine for a customer. The manager has identified a number of potential costs and revenues.

Required

Identify those that are relevant to the decision as to whether to accept the contract to build the prototype.

A   The machine will require 35 hours on a specialist machine; this is approximately the number of hours available on this machine in a working week. The machine is leased on an annual basis that costs the equivalent of $800 per week.

B   The customer has offered to pay $500,000 for the machine.

C   The machine will use a special component that the company purchased three years ago at a cost of $5,000 and never used. The component will not be replaced if it is used on this contract.

D   A technical engineer will have to be taken off other work to work on this machine. The company will have to pay a consultancy $3,000 to complete the engineer's other work.

E   The company's technicians will spend a total of 500 hours on this machine. The technicians are paid by the hour, but they have a guaranteed 40-hour working week. There is sufficient slack time for them to complete this machine without having to charge overtime.

F   Most of the materials for the machine will be taken from the company's normal inventory. Nothing will have to be purchased specially but any materials used will need to be replaced.

G   The factory manager will spend a total of 12 days working on this contract. This will be during normal working hours. Deputy managers and supervisors will cover the factory manager's day-to-day tasks in addition to their normal duties. The factory manager is paid $300 per working day.

Solution

5 Sources and integrity of data

Effective decision making relies on appropriate source data which can be processed into meaningful information.

5.1 Data collection

Primary data is gathered by the organisation to meet a specific research need. Because it is unique to the project, it is more expensive and time-consuming to gather than secondary data.

Examples of primary data include questionnaires, focus groups and in-depth interviews. In each case, the interaction is planned in advance in order to meet the specific data needs.

Secondary data involves using existing data. This is much faster and cheaper than commissioning primary data, but may not be sufficiently bespoke to the information needs of the specific project.

For example, a committee may use existing internal management information to forecast the cost of a new project. It may also collect external information which is publicly available (eg from the UK Office of National Statistics) or purchase existing data from specialist providers (eg Experian).

Activity 3: Data types

Fruit Tree Ltd is a small business that manufactures organic soft drinks. Its traditional approach to drink-making is labour intensive but enables it to stand out in a highly competitive market place. It sells its products in two local farm shops and is now considering whether to build a new production facility in order to double production. The directors are seeking further data to inform their decision making.

Required

Which two of the factors below are likely to encourage Fruit Tree Ltd to use secondary data to inform their decision making as opposed to primary data?

A   An ideal site has become available but the lease would need to be signed quickly.

B   Fruit Tree prides itself on a range of drinks which are 'unlike anything else on the market'.

C   Fruit Tree will struggle to secure the money needed for this investment.

D   The local drinks market has been disrupted by the recent arrival of a new competitor.

Solution

5.2 Information analysis and presentation

The source data needs to be processed in order to create information which possess a number of qualities. These are often known as the qualities of good information:

Accurate: Is the information free from error?

Complete: Does the information include all the data required?

Cost-beneficial: Do the benefits of the information exceed the costs of obtaining it?

User-targeted: Is the information presented in a manner that it appropriate for the user?

Relevant: Can the information be used to inform decision making?

Authoritative: Does the information come from a reliable, credible source?

Timely: Is the information received in time to inform decision making?

Easy to use: Can the information be accessed and viewed without difficulty?

 Illustration 1: Information

Fruit Tree Ltd (see the previous activity) has decided to use secondary data to inform its capital investment decision making. Having typed 'data for business decision making' into a popular search engine, it has found a website, data4u.co.uk, which advertises 'data for all your business decisions'. Data4u has offered to provide market information about the soft drink industry to Fruit Tree Ltd's precise specification for a very low fee within two working days.

Given a looming deadline and a lack of funds, Fruit Tree's directors have decided to purchase Data4u's information.

Required
To what extent will Data4u's data meet the qualities of good information?

Solution

The correct answer is:

Assuming that Data4u honours its commitment, the information will be timely and user-targeted. However, the information is **not authoritative** as Fruit Tree Ltd has no information about Data4u's reputation or reliability. As a result, there is a risk that the information will **be inaccurate, incomplete, irrelevant and difficult to use.** On that basis, the information is **unlikely to be cost-beneficial** as, in spite of a low cost, the benefits may be non-existent.

Exam focus

The characteristics of data and information are likely topics to be examined.

6 Business intelligence systems

Business intelligence systems: Business intelligence (BI) systems aim to provide forward looking analysis to support decision making, based on a combination of financial and non-financial data. BI systems will assemble information from all of an organisation's information systems across its whole value chain. As such they will be underpinned by a **data warehouse** (a large relational database).

6.1 Main stages

BI systems follow four main stages:

(a) **Collect data**

The analysis of data to identify patterns and relationships is sometimes described as **data mining**. The more robust this source data is, the more reliable the output will be. For that reason, BI systems normally focus on an organisation's internal data, which has been expertly prepared and tested. However, BI systems can also incorporate data from outside the organisation. BI systems can achieve this through the use of complex statistical algorithms.

(b) **Prepare data for analysis**

BI systems can process both structured data (content presented in standard, normally tabular, format) and unstructured data (content not in a standard format such as interviews, pictures, videos, etc); the term data lake is often used to describe a collection of unprocessed, unstructured data.

This makes BI systems superior to traditional business analytics software which is limited to structured data.

(c) **Run queries**

Having processed the data, BI systems can run complex queries that predict outcomes depending on a wide range of variables (sometimes referred to as 'what if' analysis).

(d) **Provide visualisations**

The BI system's visualisations are presented in a user-friendly manner. This is often in a dashboard format which presents the main headlines using clear graphics and allows users to drill down into the data if required.

BI systems are especially useful in quickly producing ad-hoc, non-standardised reports. BI systems have been applied successfully in many commercial fields, including:

- **Customer behaviour analysis**: what do customers prefer, what profit margins do we make on their account?
- **Contract negotiation**: real-time information on similar contracts with suppliers or customers
- **Impact of marketing campaigns**: tracking effectiveness, ensuring money is spent most effectively
- **Internal benchmarking**: comparing the operational processes of different divisions.

Real life example

The oil firm Shell uses complex machinery to extract oil from underground, both on land and at sea. These machines are used intensively in harsh environments and, at some point, break down. The longer each machine is out of action, the more money is wasted.

Shell therefore used BI systems to reduce downtime. It started by fitting sensors to key machine parts so that detailed data could be extracted and analysed. This analysis enabled predictions to be made about which parts were likely to be nearing the end of their useful lives, allowing the purchase of spare parts to be made proactively rather than reactively. This resulted in the average wait for a spare part to fall from 48 hours to less than 45 minutes.

Chapter summary

Data for decision making

The decision-making process

- Creation phase
- Qualitative (non-financial) analysis
- Financial analysis
- Implementation

Qualitative analysis

- Does the investment help the organisation to meet its objectives?
- What impact will the investment have on relevant stakeholders?

Relevant cash flows

- Relevant cash flows
- Opportunity costs
- Avoidable costs
- Non-relevant costs

Sources and integrity of data

- Primary data
- Secondary data
- Qualities of good information: **accurate**

Business intelligence systems

1. Collect data
2. Prepare data for analysis
3. Run queries
4. Provide visualisations

Key terms

Relevant cash flows: When assessing the financial viability of a capital project, only cash flows that arise as a consequence of the investment should be considered. These are described as **relevant cash flows**.

Business intelligence systems: Business intelligence (BI) systems aim to provide forward looking analysis to support decision making, based on a combination of financial and non-financial data. BI systems will assemble information from all of an organisation's information systems across its whole value chain. As such they will be underpinned by a **data warehouse** (a large relational database).

Activity answers

Activity 1: Qualitative analysis

The correct answer is:

(a) and (b) only

Qualitative analysis may identify reasons why a financially attractive project is not appropriate (eg adverse impact on a key stakeholder). It should consider internal stakeholders (eg staff) as well as external ones (eg customers).

Qualitative analysis is appropriate for all organisations, even those with a primary objective to maximise shareholder wealth. Where there is a conflict between the organisation's objectives and the project's impact, the organisation's objectives take priority and should not be compromised.

Activity 2: Relevant costing

The correct answers are:

- The customer has offered to pay $500,000 for the machine.
- A technical engineer will have to be taken off other work to work on this machine. The company will have to pay a consultancy $3,000 to complete the engineer's other work.
- Most of the materials for the machine will be taken from the company's normal inventory. Nothing will have to be purchased specially but any materials used will need to be replaced.

The other factors are not relevant because they do not involve future, incremental cash flows.

Activity 3: Data types

The correct answers are:

- An ideal site has become available but the lease would need to be signed quickly.
- Fruit Tree will struggle to secure the money needed for this investment.

Secondary data is faster and cheaper to source than primary data and would therefore be helpful in these circumstances.

On the other hand, Fruit Tree's unique product and the upheaval caused by the arrival of a new competitor will make it harder to relate secondary data to this project and therefore make primary data more attractive.

Test your learning

1 Two key considerations at the qualitative analysis stage of investment appraisal are:

- Does the investment help the organisation to meet its objectives?
- What impact will the investment have on relevant stakeholders?

Required
Is the above statement true or false?

A True

B False

2 Eagle Ltd has identified a project which requires 200 kg of material X. There is currently 500 kg of material X in inventory, which was purchased for $5,000 two years ago. Any material not used on the project will need to be disposed of professionally at a cost of $1/kg.

Required
What is the relevant cash flow associated with materials?

The relevant cash flow is $ [   ]

Is this a cost or a saving? [   ]

3 **Required**
Is the following an example of a relevant cost?

The cost of market research which is about to be commissioned as part of a project

A Yes

B No

4 **Required**
Is the following an example of a relevant cost?

Depreciation on the new machine being purchased for a project

A Yes

B No

5 **Required**
Is the following an example of a relevant cost?

Interest to be paid on a company loan which will be used to fund a project

A Yes

B No

6 **Required**
Is the following an example of a non-relevant cost?

Labour costs for staff being recruited especially to work on a project

A Yes

B No

5

Project appraisal

Syllabus learning outcomes

Having studied this chapter, you will be able to work through the following syllabus outcomes:

Syllabus area B: Capital investment decision making	
1	Data required for decision-making (continued)
a	Relevant cash flows (continued)
2	Steps and pertinent issues in the decision-making process (continued)
b	Discounting
3	Investment appraisal techniques
a	Payback
b	ARR
c	IRR
d	NPV

Exam context

In the exam, you will be expected to demonstrate competence in the following representative task statements:

- Calculate relevant cash flows taking account of tax, inflation, and working capital, and the use of perpetuities to derive final project value
- Determine the financial consequences of dealing with medium-term projects, in particular the importance of accounting for time value of money
- Calculate ARR, payback, NPV, IRR, modified IRR (modified IRR is covered in Chapter 6)
- Analyse the relative strengths and weaknesses of ARR, payback, NPV, IRR, modified IRR (Chapter 6)
- Use NPV, IRR, and payback to analyse financial aspects of projects and prioritise accordingly
- Use investment appraisal techniques for prioritisation of projects that are mutually exclusive.

Chapter overview

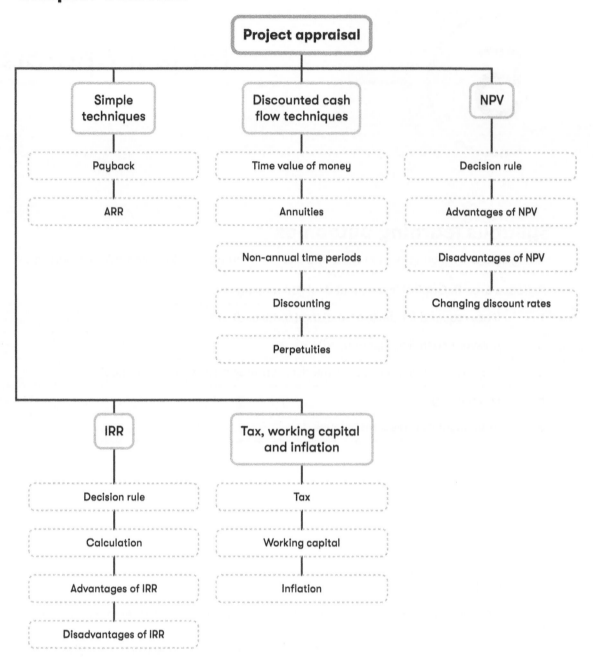

Project appraisal

Simple techniques
- Payback
- ARR

Discounted cash flow techniques
- Time value of money
- Annuities
- Non-annual time periods
- Discounting
- Perpetuities

NPV
- Decision rule
- Advantages of NPV
- Disadvantages of NPV
- Changing discount rates

IRR
- Decision rule
- Calculation
- Advantages of IRR
- Disadvantages of IRR

Tax, working capital and inflation
- Tax
- Working capital
- Inflation

1 Introduction

The decision whether to invest in projects often involves the outlay of large sums of money and expected benefits may take several years to accrue. It is critical that these decisions are subject to rigorous appraisal and control.

In this **important and commonly examined** chapter we will cover the essential techniques used in the investment appraisal process.

2 Simple project evaluation techniques

2.1 Payback

> **Payback period**: The time required for the **cash inflows** from a capital investment project to equal the cash outflows (*CIMA Official Terminology*).

Payback should be an **initial** screening process, and if a project gets through the payback test it should be **evaluated using a more sophisticated project appraisal technique**.

A project should not be evaluated on the basis of payback alone.

Payback is based on **cash flows** so any **non-cash flow cost items** (eg depreciation) should be **ignored**.

2.1.1 Decision rule

A project is **rejected** if its payback period is **longer** than the company's **target** payback.

Activity 1: Payback period

An asset costing $120,000 is to be depreciated over 10 years to a nil residual value. Forecast profits after depreciation for the first 5 years are as follows.

Year	$
1	12,000
2	17,000
3	28,000
4	37,000
5	8,000

Required

How long is the payback period to the nearest month?

A   3 years 7 months

B   3 years 6 months

C   3 years

D   The project does not pay back in 5 years

Solution

2.1.2 General advantages and disadvantages of payback

Advantages	Disadvantages
Simple to understand	Cash flows received/paid after payback are ignored
Quick for initial screening of projects	No account is taken of the time value of money within the payback period
Considers uncertainty (later cash flows are more uncertain)	The choice of any cut-off payback period by an organisation is arbitrary

2.1.3 Discounted payback period

Payback can be based on discounted cash flows (covered in Section 3), which is called discounted payback period. Aside from being based on discounted cash flows the calculation is the same.

2.2 Accounting rate of return (ARR)

Formula to learn

$$ARR = \frac{Average\ annual\ PBIT}{Initial\ or\ average\ investment}$$

PBIT = **profits** before interest and tax

(remember that profit is **after depreciation**)

Average investment =

$$\frac{Initial\ outlay +\ scrap\ value}{2}$$

2.2.1 Decision rule

Accept all projects with an ARR **above** the company's **target** ARR.

 Illustration 1: ARR

An asset costing $120,000 is to be depreciated over 10 years to a nil residual value. Profits after depreciation for the first 5 years are as follows.

Year	$
1	12,000
2	17,000
3	28,000
4	37,000
5	8,000

Required

What is the average accounting rate of return for this project? (Give your answer to the nearest percentage.)

[ ] %

Solution

The correct answer is:

34%

Average investment = [$120,000 (start) + $0 (end)] ÷ 2 = $60,000

Average profits = [12,000 + 17,000 + 28,000 + 37,000 + 8,000] ÷ 5 (years) = $20,400

Average ARR = $20,400 ÷ $60,000 = <u>34%</u>

2.2.2 General advantages and disadvantages of ARR

Advantages	Disadvantages
Easy to understand (use of profits and percentages)	No account is taken of time value of money
Looks at the whole project life	Profits can be manipulated

Exam focus

Accounting rate of return is the only project appraisal technique that is based on profit instead of cash flow. So in this technique (only) you will need to include depreciation in your calculations.

3 Discounted cash flow techniques

3.1 Time value of money

The idea that receiving $100 in the future is **worth less** than having $100 today is an example of the concept of money having a 'time value'. You will have covered this concept in earlier studies (eg Certificate level paper BA1) and the concept is briefly re-introduced in this section.

3.1.1 Worked example

If a project involved the outlay of $20,000 today and provided a definite return of $21,000 in one year's time, would you accept it if you could get a return of 6% on investments of similar risk?

We can look at this in two ways:

Firstly, If you had $20,000 today and invested it for one year at 6% then you would have $20,000 × 1.06 = $21,200 (this approach is called **compounding**). This is more than is generated by the project so the **project is not acceptable**.

Alternatively we can multiply $21,000 by

$$\frac{1}{1.06}$$

which gives a value of $19,811.

This shows the **value today**, or **present value**, of receiving $21,000 in one year's time to reflect the return available to investors. Again, we can see that the **project is unacceptable** because this present value is below the cost of the project of $20,000. We could express this as a **net present value** of $19,811 – $20,000 = **($189).**

A negative net present value is not attractive so again we **reject the project.**

KEY
TERM

> **Present value:** The cash equivalent now of a sum of money receivable or payable at a future date (*CIMA Official Terminology*).
>
> **Net present value (NPV):** The present value of cash inflows less the present value of cash outflows. If the NPV of an investment is positive then the project delivers a return that is above the cost of capital and should be accepted.
>
> **Cost of capital**: The annual cost of using capital. This reflects the return expected by the providers of capital.

3.2 Discounting project cash flows

The process of discounting future cash flows back to their value today to reflect the return that investors could get elsewhere is called **discounting the cash flows or DCF.**

Many projects involve investing money now and **receiving returns over many different time periods in the future.** DCF is an important tool in assessing whether the future cash inflows generated by a project offer a better return than an investor could get by investing elsewhere.

3.2.1 Discount factors

In the previous worked example the future cash flow was adjusted to a present value by multiplying by $\frac{1}{1.06}$.

This is the same as multiplying by 0.943 and this figure is an example of a **discount factor.**

This discount factor reflects the investor's required return (also referred to as a cost of capital) of 6% and the timing of the future cash flow (in one year's time).

In the exam you are provided with a **table of discount factors** to apply depending on the rate of return expected and the timing of the future cash flow. These are shown in the **Appendix** of this Course Book as a **present value table.**

As well as including a wide range of discount factors, this table also shows the formula for calculating any discount factor.

Formula provided

Discount factor = $(1 + r)^{-n}$
Where r = discount/interest rate and n = time period of cash flow

Exam focus

Discount tables are provided in the assessment, but they cover only integer values of r. If you need to use a discount rate that is not an integer (eg 10.5%) or is not in the range of values covered by the tables, you will need to use the discounting formula provided.

3.2.2 Conventions used in DCF

As a general rule, the following guidelines should be applied.

(a) It is usual to assume that time 0 is a day, ie the first day of a project. Time 1 is the last day of the first period (normally a year).

(b) A cash outlay to be incurred at the beginning of an investment project ('now') occurs in **time 0**. The present value of $1 now, in time 0, is $1 regardless of the value of the discount rate r.

(c) A cash flow which occurs during the course of a time period is assumed to occur all at once **at the end of the time period** (at the end of the year).

(d) A cash flow which occurs at the beginning of a time period is taken to occur at **the end of the previous time period**. So, a cash outlay of $5,000 at the beginning of time period 2 is taken to occur at the end of time period 1.

3.3 Annuities

If a project involves **equal annual cash flows** (or annuities) then each future cash flow can be discounted separately back to a present value, but it is quicker to use a single discount factor (called an annuity factor or a cumulative discount factor).

> **Annuity:** A cash flow that recurs over a number of consecutive time periods.

3.3.1 Worked example

If a project involved the outlay of $20,000 today and provided a definite return of $8,000 per year **for three years** would you accept the project? (Again assume that you could get a return of 6% on investments of similar risk.)

This can be analysed as a series of individual calculations:

Time	0	1	2	3
Cash flow	(20,000)	8,000	8,000	8,000
Discount factors (from present value table)		0.943	0.890	0.840
Present value	(20,000)	7,544	7,120	6,720
Net present value				**+1,384**

Alternatively this can be analysed by using a single discount factor provided in the Appendix to this Course Book. This is called an **annuity factor, or a cumulative discount factor.**

This approach is quicker but can only be applied to a series of **equal cash flows.**

Time	0	1 to 3
Cash flow	(20,000)	8,000
Cumulative discount factor (see **cumulative** present value table)		2.673
Present value	(20,000)	21,384
Net present value		**+1,384**

The cumulative discount factor represents the addition of the individual discount factors used in the first method. It is calculated using this formula:

 Formula provided

$$\frac{1}{r}\left[1 - \frac{1}{(1+r)^n}\right]$$

3.4 Perpetuities

If the series of cash flows does not have an end date – ie it is expected for the foreseeable future – then this is called a **perpetuity**. Again this can be dealt with by applying a single discount factor which is calculated using this formula (provided on the formula sheet):

 Formula provided

$$\frac{1}{r}$$

 Perpetuity: An annuity that occurs for the foreseeable future.

3.4.1 Worked example

If a project involved the outlay of $20,000 today and provided a definite return of $3,000 per year **for the foreseeable future** would you accept the project? (Again assume that you could get a return of 6% on investments of similar risk.)

The perpetuity factor here is:

$$\frac{1}{1.06}$$

So the present value of the future cash flows is $3,000 $\times \frac{1}{0.06}$ = $50,000

And the net present value of the project is $50,000 – $20,000 = +$30,000

So the project is acceptable.

 Activity 2: DCF 1

Required

Calculate the present value of $100,000 received in seven years' time, if the cost of capital is 12%. (Give your answer to the nearest $100.)

$ [   ]

Solution

Activity 3: DCF 2

Required

What is the value of $3,000 per year in perpetuity, when the cost of capital is 12%? (Give your answer to the nearest $.)

$ [   ]

Solution

3.5 Non-standard annuities and perpetuities

The approaches demonstrated in the previous sections for annuities and perpetuities **assume that the cash flows begin in time 1** and value these annuities or perpetuities from the perspective of the preceding time period to when the cash flows begin (ie time 0, a present value).

3.5.1 Worked example

If a project involved the outlay of $20,000 today and provided a definite return of $3,000 per year for the foreseeable future **starting in three years' time** would you accept the project? (Again assume that you could get a return of 6% on investments of similar risk.)

As before, the perpetuity factor here is: $\dfrac{1}{0.06}$

So the value of the future cash flows is $50,000.

However, this values the cash flows from the perspective of the preceding time period to when the cash flows begin and here the cash flows begin at time 3 so the value is from the perspective of **time 2** (the preceding time period).

BPP
LEARNING
MEDIA

To adjust this delayed perpetuity to a present value (time 0) we treat this as a one-off cash flow received in time 2 and multiply by the discount factor from the present value table for period 2 at 6% of 0.890.

$50,000 × 0.890 = $44,500

This is now a present value and can be netted off against the investment (today) of $20,000 to give a net present value of +$24,500.

The same approach can be used for delayed **annuities**.

3.5.2 Annuity or perpetuity received in advance

If the annuity or perpetuity is received from time 0 – ie immediately from the **start** of the first year – then delayed, then the normal approach is followed and then adjusted by adding the value of the cash received at the start of the year (which is not discounted as it is received now).

For example, what is the value of four cash inflows received at the **start of each year** of $8,000? (Again assume a cost of capital of 6%.)

This can be pictured as a normal annuity (cash received at the end of the year) over three years **plus an upfront receipt of $8,000 at time 0.** The overall present value is therefore:

Time	0	1 to 3
Cash flow	8,000	8,000
Cumulative discount factor (for 3 years)		2.673
Present value	8,000	21,384
Total present value		**29,384**

Activity 4: Annuities 1

A firm has arranged a 10-year lease at an annual rent of $17,264. The first rental payment has to be paid immediately, and the others are to be paid at the end of each year.

Required
What is the present value of the lease at 12%? (Give your answer to the nearest $.)

$ [   ]

Solution

Activity 5: Annuities 2

An annuity of $3,000 per annum for eight years starts at the end of the third year and finishes at the end of the tenth year.

Required

What is the present value of the annuity if the discount rate is 6%? (Give your answer to the nearest $.)

$ [_____]

Solution

3.6 Dealing with non-annual periods

3.6.1 Calculating non-annual discount factors

Occasionally you may be asked to discount the value of a cash flow that is not received annually. Instead the cash flow might be received every quarter or every month, for example.

If you are given an **annual** cost of capital, you can calculate the appropriate cost of capital for a non-annual period as follows:

> **Formula to learn**
>
> $$(1 + \text{non - annual return}) = (1 + \text{annual return})^{(1 \div \text{ number of periods in a year})}$$

Activity 6: Non-annual rates

Required

If the annual rate is 21%, what is the discount rate to apply to calculate the present value of a cash flow received every six months? (Give your answer to the nearest percentage.)

[_____] %

Solution

3.6.2 Calculating annual rates

Occasionally you may be asked to calculate the annual percentage rate (APR) from a non-annual cost of capital. This can be done by adapting the approach used to calculate a non-annual rate.

Formula to learn

$$(1 + APR) = (1 + \text{non - annual rate})^{(\text{number of periods in a year})}$$

So if the six-month required return is 10%, there are two six-month periods in a year and therefore the annual discount rate (APR) is:

$1.1^2 = 1.21 = 1 + \text{annual rate}$

So the annual rate = 0.21 ie 21%.

4 Net present value (NPV)

The concept of NPV has already been introduced and is developed further here.

The NPV method **compares the present value of all the cash inflows** from a project **with the present value of all the cash outflows** from a project. The difference, the NPV, represents the **change in wealth** of the investor as a result of investing in the project.

- If the **NPV is positive**, it means that the present value of the cash inflows from a project is greater than the present value of the cash outflows. The **project should therefore be undertaken.**
- If the **NPV is negative**, it means that the present value of cash outflows is greater than the present value of inflows. The **project should therefore not be undertaken.**
- If the **NPV is exactly zero**, the present value of cash inflows and cash outflows are equal and the **project will be only just worth undertaking.**

4.1 Decision rule

A project is acceptable if the **NPV is zero or above.**

Illustration 2: NPV

Slogger has a cost of capital of 15% and is considering a capital investment project, where the estimated cash flows are as follows.

Time	Cash flow ($)
0 (ie now)	(100,000)
1	60,000
2	80,000
3	40,000
4	30,000

Required

Calculate the NPV of the project, and assess whether it should be undertaken.

$ [   ]

Solution

The correct answer is:

$56,160

Year	Cash flow	Discount factor	Present value
	$	15%	$
0	(100,000)	1.000	(100,000)
1	60,000	$1/(1.150) = 0.870$	52,200
2	80,000	$1/1.15^2 = 0.756$	60,480
3	40,000	$1/1.15^3 = 0.658$	26,320
4	30,000	$1/1.15^4 = 0.572$	17,160
			NPV = 56,160

Note. The **discount factor for any cash flow 'now' (time 0) is always 1**, whatever the cost of capital.

The **PV of cash inflows exceeds the PV of cash outflows** by $56,160, which means that the project will earn a DCF yield in excess of 15%. It should therefore be **undertaken**.

4.2 General advantages and disadvantages of NPV

Advantages	Disadvantages
Takes into account the time value of money	The need to estimate a cost of capital
Gives an absolute measure, allowing for comparison of projects	Difficulty in obtaining all relevant costs/benefits
Considers cash flows in the whole life of the project	Assumes cash flows occur at annual intervals

4.3 Changing discount rates

A possible complication is that the cost of capital is not constant through the life of a project. This will complicate the calculation of the discount rates.

4.3.1 Worked example

If a project lasts two years and the cost of capital is 6% then the discount rate for time 2 (from the present value tables) is 0.890.

This has been calculated using the formula:

$$(1+r)^{-n}$$

Here this is $(1.06)^{-2}$ which is the same as $\dfrac{1}{1.06 \times 1.06}$

If the cost of capital changes so that it is 6% in year 1 and then 10% in year 2 (for example due to higher inflation in year 2) then the discount factor for year 2 is calculated using the cost of capital in year 1 **and** year 2. The discount factor for year 2 becomes:

$$\dfrac{1}{1.06 \times 1.1} = 0.858$$

5 Internal rate of return (IRR)

Internal rate of return: 'The annual percentage return achieved by a project, at which the sum of the discounted cash inflows over the life of the project is equal to the sum of the discounted cash outflows' (*CIMA Official Terminology*).

As the cost of capital rises the present value of cash inflows from a project falls and eventually will fall to zero. The cost of capital that causes this to occur is called the internal rate of return and is illustrated in the graph below:

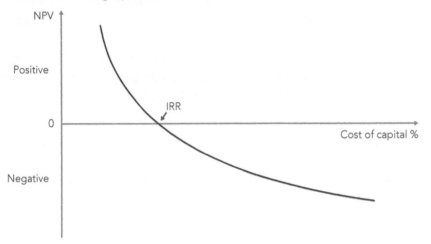

The IRR of a project is the **cost of capital at which the NPV of a project would be $0.**

It can also be defined as the **rate of return that is actually achieved by an investment.**

5.1 Decision rule

Accept project if IRR > cost of capital.

5.2 Interpolation method

Without a computer or calculator program, an estimate of the IRR is made using a hit and miss technique known as the **interpolation method.**

Step 1 – Calculate NPV at given cost of capital.

Step 2 – Calculate NPV using a second discount rate.

Step 3 – Estimate the IRR using the following formula:

Formula to learn

$$a + \dfrac{NPVa}{NPVa - NPVb}(b-a)$$

Where 'a' is the first discount rate giving NPVa, and 'b' is the second discount rate giving NPVb.

Note that if NPVb is negative then we effectively end up adding in the denominator, as subtracting a negative is the same as adding a positive.

5.2.1 Worked example

A company is trying to decide whether to buy a machine for $80,000 which will save costs of $20,000 per annum for five years and which will have a resale value of $10,000 at the end of year 5.

Required

If it is the company's policy to undertake projects only if they are expected to yield a DCF return of 10% or more, estimate the IRR using the interpolation method (using 9% and 12% in your estimates) and recommend whether this project should be undertaken.

- **Step 1.** NPV at 9%

Year	Cash flow	PV factor	PV of cash flow
	$	9%	$
0	(80,000)	1.000	(80,000)
1–5	20,000	3.890	77,800
5	10,000	0.650	6,500
			NPV = 4,300

- **Step 2.** NPV at 12%

Year	Cash flow	PV factor	PV of cash flow
	$	12%	%
0	(80,000)	1.000	(80,000)
1–5	20,000	3.605	72,100
5	10,000	0.567	5,670
			NPV = (2,230)

Step 3. So, IRR =

$$9 + [\frac{4,300}{4,300 + 2,330} \times (12-9)] = 11\%$$

If it is company policy to undertake investments which are expected to yield 10% or more, this project would be undertaken.

Activity 7: IRR

Using IRR, the project shown below should be accepted if the company requires a minimum return of 17%.

Time		$
0	Investment	(4,000)
1	Receipts	1,200
2	Receipts	1,410
3	Receipts	1,875
4	Receipts	1,150

Required

True or false?

A   True

B   False

Solution

5.3 General advantages of IRR

Like NPV, IRR recognises the time value of money and considers all the time periods of a project.

In addition:

- Because it is expressed as a percentage, the information it provides is more **easily understood** by managers, especially non-financial managers
- A **discount rate does not have to be specified** before the IRR can be calculated; a hurdle discount rate is simply required to which the IRR can be compared

5.4 Disadvantages of IRR

5.4.1 Ignores the relative size of investments

For example, both projects below have an IRR of 18%.

	Project A	Project B
	$	$
Cost, year 0	350,000	35,000
Annual savings, years 1–6	100,000	10,000

Clearly, project A is bigger (ten times as big) and so more 'profitable', but if the only information on which the projects were judged were to be their IRR of 18%, project B would be made to seem just as beneficial as project A, which is not the case.

5.4.2 Non-conventional cash flows

The projects we have considered so far have had **conventional cash flows (an initial cash outflow followed by a series of inflows)**. When flows vary from this they are termed 'non-conventional'.

In general, if the sign of the net cash flow changes in successive periods (inflow to outflow or vice versa), it is possible for the calculations to produce **as many IRRs as there are sign changes**.

Worked example

The following project has non-conventional cash flows.

Year	Project X
	$'000
0	(1,900)
1	4,590
2	(2,735)

Project X above has two IRRs as shown by the diagram which follows.

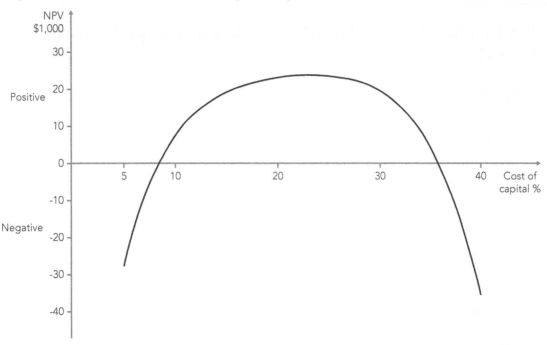

Suppose that the required rate of return on project X is 10% but that the IRR of 7% is used to decide whether to accept or reject the project. The project would be rejected since it appears that it can only yield 7%.

The diagram shows, however, that **between rates of 7% and 35% the project should be accepted**. Using the IRR of 35% would produce the correct decision to accept the project.

Lack of knowledge of multiple IRRs could therefore lead to serious **errors in the decision** of whether to accept or reject a project.

The use of the **IRR** is therefore **not recommended** in circumstances in which there are **non-conventional cash flow patterns**. The NPV method, on the other hand, gives clear, unambiguous results whatever the cash flow pattern.

5.4.3 Re-investment assumption

An assumption underlying the **NPV method** is that any net cash **inflows generated** during the life of the project will be **reinvested** elsewhere **at the cost of capital** (that is, the discount rate).

The **IRR method,** on the other hand, **assumes** these **cash flows** can be **reinvested** elsewhere to earn a **return** equal to the **IRR** of the original project.

If this assumption is not valid, the IRR method overestimates the project's actual return (this is considered further in Chapter 6 in the context of modified IRR).

5.5 Conflict between IRR and NPV

There are occasions when the results from a NPV and IRR calculation provide conflicting information. Having noted the many drawbacks of IRR, if the two approaches give conflicting results, accept the NPV result because it is intrinsically more reliable.

> ### Exam focus
>
> Make sure you know the strengths and weaknesses of each method of investment appraisal and consider their relevance to the question (eg an advantage of IRR compared to ARR is that IRR takes into account the time value of money; however, this advantage would not be true if comparing to NPV which also takes into account the time value of money).

6 Taking account of taxation, working capital and inflation

6.1 Taxation

Taxation has two effects on DCF analysis:

- **Tax payments** on operating profits (or tax saved on losses)
- **Tax savings** resulting from tax allowable depreciation (capital allowances) on capital expenditure

6.1.1 Tax allowable depreciation (TAD)

A business can claim tax allowances, also called tax allowable deprecation (or capital allowances), on certain purchases or investments. Where these are present you will need to:

(a) Calculate TAD each year (generally reducing balance but check the question for detail).

(b) Calculate tax saved each year due to TAD (calculated as TAD tax rate) and when these occur (again check the question for details).

(c) In **the final year** calculate whether the net capital outlay (capital outlay less any scrap value) has been fully reclaimed by TAD/capital allowances:

  (i) A **balancing allowance** is claimed if TAD/capital allowances claimed < net capital outlay

  (ii) A **balancing charge** is due if TAD/capital allowances claimed > net capital outlay

6.1.2 Worked example

Bingo plc is considering an investment programme which has a capital cost of $3.88 million, of which $3.13 million is to be spent on land and buildings and $0.75 million on fittings and equipment.

The following schedule of expected cash flows has been prepared for analysis.

Time	1	2	3	4
	$'000	$'000	$'000	$'000
Gross revenue	1,000	1,750	2,500	3,200
Direct costs	1,030	1,410	1,760	1,860
Net operating cash flows (before tax)	(30)	340	740	1,340

Bingo plc expects to be able to sell the chain at the end of Year 4 for $4.5 million (including resale proceeds of $200,000 for the fittings and equipment).

The company's after-tax cost of capital is 7% per year.

Bingo plc **pays tax at a rate of 30% on profits**. Tax is payable in the year that profits are earned.

The fittings and equipment ($750,000) qualify for tax depreciation at the rate of 20% per year on a reducing balance basis.

Tax depreciation is not available on land and buildings.

Expenditure on the investment programme will take place in January, Bingo's year end is 31 December.

Required

Incorporate the corporation tax flows into the DCF calculation.

Solution

Time	0	1	2	3	4
	$'000	$'000	$'000	$'000	$'000
Net operating cash flows		(30)	340	740	1,340
Taxation @ 30%		9	(102)	(222)	(402)
Fittings and equipment	(750)				200
Sale of business					4,300
Land and buildings	(3,130)				
Tax benefit of TAD (W1)		45	36	29	55

Tax workings:

Tax on profits are calculated as the tax rate × net operating cash flows.

In time 1 there is a tax saving as losses have been made.

Tax allowable depreciation working:

(W1) *Calculation of tax benefit on TAD:*

Calculated as the tax rate × the capital allowance (or writing down allowance, WDA).

Time of claim	Asset cost	Tax saved	Timing of tax saving
	$'000	30%	
1	750		
20% TAD	(150)	45	1
2	600		
20% TAD	(120)	36	2
3	480		
20% TAD	(96)	29	3
4	384		
Proceeds	(200)		
Balancing allowance	184	55	4
		165	

Exam focus

In exam questions you can assume (unless otherwise stated) that the organisation in question generates enough profit from other projects to absorb any tax benefits in the year to which they relate.

6.2 Working capital

Major projects will need the injection of funds to finance the level of working capital required (eg inventory).

The effect on cash flows is due to the change in working capital required during the life of the project.

The relevant cash flow associated with working capital is **the change in working capital.**

- An **increase in working capital required will cause a cash outflow.**
- A decrease in working capital required will cause a cash inflow.

Exam focus

At the end of the project, when there is no further requirement for working capital in the project, the full amount of working capital invested will be released, creating a positive cash flow.

Activity 8: Working capital

Bingo plc (from the previous example) expects the following working capital requirements during each of the four years of the investment programme (all figures in $'000).

Year 1	Year 2	Year 3	Year 4
250	300	375	350

Required

Insert the relevant cash flows and the timings of these cash flows into the following table.

Year	Annual working capital requirement	Incremental cash flow	Timing
1	250		
2	300		
3	375		
4	350		
All released			

Solution

6.2.1 Completed worked example

The following shows the **complete solution** for the Bingo plc example incorporating tax and working capital and the final NPV. This is for interest only.

Time	0	1	2	3	4
	$'000	$'000	$'000	$'000	$'000
Net operating cash flows		(30)	340	740	1,340
Taxation @ 30%		9	(102)	(222)	(402)
Fittings and equipment	(750)				200
Sale of business					4,300
Land and buildings	(3,130)				
Tax benefit of TAD					
		45	36	29	55
Working capital	(250)	(50)	(75)	25	350
Net cash flow	(4,130)	(26)	199	572	5,843
7% discount factors	1	0.935	0.873	0.816	0.763
Present value	(4,130)	(24.3)	173.7	466.8	4,458.2

NPV = +$944,400

6.3 Inflation

Key terms	Explanation
Real terms or current prices	Ignoring inflation
Nominal or money	Including inflation

Inflation has two impacts on NPV:

Time	0	1 onwards

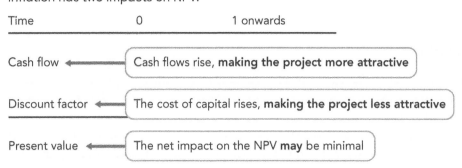

Cash flow ← Cash flows rise, **making the project more attractive**

Discount factor ← The cost of capital rises, **making the project less attractive**

Present value ← The net impact on the NPV **may** be minimal

6.3.1 One rate of inflation

If there is one rate of inflation, inflation has no net impact on the NPV. In this case it is normally **quicker to ignore inflation** in the cash flows (ie real cash flows) and to use an uninflated (real) cost of capital.

6.3.2 More than one rate of inflation

If there is more than one rate of inflation, inflation will have an impact on profit margins and therefore needs to be included in the NPV. In this case **the cash flows must be inflated, and inflation must also be incorporated into the cost of capital** (ie a money or nominal rate should be used).

To incorporate inflation into the cost of capital the following equation must be learnt (this formula is known as the **Fisher effect**):

Formula to learn

[1 + real cost of capital] × [1 + general inflation rate] = [1 + nominal (inflated) cost of capital]

The general inflation rate may be given as the retail price index (RPI) or consumer price index (CPI).

Illustration 3: Fisher effect

A company's money cost of capital is 11%. The expected annual rate of inflation is 5%.

Required
What is the real cost of capital?

A   16.6%

B   6.0%

C   16.0%

D   5.7%

Solution

The correct answer is:

5.7%

$(1 + r)(1 + i) = (1 + m)$

$(1 + r)(1 + 0.05) = (1 + 0.11)$

$(1 + r)(1.05) = (1.11)$

$(1 + r) = 1.11/1.05$

$1 + r = 1.057$

$r = 1.057 - 1 = 0.057$ or 5.7%

Activity 9: Inflation

Bistro Ltd is a brewing company trying to decide whether to buy a new bottling machine for $10 million to save on rental costs which are currently $6.6 million p.a. Running costs for the new machine would be $1.2 million p.a.

All cash flows except rental cost are quoted in current terms and are expected to rise in line with the consumer price index at 5.3% p.a. Rental costs were expected to increase at 2% p.a.

The bottling machine has no resale value. Bistro's **real** cost of capital is 14%.

Ignore tax.

Required
Evaluate the NPV of the new bottling machine if its life is expected to be three years. (Give your answer in $m to two decimal places.)

$  million

Solution

Chapter summary

Project appraisal

Simple techniques

Payback
- Time taken for cash inflows to equal cash outflows
- Ignores time value of money and cash flows after the payback period

Accounting rate of return
- Normally average profit/average investment
- Ignores time value of money

Discounted cash flow techniques

Time value of money
Money received in the future is worth less than money received today

Annuities
- Annuities are an equal cash flow each year
- The treatment of annuities needs to be adjusted if they are in advance or delayed

Non-annual time periods
- Discount rates, if given in annual terms, need to be adjusted if the cash flows are not received or paid annually
- Alternatively if a cost of capital is given in non-annual terms, it may need to be annualised if cash flows are received or paid annually

Discounting
Money received in the future is discounted back to a present value using discount factors (for a single cash flow) or cumulative discount factors (if an annuity or equal cash flow)

Perpetuities
- Cash flows received or paid every year for the foreseeable future
- Discount by multiplying by $1/r$

Net present value

Decision rule
An NPV of zero or above indicates that a project is attractive

Advantages of NPV
- Absolute value, so good for comparing projects
- Takes into account time value, and the whole project

Disadvantages of NPV
- Need to estimate cash flows and cost of capital
- Assumes cash flows occur at annual intervals

Changing discount rates
If this happens then discount factors will need to be calculated, and not extracted from the discount tables

Internal rate of return

- The cost of capital at which the NPV of a project is zero
- Alternatively, IRR is the return provided by a project

Decision rule

A project is accepted if the IRR is above the cost of capital

Calculation

Calculate using two estimates of NPV and then applying the formula

Advantages of IRR

Percentage measure so easy to understand

Disadvantages of IRR

- Ignores the relative size of investments
- Distorted if cash flows are non-conventional
- Assumes cash flows are re-invested in projects with the same IRR
- Inferior to NPV

Tax, working capital and inflation

Tax

- Tax payments on profits affect project cash flows
- Tax saved from tax allowable depreciation also needs to be taken into account
- Tax rules are given in exam questions where relevant

Working capital

- Changes in working capital create cash flows
- Increases in working capital create a cash outflow
- Decreases in working capital create a cash inflow

Inflation

- Use a real cost of capital to discount real cash flows
- Use a nominal cost of capital to discount nominal cash flows
- A nominal approach needs to be used if there is more than one rate of inflation

Key terms

Payback period: The time required for the **cash inflows** from a capital investment project to equal the cash outflows (*CIMA Official Terminology*).

Present value: The cash equivalent now of a sum of money receivable or payable at a future date (*CIMA Official Terminology*).

Net present value (NPV): The present value of cash inflows less the present value of cash outflows. If the NPV of an investment is positive then the project delivers a return that is above the cost of capital and should be accepted.

Cost of capital: The annual cost of using capital. This reflects the return expected by the providers of capital.

Annuity: A cash flow that recurs over a number of consecutive time periods.

Perpetuity: An annuity that occurs for the foreseeable future.

Internal rate of return: 'The annual percentage return achieved by a project, at which the sum of the discounted cash inflows over the life of the project is equal to the sum of the discounted cash outflows' (*CIMA Official Terminology*).

Activity answers

Activity 1: Payback period

The correct answer is:

3 years 7 months

Profits before depreciation should be used as an approximation to cash flow.

Year	Profit after depreciation $'000	Depreciation $'000	Profit before depreciation/ cash flow $'000	Cumulative cash flow $'000
1	12	12	24	24
2	17	12	29	53
3	28	12	40	93
4	37	12	49	142
5	8	12	20	

So payback period = 3 years +

$$\left[\frac{(120-93)}{(142-93)} \times 12 \, months\right]$$

= 3 years 7 months

Activity 2: DCF 1

The correct answer is:

$45,200

$100,000/(1 + 0.12)^7 = 45,234$ or $45,200 to the nearest $100

Or using tables:

100,000 × 0.452 = $45,200

Activity 3: DCF 2

The correct answer is:

$25,000

3,000/0.12 = $25,000

Activity 4: Annuities 1

The correct answer is:

$109,247

Use cumulative present value tables

r = 12%

n = 9 (1st payment now, 10th payment at the end of year 9)

PV = 17,264 + (5.328 × 17,264) = 109,247

Activity 5: Annuities 2

The correct answer is:

$16,581

CDF for 8 years = 6.210

PV = 3,000 × 6.210 = $18,630

This is a value from the perspective of the preceding time period to the annuity (time 2).

Discount at time 2 discount factor of 0.890 gives 18,630 × 0.890 = $16,581.

Alternatively

CDF for years 3–10 = (CDF for years 1–10) – (CDF for years 1–2)

= 7.360 – 1.833 = 5.527

PV = 3,000 × 5.527 = $16,581

Activity 6: Non-annual rates

The correct answer is:

10%

There are two six-month periods in a year, so the six-month discount rate is:

$1.21^{0.5}$= 1.1 = 1 + non-annual rate

So the non-annual rate = 0.1 ie 10%

Activity 7: IRR

The correct answer is:

False

A quick approach is discount the project at 17% and you will see that the NPV is negative. This implies that the project return is below 17% and so the statement is false.

If you calculate the IRR, it is approximately 15% which reinforces the fact that the statement is false.

			Try 17%		Try 16%
Time	Cash flow	Discount factor	PV	Discount factor	PV
	$		$	16%	$
0	(4,000)	1.000	(4,000)	1.000	(4,000)
1	1,200	0.855	1,026	0.862	1,034
2	1,410	0.731	1,031	0.743	1,048
3	1,875	0.624	1,170	0.641	1,202
4	1,150	0.534	614	0.552	635
		NPV	(159)	NPV	(81)

The **IRR must be less than 16%, and also less than 14%**. The NPVs at these two costs of capital will be used to estimate the IRR.

Use the **interpolation formula:**

$$IRR = 16 + \frac{-81}{-81 + 159}(17-16) = 16-1 = 15\%$$

The project should be **rejected** as the **IRR is less than the minimum return demanded.**

Activity 8: Working capital

The correct answer is:

Year	Annual working capital requirement	Incremental cash flow	Timing
1	250	(250)	0
2	300	(50)	1
3	375	(75)	2
4	350	25	3
All released		350	4

Activity 9: Inflation

The correct answer is:

$1.64 million

In this case there is more than one rate of inflation, so the method that includes inflation needs to be used. The savings on rental costs are lower than the rate of inflation so the NPV of the project will fall.

1 + inflated (nominal) cost of capital = (1 + 0.14) × (1.053) = 1.20 ie 20%

Time	0	1	2	3
Running costs (5.3%)		(1.26)	(1.33)	(1.40)
Savings (2%)		6.73	6.87	7.00
Purchase costs	(10.00)			
Net	(10.00)	5.47	5.54	5.60
DF @ 20%		0.833	0.694	0.579
PV	(10.00)	4.56	3.84	3.24
NPV	**+$1.64m**			

If there is more than one rate of inflation then **inflation needs to be included** in the cash flows and in the discount factor.

Test your learning

1 **Required**

Which of these two methods include depreciation as a cost?

A   Internal rate of return (IRR)

B   Accounting rate of return (ARR)

2 **Required**

What is the present value of a cash inflow of $3,000 each year from Years 2 to 6, when the required return on investment is 12%? (Give your answer to the nearest $100.)

$ _____

3 For a certain project, the net present value at a discount rate of 15% is $3,670, and at a rate of 18% the net present value is negative at ($1,390).

Required

What is the internal rate of return of the project? (Give your answer to one decimal place.)

_____ %

4 **Required**

Which one of the following items is included in the cash flows when determining the net present value of a project?

A   The disposal value of equipment at the end of its life

B   Depreciation charges for the equipment

C   Research costs incurred prior to the appraisal

D   Interest payments on the loan to finance the investment

5 The money cost of capital is 11%.

The expected annual rate of inflation is 5%.

Required

What is the real cost of capital?

A   16.6%

B   6.0%

C   16.0%

D   5.7%

6 A company wants a minimum real return of 3% a year on its investments. Inflation is expected to be 8% a year.

Required

What is the company's minimum money cost of capital?

A   4.9%

B   11.24%

C   5.0%

D   11.0%

6

Further aspects of project appraisal

Syllabus learning outcomes

Having studied this chapter, you will be able to work through the following syllabus outcomes:

Syllabus area B: Capital investment and decision making	
2	Explain the steps and pertinent issues in the decision-making process.
b	Discounting (continued)
c	Capital investments as real options
3	Apply investment appraisal techniques to evaluate different projects.

Exam context

In the exam, you will be expected to demonstrate competence in the following representative task statements:

- Use discounting, including the use of annuities in comparing projects with unequal lives
- Use profitability index in capital rationing situations
- Determine capital investment real options (ie to make follow-on investment, abandon, or wait decisions)
- Calculate, and analyse the relative strength of, modified IRR (based on a project's terminal value)

Chapter overview

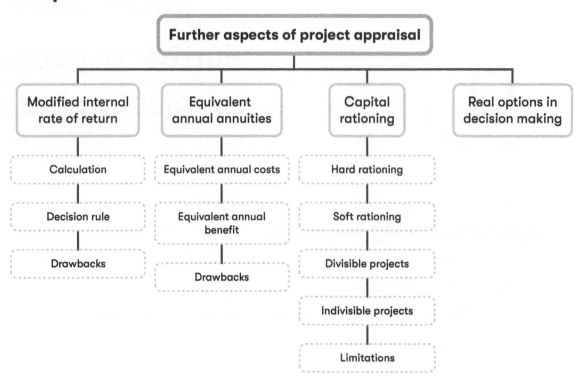

BPP
LEARNING
MEDIA

1 Introduction

This chapter continues to look at techniques used in the investment appraisal process, and focuses on:

- More sophisticated techniques such as modified internal rate of return (Section 2) and real option evaluation (Section 5)
- Specific scenarios where net present value (NPV) analysis needs to be adjusted (equivalent annual costs in Section 3 and capital rationing in Section 4)

2 Modified internal rate of return (MIRR)

As we have seen, the internal rate of return (IRR) assumes that the cash flows after the investment phase are **reinvested at the project's IRR**. If the project's IRR is high this may be unrealistic.

In addition, we have seen that if there are changes in the direction of the project cash flows there may be **more than one IRR**, which can cause confusion.

MIRR removes some of the drawbacks of IRR (reinvestment assumption and multiple IRRs) by **modifying** the reinvestment assumption so that it is assumed that cash inflows are **reinvested at the company's cost of capital**.

2.1 Calculating MIRR

Calculating MIRR involves two steps:

Step 1

Calculate the terminal values of the cash flows using the given cost of capital.

Step 2

Calculate the annual return by comparing the terminal value (the value of the cash flows at the **end** of the project assuming they have been reinvested and have earned a return equivalent to the cost of capital) to the present value of the amount invested in the project.

> **Formula to learn**
>
> $$\left(\frac{\text{Terminal value of cash inflows}}{\text{Present value of cash outflows}}\right)^{\frac{1}{n}} - 1$$
>
> or
>
> $$\sqrt[n]{\left(\frac{Terminal\ value\ of\ cash\ inflows}{Present\ value\ of\ cash\ outflows}\right)} - 1$$
>
> where n is the number of periods of growth.

Illustration 1: MIRR

Consider a project requiring an initial investment of $24,500, with cash inflows of $15,000 in Years 1 and 2 and cash inflows of $3,000 in Years 3 and 4. The cost of capital is 10%.

The IRR can be estimated as follows:

Time	Cash flow $	Discount factor 10%	Present value $	Discount factor 25%	Present value $
0	(24,500)	1.000	(24,500)	1.000	(24,500)
1	15,000	0.909	13,635	0.800	12,000
2	15,000	0.826	12,390	0.640	9,600
3	3,000	0.751	2,253	0.512	1,536
4	3,000	0.683	2,049	0.410	1,230
			5,827		(134)

IRR =

$$10\% + [\frac{5827}{5827 + 134} \times (25\%-10\%)] = 24.7\%$$

However, MIRR is calculated on the basis of **investing the inflows** at the company's **cost of capital**.

The following table shows the **values of the inflows if they were immediately reinvested at 10%;** eg the $15,000 received at the end of Year 1 could be reinvested for three years at 10% p.a. (multiply by 1.1 × 1.1 × 1.1 = 1.331).

Time	Cash inflows	Interest rate multiplier	Amount when reinvested
	$		$
1	15,000	1.331	19,965
2	15,000	1.21	18,150
3	3,000	1.1	3,300
4	3,000	1.0	3,000
			44,415

Required

From this information, what is the project's MIRR?

[   ] %

Solution

The correct answer is:

16%

We can calculate the MIRR as follows.

Total return =

$$\frac{44,415}{24,500} = 1.813$$

MIRR =

$$\sqrt[4]{1.813} \ or \ 1.813^{\frac{1}{4}}-1 = 0.16 \ or \ 16\%$$

Alternative solution:

For the terminal value at time 4 of $44,415 to have a present value that is the same as the outlay of $24,500 would require a time 4 discount factor of 24,500/44,415 = 0.552.

By looking along the Year 4 row in present value tables you will see that this gives a return of 16%. This means that the $44,415 received in Year 4 is equivalent to $24,500 in Year 0 if the discount rate is 16%.

Because **the return from the project is above the cost of capital**, this project should be accepted.

The MIRR of 16% will be a **better measure of the return delivered by the project** than the IRR of 24.7%.

Activity 1: MIRR

A project has the following estimated cash flows.

Time	0	1	2	3	4	5
$'000	(4,140)	743	920	811	5,527	(345)

Required

Assuming that the cost of capital is 12%, calculate the modified IRR. (Give your answer to one decimal place.)

☐ %

Solution

2.2 Decision rule

Accept a project if its MIRR is above the cost of capital.

2.3 Drawbacks of MIRR

Although MIRR removes some of the drawbacks of IRR, the reinvestment assumption may not be valid (depending on whether any other projects are available and what return they offer).

In addition, IRR still not does not measure the absolute amount of wealth created by a project and therefore is still inferior to NPV when choosing between projects.

Activity 2: MIRR 2

Required

Which of the following statements is true in relation to MIRR?

A   It is superior to NPV when evaluating mutually exclusive projects.

B   It measures the yield of an investment assuming that any cash flows are reinvested at the deposit rate of interest that can be obtained from the company's bank.

C   It gives a consistent answer to NPV when evaluating mutually exclusive projects.

D   It represents the maximum cost of capital that could be sustained and the project still be worthwhile.

Solution

3 Equivalent annual annuities

When mutually exclusive projects have different expected lives it can help to convert their total lifetime costs (or benefits) into an **annuity ie cost (or benefit) per year;** this makes it easier to compare the projects and to choose between them.

3.1 Equivalent annual costs

Where an investment is being evaluated on the basis of cost, and the aim is to choose the lowest cost investment, it can help to evaluate the investment using the concept of **equivalent annual cost**.

> **Formula to learn**
>
> $$\text{Equivalent annual cost (EAC)} = \frac{\text{Present Value of costs over } n \text{ years}}{n \text{ year annuity factor}}$$

3.1.1 Projects with different expected lives

Companies considering the **replacement of an asset** may be faced with alternatives where the life spans of the various assets differ. The options must be evaluated over a comparable number of years. In order to compare like with like we need to calculate an **equivalent annual cost** (EAC).

The PV of the costs for each project must therefore be **divided** by the **annuity factor** for the number of years of the project.

This calculates an **equivalent annual cost**.

Illustration 2: EAC

F Co has decided to replace its delivery trucks.

Two alternative types of truck are available, Truck X and Truck Y. Details of both are as follows:

	Expected life	Initial cost	Running costs per year	Residual value
Truck X	3 years	$24,000	$4,000	0
Truck Y	2 years	$15,000	$6,000	0

The total NPV of these costs, at a cost of capital of 10%, has been calculated (rounded to the nearest $100) as follows:

Truck X $33,900

Truck Y $25,400

Required
Which truck should be selected?

Truck [   ]

Solution

The correct answer is:

Truck X

Although Truck X is more expensive, it also provides a year of extra life.

Using the concept of equivalent annual cost we can calculate the cost per year of each truck by dividing by the annuity factor (3 years for Truck X = 2.487, 2 years for Truck Y = 1.736).

Equivalent annual cost for Truck X = $33,900/2.487 = $13,631

Equivalent annual cost for Truck Y = $25,400/1.736 = $14,631

On an annualised basis **Truck X, despite being more expensive to purchase, offers a lower annualised cost and should be selected.**

Note. The same conclusion could be obtained by evaluating both investments over a six-year period. This accommodates two replacement cycles for Truck X and three for truck Y – this is sometimes called the lowest common multiple method.

3.1.2 Replacement cycles

This method can also be used to assess when and **how frequently** an asset should be replaced.

Step 1	Calculate the **present value of costs** for each **replacement cycle** over **one cycle only**. These costs are not comparable because they refer to different time periods, whereas replacement is continuous.
Step 2	**Turn the present value** of costs for each replacement cycle into an **equivalent annual cost** (an annuity) by dividing by the cumulative present value factor for the number of years in the cycle.

Activity 3: Replacement cycles

Naurfold requires a new machine on a regular basis. The following information is available.

The new machine costs $30,000.

Year	Running costs	Resale value at end of year
1	$3,000	n/a
2	$4,000	$7,000
3	$5,000	$4,000

Naurfold's cost of capital is 15%. The machine will be kept for at least two years.

Required

Identify the EAC of the optimal replacement cycle of the new asset. Ignore taxation and inflation. (Give your answer to the nearest $100.)

The EAC of the optimal replacement cycle is $ ☐ .

Solution

3.2 Equivalent annual benefit

A similar approach can be applied to evaluating investments with different life cycles on the basis of the costs **and revenue** generated over their life cycle. This will only be relevant if a company is planning to repeat the same projects into perpetuity, which is **unlikely**.

The calculation is almost identical but uses the NPV of the project instead of the PV of the costs of the project (which was the approach used for EAC).

Formula to learn

$$\text{Equivalent annual benefit (EAB)} = \frac{\text{NPV of project over } n \text{ years}}{n \text{ year annuity factor}}$$

3.3 Drawbacks

The equivalent annual annuity method ignores the risk that by selecting assets with longer lives, or by selecting longer replacement cycles, an organisation may be more likely to incur quality problems in the later years of the assets' lives (or that they become obsolete as new technology emerges or new markets emerge).

4 Capital rationing

> **Capital rationing:** Capital rationing is a restriction on an organisation's ability to invest capital funds, caused by an internal budget ceiling being imposed on such expenditure by management (**soft capital rationing**), or by external limitations being applied to the company, as when additional borrowed funds cannot be obtained (**hard capital rationing**). *(CIMA Official Terminology)*

If an organisation is in a capital rationing situation it will not be able to invest in all available projects which have positive NPVs because there is not enough capital for all of the investments.

Capital is a **limiting factor**.

4.1 Hard capital rationing

- Investors are unwilling or unable to invest more equity finance.
- Lending institutions consider an organisation to be too **risky** to be granted funds.

4.2 Soft capital rationing

Soft capital rationing is an internal management decision to restrict capital spending and may occur for a range of reasons.

(a) Management may be **reluctant to issue additional share capital** because of a concern that this may lead to outsiders gaining control of the business or due to the dilutive impact on earnings per share.

(b) Management may **not want to raise additional debt capital** because they do not wish to be committed to large fixed interest payments.

(c) Creating **competition for a limited pool of funds** encourages divisions to search for the very best possible projects.

Note that whenever an organisation adopts a policy that restricts funds available for investment, such a policy may be less than optimal as the organisation may reject projects with a positive NPV and forgo opportunities that would have enhanced the market value of the organisation.

4.3 Divisible and non-divisible projects

> **Divisible projects:** Divisible projects are those which can be done in part or as a whole.
>
> **Indivisible projects:** Indivisible projects are those which must be undertaken completely or not at all. It is not possible to invest in a fraction of the project.

> ### Exam focus
>
> The technique that needs to be applied depends on whether projects are divisible or not, so look out for this in assessment questions.

4.3.1 Capital rationing with divisible projects

With **single period capital rationing**, investment funds are a limiting factor and management should follow the decision rule of maximising the return per unit of the limiting factor ie by selecting the projects whose cash inflows have the highest NPV per $1 of capital invested.

This is measured by the profitability index **(PI)**.

> ### Formula to learn
>
> $$PI = \frac{\text{NPV of project}}{\text{Initial cash outflow}}$$
>
> (By this method a value of zero or above is acceptable.)

$$\text{Alternatively PI} = \frac{\text{PV of project cash inflows}}{\text{Initial cash outflow}}$$

(By this method a value of 1 or above is acceptable.)

 ## Illustration 3: PI

Short O'Funds has capital of $95,000 available for investment in the forthcoming period. Details of three projects under consideration (P, Q and R) are as follows. All projects are independent and **divisible.**

Project	Investment required	NPV
	$'000	$'000
P	40	16.5
Q	50	17.0
R	30	18.8

Required

Calculate the NPV from investing in the optimal combination of projects. (Give your answer in $m to one decimal place.)

$m [   ]

Solution

The correct answer is:

$m 43.8

The first step is to rank the projects according to the return achieved from the limiting factor of investment funds.

Project	NPV	Investment	PV per $1 invested	Ranking
	$'000	$'000	$	
P	16.5	40	0.41	2
Q	17.0	50	0.34	3
R	18.8	30	0.63	1

The available funds of $95,000 can now be allocated.

Project	Investment		PV
	$'000		$'000
R	30		18.8
P	40		16.5
Q (balance, only 50% of the project can be afforded)	25	(50% of project NPV)	8.5
	95	Maximum PV =	43.8

Only half of project Q can be afforded.

4.3.2 Capital rationing with non-divisible projects

If the projects are **not divisible** then **the PI method cannot be applied** since it does not make sense to recommend investing in a fraction of a project if it is not divisible.

In this situation, the combinations of projects that are affordable need to be identified and assessed to identify the NPV from different combinations of projects.

The combination of projects that delivers the highest NPV will be selected.

Illustration 4: PI (cont)

Short O'Funds (from the previous illustration) has funds of $95,000 for future investments in the next period. The same three projects are available, but these have now been assessed as being **non-divisible**.

Required

Calculate the NPV from investing in the optimal combination of projects. (Give your answer in $m to one decimal place.)

$m [   ]

Solution

The correct answer is:

$m 35.8

The investment combinations we need to consider are the various affordable pairs of Projects P, Q and R.

Projects	Required investment	NPV from projects
	$'000	$'000
P and Q	90	33.5
P and R	70	35.3
Q and R	80	35.8

The highest NPV – of $35.8 million – is achieved by undertaking Projects Q and R.

 Activity 4: Capital rationing

A company has maximum capital to invest of $50,000. Four capital projects have been identified which are of a similar degree of risk. The initial step of calculating the NPVs has been completed and the details are as follows.

Project	Required initial outlay	NPV
1	$50,000	$100,000
2	$10,000	($50,000)
3	$10,000	$84,000
4	$15,000	$45,000

Projects cannot be postponed and multiples of the same project are not allowed.

Required

How much higher is the NPV from the optimal combination of projects if the projects are divisible compared to if they are indivisible? (Give your answer in $'000 to the nearest $'000.)

$ [   ] (000)

Solution

4.4 Limitations

The methods used for dealing with capital rationing make a number of assumptions. These can be regarded as limitations, as follows:

- Capital rationing is considered for a **single period** only
- Projects are **independent** so that the success of one project is not affected if another project does not proceed
- It is **not possible to delay** any projects
- **Multiples** of a single project are **not allowed**
- It is **not possible to share the investment** in any projects with another organisation (eg forming a joint venture)

Exam focus

The limitations of the techniques use are important – do not only focus on the calculations. Also, the profitability index can be applied using either approach unless otherwise stated in a question.

5 Real options in decision making

As part of the process of project control, projects should be analysed as to how easily they can adapt to different business scenarios.

Higher flexibility adds to the attractiveness of a project, a point that is sometimes ignored using traditional project appraisal techniques.

Where a project can adapt to different scenarios it is said to have 'real options'. These options can be **valued** using the Black–Scholes option pricing model, but **this numerical aspect of real options is not examinable in P2**.

5.1 Types of real option

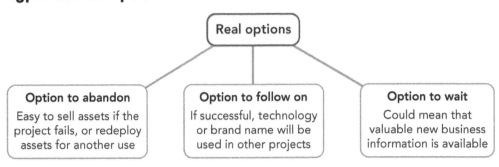

Illustration 5: Real options: Entraq

Entraq Co is considering two proposals to invest in the manufacture of solar panels.

Proposal 1 – to build a customised plant with specialist staff in a low-cost area with few other industrial employers, which can only be used to construct solar panels. This proposal would significantly enhance Entraq's profile in the solar panel industry.

Proposal 2 – to use more expensive machinery in Entraq's existing premises in a highly industrialised area that could be adapted to produce components for the wind power industry.

A political election is expected next year that could result in a change in government. This will affect the likely growth of the solar panel industry.

Required
Identify if any real options are present in these investments.

Solution

The correct answer is:

	Option type		
	To abandon	**To follow on**	**To wait**
Proposal 1	No	Higher profile in the industry may allow Entraq to move into new geographical markets/related product areas.	Better information on which to make this decision will be available after the election.
Proposal 2	Assets can be redeployed. Land should be easy to sell.	No	Better information on which to make this decision will be available after the election.

Chapter summary

Further aspects of project appraisal

Modified internal rate of return

Calculation

$n\sqrt{(\text{Terminal value}/\text{Cash outflow in Y0})}$

Decision rule

Accept the project if MIRR exceeds the cost of capital

Drawbacks

- Reinvestment assumption may not always be valid
- Not suitable for comparing projects because not an absolute value

Equivalent annual annuities

Equivalent annual costs

- Hard to compare assets with different lives using NPV
- Equivalent annual cost (EAC) takes into account the life of the project
- Alternatively a lowest common multiple approach may be used
- EAC is also useful to evaluate costs over different replacement cycles

Equivalent annual benefit

For comparing income generating projects with different life cycles, which are repeated into perpetuity

Drawbacks

Focus on cost ignores potential quality problems if an asset is used over a longer period of time

Capital rationing

Hard rationing

Unable to obtain finance

Soft rationing

Internal decision to restrict finance

Divisible projects

Evaluate using the profitability index

Indivisible projects

Combinations of affordable projects are assessed to identify the NPV from different combinations of projects

Limitations

- Only considers a single period
- Projects are independent so that the success of one project is not affected if another project does not proceed
- Ignores possibility of delaying any projects

Real options in decision making

- Option to abandon
- Option to follow on
- Option to wait

Key terms

Capital rationing: Capital rationing is a restriction on an organisation's ability to invest capital funds, caused by an internal budget ceiling being imposed on such expenditure by management (**soft capital rationing**), or by external limitations being applied to the company, as when additional borrowed funds cannot be obtained (**hard capital rationing**). *(CIMA Official Terminology)*

Divisible projects: Divisible projects are those which can be done in part or as a whole.

Indivisible projects: Indivisible projects are those which must be undertaken completely or not at all. It is not possible to invest in a fraction of the project.

Activity answers

Activity 1: MIRR

The correct answer is:

17.6%

Time	1	2	3	4	5
$'000	743	920	811	5,527	−345
Reinvest to time 5 at 12%	× 1.12^4	× 1.12^3	× 1.12^2	× 1.12	× 1
Value at time 5	1,169	1,293	1,017	6,190	−345
Total time 5 value	9,324				

The total return is 9,324/4,140 = 2.252

Modified IRR = $\sqrt[5]{2.252}$ = 1.176 ie **17.6%**

Alternatively, for the terminal value at time 5 of $9,324 to have a present value that is the same as the outlay of $4,140 would require a time 5 discount factor of 4,140/9,324 = 0.444.

By looking along the Year 5 row in present value tables you will see that this gives a return of about half way between 17% and 18%.

Activity 2: MIRR 2

The correct answer is:

It represents the maximum cost of capital that could be sustained and the project still be worthwhile.

Response option	Explanation
It is superior to NPV when evaluating mutually exclusive projects.	Not true; MIRR may still prioritise smaller projects that create less wealth (NPV) but deliver a higher percentage return on the funds invested over larger projects with a higher NPV that deliver a smaller percentage return.
It measures the yield of an investment assuming that any cash flows are reinvested at the deposit rate of interest that can be obtained from the company's bank.	Not true; the assumed reinvestment rate is the company's expected return on capital (cost of capital) which will be well above the deposit rate on a bank account.
It gives a consistent answer to NPV when evaluating mutually exclusive projects.	Not true, as per the first incorrect answer.
It represents the maximum cost of capital that could be sustained and the project still be worthwhile.	

Activity 3: Replacement cycles

The correct answer is:

The EAC of the optimal replacement cycle is $15,900.

Year	Replace every two years		Replace every three years	
	Cash flow	PV at 15%	Cash flow	PV at 15%
	$	$	$	$
0	(30,000)	(30,000)	(30,000)	(30,000)
1	(3,000)	(2,610)	(3,000)	(2,610)
2	3,000	2,268	(4,000)	(3,024)
3		–	(1,000)	(658)
		(30,342)		(36,292)
CDF		÷ 1.626		÷ 2.283
Equivalent annual annuity		18,661		15,897

The new machine should be replaced every three years, as a three-year replacement cycle gives the lowest EAC. The EAC to the nearest $100 is $15,900.

Activity 4: Capital rationing

The correct answer is:

$50 (000)

If projects are divisible:

Project	Required initial outlay	NPV	Profitability index	Rank
1	$50,000	$100,000	2	3
2	$10,000	($50,000)	–	–
3	$10,000	$84,000	8.4	1
4	$15,000	$45,000	3	2

Combination of projects to undertake:

Project	Outlay	Amount of project (%)	NPV
3	$10,000	100	$84,000
4	$15,000	100	$45,000
1	$25,000	50	$50,000
	$50,000		$179,000

If projects are indivisible the affordable projects are:

Projects	Outlay	NPV
3, 4	10 + 15 = 25	84 + 45 = $129,000
1	50	$100,000

The optimal combination of projects is 3 and 4.

So, the NPV is $179,000 – $129,000 = $50,000 higher if projects are divisible compared to if they were indivisible.

Test your learning

1   **Hard capital rationing** occurs when a restriction on an organisation's ability to invest capital funds is caused by an internal budget ceiling imposed by management.

    Required
    True or false?

    A   True

    B   False

2   **Required**
    For what type of project is the profitability index (PI) applicable?

    A   Divisible

    B   Indivisible

3   **Required**
    Which of the following types of option is provided by an investment in a product with potential spin-off applications into new business areas in the future?

    A   To wait

    B   To abandon

    C   To follow on

    D   To redeploy

4   Four projects – K, L, M and N – are available to a company facing a shortage of capital over the next year; the maximum capital available is $100,000. Capital is expected to be freely available thereafter. None of the projects can be delayed.

	K	L	M	Project N
Capital required in next year ($'000)	30	15	45	60
NPV ($'000)	90	60	150	120

    Required
    What will be the best NPV attainable (to the nearest $'000) assuming that the projects are divisible?

    A $312

    B $356

    C $320

    D $270

5   Four projects – K, L, M and N – are available to a company facing a shortage of capital over the next year; the maximum capital available is $100,000. Capital is expected to be freely available thereafter. None of the projects can be delayed.

	K	L	M	Project N
Capital required in next year ($'000)	30	15	45	60
NPV ($'000)	90	60	150	120

Required

What will be the best NPV attainable (to the nearest $'000) assuming that the projects are indivisible?

A $210

B $300

C $270

D $320

7

Pricing strategies

Syllabus learning outcomes

Syllabus area B: Capital Investment Decision Making

4	Pricing strategies
a	Pricing decisions
b	Pricing strategies

Exam context

In the exam, you will be expected to demonstrate competence in the following representative task statements:

- Understand pricing decisions
- Analyse pricing strategies and the consequences of market skimming, penetration pricing, premium pricing, loss leaders, product bundling/optional extras, and product differentiation to appeal to different market segments

Chapter overview

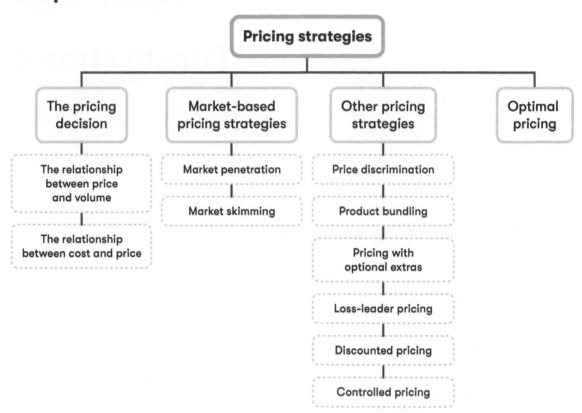

1 Introduction

The price to be charged to customers for a business's products or services is an important business decision.

Where there is not a prevailing market price, a business will have to select its chosen selling price using techniques and strategies that we will cover in this chapter.

The estimated selling price is also an important influence on the investment decision, because it influences the cash inflows resulting from new investments, so this chapter links to the other chapters in syllabus section B (Chapters 4–6).

2 The pricing decision

A key driver of the current profit made by an organisation, and the potential attraction of future investment opportunities, is the interaction between **cost, price and volume of sales**.

By considering the relationship between these variables we can introduce some of the main influences on the pricing decision.

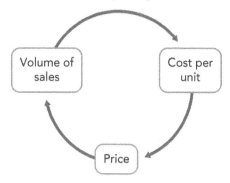

2.1 Relationship between price and volume

Price impacts volume sold, since a higher price will normally lower the quantity sold.

Despite this, organisations may consider increasing revenue if the fall in volume sold (as a percentage) is lower than the increase in the price (as a percentage).

Where this is the case, demand is said to be unresponsive to price changes or is **price-inelastic**.

KEY TERM

> **Price elasticity of demand (PED):** Price elasticity of demand measures the extent of the change in market demand for a good **in response to a change in its price**.

> **Formula to learn**
>
> $$\frac{\% \, change \, in \, demand}{\% \, change \, in \, price}$$

The **value of elasticity** may be anything from zero to infinity.

Demand is referred to as **inelastic** if the percentage change in demand is **lower** than the percentage change in price; this gives an absolute value of **less than 1** (ignoring the negative sign, which is normal because PED is expected to be negative since demand will fall if price rises and vice versa).

Demand is referred to as **elastic** if the percentage change in demand is **higher** than the percentage change in price; this gives an absolute value of **more than 1** (ignoring the negative sign).

Illustration 1: Price elasticity of demand

The price of a good is $1.20 per unit and annual demand is 800,000 units. Market research indicates that an increase in price of 10 cents per unit will result in a fall in annual demand of 75,000 units.

Required

What is the price elasticity of demand? (Ignore the negative sign and work to three decimal places.)

[   ]

Solution

The correct answer is:

1.125

Annual demand at $1.20 per unit is 800,000 units.

Annual demand at $1.30 per unit is 725,000 units.

% change in demand = (75,000/800,000) × 100% = 9.375%

% change in price = ($0.10/ $1.20) × 100% = 8.333%

Price elasticity of demand = (–9.375/8.333) = –1.125 or 1.125 ignoring the negative sign

Since the demand goes up when the price falls, and goes down when the price rises, the elasticity has a negative value, but it is usual to ignore the minus sign.

Ignoring the minus sign, price elasticity is 1.125.

The demand for this good, at a price of $1.20 per unit, would be referred to as **elastic** because the **price elasticity of demand is greater than 1**.

A price rise will therefore cause a **fall in revenue**.

Revenue before the price rise = $1.20 × 800,000 = $960,000

Revenue after the price rise = $1.30 × 725,000 = $942,500

2.1.1 Factors determining price elasticity of demand

Factor	How it might act to reduce elasticity
Income	If a good takes up a low percentage of customer income then customers will be less sensitive to price rises.
Degree of necessity	An essential item (eg medicine) will still have to be bought even if the price rises.
Availability of alternative products	If there are few alternative substitute goods or services then there will be a smaller fall in demand if price rises.

We return to consider the relationship between price and demand in more detail in the final section of this chapter, which covers **optimal pricing**.

Activity 1: Elasticity of demand

Company X is considering increasing its prices to $12 from $8. As a result, demand is expected to fall from 15,000 units per month to 12,000.

Required

Which of the following statements is true?

A   Price elasticity of demand is 0.4 and Company X's revenue will fall

B   Price elasticity of demand is 2.5 and Company X's revenue will fall

C   Price elasticity of demand is 0.4 and Company X's revenue will rise

D   Price elasticity of demand is 2.5 and Company X's revenue will fall

Solution

2.2 Relationship between cost and price

Cost per unit will impact the price a business seeks to charge (we have already touched on this in the discussion of ABC in Chapter 1); **in practice, cost is one of the most important influences on price**.

In a traditional cost-based pricing **approach,** the price is set as cost per unit + expected mark-up.

If the cost per unit includes overheads this is referred to as **full cost plus** pricing.

Cost-based pricing is intuitively logical; a business clearly needs to cover its costs in order to survive. In addition, it is based on internal costing data which a company should be able to access **quickly and easily.**

It should also ensure that **adequate profits** are made for shareholders and can also ensure that an organisation can justify to customers or regulators that **excessively high prices are not being set.**

 Illustration 2: Cost plus pricing

A product's full cost is $4.75 and it is sold at full cost plus 70%. A competitor has just launched a similar product selling for $7.99.

Required

Fill in the gap in the sentence below.

To match the pricing of the competitor's product, the cost-plus percentage will need to be

reduced by [   ] %.

Solution

The correct answer is:

To match the pricing of the competitor's product, the cost-plus percentage will need to be reduced by 2%.

Profits = $(7.99 – 4.75) = $3.24

Mark-up = ($3.24/$4.75) × 100% = 68%

So the % needs to be reduced by (70 – 68)% = 2%

2.2.1 Problems with full cost plus pricing

Full cost plus pricing can mean that at the **start** of a product's life, cost per unit is high because demand is low, and there are therefore few units to spread an organisation's fixed cost over.

A high cost per unit will then result in a **high price** being set **at the start of a product's life**.

As a result of price being high, **demand remains low**, in which case a product may not gain a foothold in the marketplace.

Other problems include:

- **Inaccurate apportionment** of overheads to products (less of a problem if ABC is being used).
- If actual volume is lower than expected volume, then **overheads may not be fully recovered** (not enough units are sold to pay for total fixed overhead costs).
- Can result in a **loss of focus on competitor pricing** strategies.
- Overlooks **market factors** (how much the customer is prepared to pay) and how these may vary at different stages of the **product life cycle** (see section 3).

2.2.2 Marginal cost plus pricing

To avoid the problems surrounding overhead allocation, an organisation may choose to base its pricing on the marginal or variable cost of a product.

The mark-up will be set at a level that delivers **sufficient contribution** to meet the organisation's objectives and to reflect competitive pressures.

Activity 2: Marginal cost plus pricing

A product has the following costs:

Cost type	$
Direct materials	5
Direct labour	3
Variable overheads	7

Fixed overheads are $10,000 per month. Budgeted sales per month are 400 units to allow the product to break even.

Required

Fill in the blank in the sentence below.

The mark-up which needs to be added to **marginal** cost to allow the product to break even is

[   ] % (to two decimal places).

Solution

2.2.3 Relevant cost plus pricing

For one-off contracts that are of a significant value, an organisation will often want to understand precisely what cash flows are being incurred as a result of the contract to establish the **minimum price** required to cover these costs, and then to apply a reasonable mark-up to ensure that profit is made.

This involves identifying the **relevant costs** of the contract (see Chapter 4).

Activity 3: Relevant cost plus pricing

Markup Co has been requested to produce a one-off order for a major customer. The following cost estimates have been made.

Cost type	$
Direct materials	27
Direct labour: 4 hours at $5 per hour	20
Variable production overheads: machine related, 0.5 hours at $6 per hour	3
	50

Because of the shortage of available machining capacity, the company will be restricted to 10,000 hours of machine time per month.

It is estimated that the company could obtain a minimum contribution of $10 per machine hour on producing items other than product X.

The direct cost estimates are not certain as to material usage rates and direct labour productivity, and it is recognised that the estimates of direct materials and direct labour costs may be subject to an error of +/−15%. Machine time estimates are similarly subject to an error of +/− 10%.

The company wishes to make a mark-up of 20% on the relevant cost of this order.

Required

What is the relevant cost-plus based price that ensures that the required mark-up is achieved? (Give your answer to two decimal places.)

$ [   ]

Solution

2.2.4 Relationship between price and required (target) cost

The **market price** at which a firm wishes to (or must) sell can also impact the **required (target) cost per unit**. Here the target cost is set by subtracting the required margin (the percentage of selling price) from the target price.

Target costing was already covered in Chapter 3.

3 Market-based pricing strategies

Cost is only one factor in determining product prices, another key factor involves assessing market factors and how these may vary at different stages of the product life cycle (PLC).

The product life cycle was introduced in Chapter 3. The diagram below is a reminder of the key stages in the PLC.

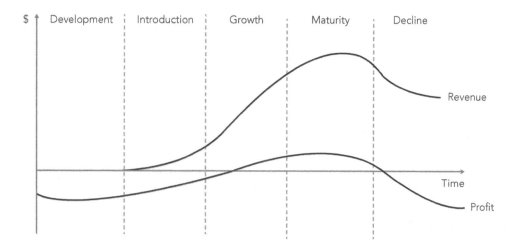

3.1 Market penetration

A policy of **low prices** when the product is first launched to **obtain sales volume and market share**.

Circumstances in which a penetration policy may be appropriate include:

- If the firm wishes **discourage new entrants** into the market
- If the firm wishes to **shorten the initial period of the product's life cycle** in order to enter the growth and maturity stages as quickly as possible
- If there are **significant economies of scale** to be achieved **from a high volume of output**, so that quick penetration into the market is desirable in order to gain unit cost reductions
- If **demand is highly elastic** and so would respond well to low prices

Penetration prices are prices which aim to **secure a substantial share** in a substantial total market. A firm might therefore **deliberately build excess production capacity** and set its prices very low.

As demand builds up, the spare capacity will be used up gradually and unit costs will fall; the firm might even reduce prices further as unit costs fall. In this way, early losses will enable the firm to dominate the market and have the lowest costs.

3.2 Market skimming

Involves charging **high prices** when a product is first launched and spending heavily on advertising and sales promotion to obtain sales.

As the product moves into the **later stages** of its life cycle (growth, maturity and decline) **progressively lower prices will be charged**.

The aim of market skimming is to gain **high unit profits early in the product's life**.

Circumstances in which such a policy may be appropriate include:

- Where the product is **new and different**, so that customers are prepared to pay high prices so as to be one up on other people who do not own it.
- Where the **strength** of demand and the **sensitivity of demand** to price are **unknown**. It is better from the point of view of marketing to start by charging high prices and then reduce them if the demand for the product turns out to be price elastic than to start by charging low prices and then attempt to raise them substantially if demand appears to be insensitive to higher prices.
- Where **high prices** in the early stages of a product's life might **generate high initial cash flows**. A firm with liquidity problems may prefer market-skimming for this reason.

- Where the firm can identify **different market segments** for the product, each prepared to pay progressively lower prices. If **product differentiation** can be introduced, it may be possible to continue to sell at higher prices to some market segments when lower prices are charged in others. This is **discussed further** in the section on price discrimination.
- The product has a **short life cycle** and needs to recover development costs and make a profit quickly.

Activity 4: Pricing and the life cycle

Required

Which TWO of the following circumstances favour the adoption of a penetration pricing policy?

A   Short product life cycle

B   Demand is relatively elastic

C   Scope for significant economies of scale

D   High barriers to entry for new competition

E   There are clearly identifiable market segments

Solution

Exam focus

The use of price skimming and penetration pricing are important areas that are likely to be examined.

4 Other pricing strategies

4.1 Product differentiation and price discrimination

Price discrimination: Price discrimination is the practice of charging different prices for the **same product** to different groups of buyers when these prices are not reflective of cost differences.

In certain circumstances, the **same product** can be sold at different prices to **different customers (price discrimination) or variants of** the **product** can be sold at different prices to **different customers** (product differentiation).

There are a number of bases for price discrimination and product differentiation.

Basis	Detail
By market segment	A cross-channel ferry company would market its services at different prices in England and France, for example. Services such as cinemas and hairdressers are often available at lower prices to pensioners and/or young people.
By place	Theatre seats are usually sold according to their location so that patrons pay different prices for the same performance according to the seat they occupy.
By time	This is perhaps the most popular type of price discrimination. Off-peak travel bargains, hotel prices and telephone charges are all attempts to increase sales revenue by covering variable but not necessarily average cost of provision. Railway companies are successful price discriminators, charging more to rush hour rail commuters whose demand is inelastic at certain times of the day.

Price discrimination can only be effective if a number of **conditions** hold.

- The market must be **segmentable** in price terms, and different sectors must show different intensities of demand. Each of the sectors must be identifiable, distinct and separate from the others, and be accessible to the firm's marketing communications.
- There must be little or **no** chance of a **black market** developing (this would allow those in the lower priced segment to resell to those in the higher priced segment).
- There must be little or **no** chance that **competitors** can and will undercut the firm's prices in the higher priced (and/or most profitable) market segments.
- The cost of segmenting and **administering** the arrangements should not exceed the extra revenue derived from the price discrimination strategy.

This approach to pricing is especially useful where a high proportion of the costs of providing a service are fixed, so that any extra revenue feeds directly through to generating extra profit.

4.1.1 Own-label pricing

Many supermarkets and multiple retail stores sell their 'own label' or 'private label' products, often at a lower price than established branded products. The supermarkets or multiple retailers do this by entering into arrangements with manufacturers to supply their goods under the 'own brand' label.

In many cases the own-label brand will be pitched at an economy price segment, but it can also be pitched at a premium price segment.

This is a slight variant on price discrimination since the result is that an organisation will charge customers different prices for slightly **different** products.

4.2 Premium pricing

This involves making a product **appear 'different'** through **product differentiation** so as **to justify a premium price.** The product may be different in terms of, for example, quality, reliability, durability, after-sales service or extended warranties. Heavy advertising can establish brand loyalty, which can help to sustain a premium, and premium prices will always be paid by those customers who blindly equate high price with high quality.

4.3 Product bundling

Product bundling is a variation on price discrimination which involves **selling a number of products or services as a package at a price lower than the aggregate of their individual prices.**

BPP
LEARNING
MEDIA

For example, a hotel might offer a package that includes the room, meals, use of leisure facilities and entertainment at a combined price that is lower than the total price of the individual components. This might encourage customers to buy services that they might otherwise not have purchased.

The **success** of a bundling strategy depends on the expected **increase in sales volume** and **changes in margin**. Other cost changes, such as in product handling, packaging and invoicing costs, are possible.

4.4 Pricing with optional extras

The decision here is very similar to that for product bundling. It rests on whether the **increase in sales revenue from the increased price that can be charged** is **greater** than the **increase in costs** required to incorporate extra features. Not all customers will be willing to pay a higher price for additional features if they do not want or need those features.

4.5 Loss-leader pricing

A **loss-leader** is when a company sets a very low price for one product intending to make customers buy other products in the range which carry higher profit margins. An example is selling inkjet printers at a relatively low price while selling the print cartridges at a higher profit margin. People will buy many of the high-profit items but only one of the low-profit items, yet they are 'locked in' to the former by the latter.

4.6 Discounted pricing

There are a number of reasons for using discounts to adjust prices:

- To get rid of perishable goods that have reached the end of their shelf life
- Normal practice (eg antique trade)
- To increase sales volumes during a poor sales period without dropping prices permanently
- To get cash in quickly

4.7 Controlled prices

Many **previously nationalised industries** now operate within the private sector and are **overseen by an industry regulator** (such as OFCOM Ofcom for telecommunications, in the UK).

Regulators tend to concentrate on **price** so that these near-monopolies cannot exploit their position (although the regulators are also concerned with quality of service/product).

5 Optimal pricing

It is possible to try to estimate the 'optimal' selling price by combining an analysis of both costs and demand factors; this selling price is designed to maximise short-term profitability.

5.1 Estimating the demand curve

The demand curve shows the relationship between the price charged for a product and the subsequent demand for that product. This section shows how a demand curve can be expressed as an equation.

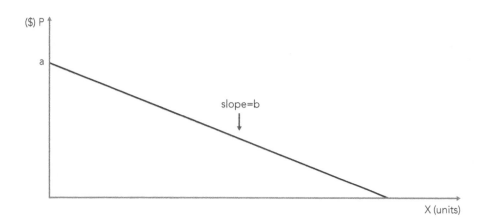

($) P

a

slope=b

X (units)

$\sqrt{x}$ Formula provided

When demand is linear the **equation for the demand curve is P = a – bx**

Where P = the selling price

x = the quantity demanded at that price

a = theoretical maximum price. If price is set at 'a' or above, demand will be zero

b = the change in price required to change demand by one unit

Illustration 3: Demand curve

The current price of a product is $12. At this price the company sells 12,000 items a month.

One month later the company decides to raise the price to $13, but only 10,000 items are sold at this price.

Required
Determine the values of a and b for use in the demand equation.

a =

b =

Solution

The correct answer is:

a = 18

b = 0.0005

Step 1: Find the gradient of the line (b) first.

This is calculated as the change in the value of the vertical axis (price) / the change in the value of the horizontal axis (X).

b = 1 / 2,000 = 0.0005

This shows the change in price needed to reduce demand by 1 unit.

Step 2: Now estimate the value of a.

If a $0.0005 change in price causes a change in demand of 1 unit then the first price at which demand falls to 0 from its current level of 10,000 can be estimated as $13 + (10,000 × $0.0005) = $18.

The demand equation can now be determined as P = a – bx

∴ P = 18 – 0.0005x

Step 3: Check your equation.

We can check this by substituting $12 and $13 for P and checking that it works (which it does as shown below).

12 = 18 – 0.0005x = 18 – (0.0005 × 12,000)

13 = 18 – 0.0005x = 18 – (0.0005 × 10,000)

Activity 5: Demand equation

Maximum demand for JL's product is 110,000 units per annum. Demand will reduce by 50 units for every $1 increase in the selling price.

JL is aiming to achieve sales for the coming year of 42,000 units.

Required

Calculate the required selling price for the product. (Give your answer to the nearest $.)

$ [   ]

Solution

5.2 Estimating marginal revenue

It is worthwhile for a company to sell further units when the increase in revenue gained from the sale of the next unit (marginal revenue) is greater than the cost of making it (marginal cost).

Marginal revenue (MR) is determined by the demand curve and can be expressed as an equation that is similar to the demand equation that we have seen already.

 Formula provided

$MR = a - 2bx$

Economic theory suggests that in order to sell more, the selling price will need to be reduced. As a result, the **marginal (extra) revenue generated by selling another unit will continually fall as output rises.**

Marginal revenue may not be the same as the **price** charged for all units up to that demand level, as to increase volumes the price may have to be reduced.

5.3 Profit maximisation

As economic theory suggests that **marginal (extra) revenue generated by selling another unit will continually fall as output rises,** then there will be a point at which it is not worth cutting the price any further because the revenue generated by selling another unit (MR) is below the marginal cost (MC) of producing it.

Profits will continue to be maximised only up to the output level where marginal cost has risen to be exactly equal to the marginal revenue.

At this point the selling price is said to be '**optimal**' because it is the price at which profits are maximised.

> **Formula to learn**
>
> Profit is maximised at the level of output where MR = MC.

5.3.1 Determining the optimal price using equations

You could be required to use the equation for **marginal revenue** to determine the optimal price.

Remember, **marginal cost** is the **extra cost of producing one extra unit; marginal revenue** is the **extra revenue from producing one extra unit**.

The following approach should be used:

Step 1 – Solve the demand function by finding b and then a.

Step 2 – Make the MR equation given equal to the value of MC. Substitute the values found for a and b in Step 1 into the MR formulae and solve.

Step 3 – Take the quantity found in Step 2 and put this into the demand function to find the price that should be charged.

Illustration 4: MC = MR

AB has used market research to determine that if a price of $250 is charged for product G, demand will be 12,000 units. It has also been established that demand will rise or fall by 5 units for every $1 fall/rise in the selling price.

The marginal cost of product G is $80.

Required

Calculate the profit-maximising selling price for product G. (Give your answer to the nearest $.)

$ ☐

Solution

The correct answer is:

$1365

Step 1 – Solve the demand function by finding b and then a.

$b = \frac{1}{5} = 0.2$

$a = \$250 + (12,000 \times 0.2) = \$2,650$

So P = 2,650 – 0.2x

Step 2 – Make the MR equation given equal to the value of MC. Substitute the values found for a and b in Step 1 into the MR formulae and solve.

Profits are maximised when MC = MR, ie when $80 = a - 2bx$

$80 = 2,650 - 0.4x$, so $0.4x = 2,650 - 80$, so $x = (2,650 - 80) / 0.4$, therefore $x = 6,425$

Profit-maximising demand = 6,425

Step 3 – Take the quantity found in Step 2 and put this into the demand function to find the price that should be charged.

Profit-maximising price = $\$(2,650 - 0.2 \times 1,285) = \$1,365$

Activity 6: Optimal pricing

A firm charges $12 per unit for its product. At this price it sells 16,000 units.

Research has shown that when prices were changed by $1 per unit sales changed by 2,500 units. The product has a constant variable cost per unit of $5.

Required
What price should be charged to maximise profit? (Give your answer to two decimal places.)

$ ☐

Solution

5.3.2 Tabulation approach to finding the optimal price

Another (simpler) approach to determining the profit-maximising production plan is to calculate the profit at different combinations of output and selling price from data that is provided to identify the optimal price.

5.4 Limitations of the optimal pricing approach

There are problems with applying the approach described above in practice for the following reasons.

(a) It assumes that the demand curve and total costs can be **identified with certainty**; this is unlikely.

(b) It ignores the **market research costs of** acquiring knowledge of demand.

(c) It assumes the firm has **no production constraint**, which could mean that the equilibrium point between supply and demand cannot be reached.

(d) It assumes the objective is **to maximise profits**. There may be other objectives (eg increasing market share).

(e) It assumes that **price is the only influence** on quantity demanded. In reality, other factors will affect demand eg advertising.

(f) It is **complicated by** the issue of **price discrimination** (the practice of charging different unit selling prices for the same product). We look at price discrimination later in the chapter.

Chapter summary

```
                        ┌─────────────────────┐
                        │  Pricing strategies  │
                        └─────────────────────┘
```

The pricing decision

Interaction between price, volume and cost per unit

The relationship between price and volume

- Price elasticity of demand
- Demand less responsive to price changes if a good is cheap relative to income, is a necessity or there are few alternatives (substitutes)

The relationship between cost and price

- Low volume at the start of a product's life can cause a high cost per unit, and a high price
- A high price can mean that volume remains low and cost per unit remains high
- Cost-based pricing ignores market factors (customers/competitors)

Market-based pricing strategies

Pricing needs to react to market factors; these will change across the life cycle of a product

Market penetration

- Low prices at the start of the life cycle
- Appropriate if demand is elastic and economies of scale exist

Market skimming

- High prices, supported by high levels of advertising
- Appropriate if the life cycle is short, the product is distinctive and demand is inelastic

Other pricing strategies

Price discrimination

- Price discrimination involves selling the same product at different prices
- The prices can differ by, for example, market segment, place or time
- The market must have different demand conditions, and each segment must be separable from the other

Product bundling

Product bundling is a variation on price discrimination which involves selling a number of products or services as a package at a price lower than the aggregate of their individual prices

Pricing with optional extras

- Similar to product bundling
- Decision considers whether the increase in sales revenue from the increased price that can be charged is greater than the increase in costs required to incorporate extra features

Loss-leader pricing

A loss-leader is when a company sets a very low price for one product intending to make customers buy other products in the range which carry higher profit margins

Discounted pricing

Discounts to adjust prices often in periods of unusually low demand

Controlled pricing

Regulators control prices so that these near-monopolies cannot exploit their position

Optimal pricing

Estimated demand curve: $P = a - bx$

Estimating $MR = a - 2bx$

$MC = MR$

Key terms

Price elasticity of demand (PED): Price elasticity of demand measures the extent of the change in market demand for a good **in response to a change in its price.**

Price discrimination: Price discrimination is the practice of charging different prices for the **same product** to different groups of buyers when these prices are not reflective of cost differences.

Activity answers

Activity 1: Elasticity of demand

The correct answer is:

Price elasticity of demand is 0.4 and Company X's revenue will rise

% change in price = (12 – 8)/8 × 100% = 50%

% change in demand = (15 – 12)/15 × 100% = 20%

Price elasticity of demand = (–20/50) = –0.4

Since the demand goes up when the price falls, and goes down when the price rises, the elasticity has a negative value, but it is usual to ignore the minus sign.

Ignoring the minus sign, price elasticity is 0.4.

The demand for this good would be referred to as **inelastic** because the **price elasticity of demand is less than 1**.

A price rise will therefore cause a **rise in revenue**.

Revenue before the price rise = $8 × 15,000 = $120,000

Revenue after the price rise = $12 × 12,000 = $144,500

Notes on incorrect answers:

Confusing the current price and the revised price – eg thinking the price move starts at 12 and moves to 8 – can result in incorrectly calculating that revenue falls.

Incorrectly calculating price elasticity of demand as a percentage change in price divided by a percentage change in quantity results in the figure of 2.5 for price elasticity of demand.

Activity 2: Marginal cost plus pricing

The correct answer is:

The mark-up which needs to be added to **marginal** cost to allow the product to break even is 166.67% (to two decimal places).

Breakeven point is when total contribution equals fixed costs.

At breakeven point, $10,000 = 400 (price – $15)

So $25 = price – $15

So $40 = price

So the mark-up = ((40 – 15)/15) × 100% = 166.67%

Activity 3: Relevant cost plus pricing

The correct answer is:

$75.42

Including machine time opportunity costs and full allowance for possible underestimates of cost:

	$	$
Direct materials	27.00	
Direct labour	20.00	
	47.00	
Possible error (15%)	7.05	
		54.05
Variable production overheads	3.00	
Possible error (10%)	0.30	
		3.30
Potential marginal cost		57.35
Opportunity cost of machine time:		

	$	$
Potential contribution forgone (½ hr × $10 × 110%)	5.50	
Adjusted relevant cost		62.85
Profit mark-up (20%)		12.57
Selling price per unit		75.42

Activity 4: Pricing and the life cycle

The correct answers are:

- Demand is relatively elastic
- Scope for significant economies of scale

Elastic demand will respond to a low price strategy.

Economies of scale will allow a company to reduce unit costs as output rises and still make profits with a low pricing strategy.

Notes on incorrect answers:

- Short product life cycle – this argues for a high price strategy to quickly recoup costs during the short life cycle
- High barriers to entry for new competition – this makes a low price strategy less necessary
- Where there are clearly identifiable market segments – this argues for a price discrimination strategy (a variant of price skimming)

Activity 5: Demand equation

The correct answer is:

$1360

Using the demand equation P = a − bx

P	=	selling price
x	=	the quantity demanded at that price
a,b	=	constants

(a) **Find the gradient of the line (b) first**

This is calculated as the change in the value of the vertical axis (price) / the change in the value of the horizontal axis (X)

b = 1 / 50 = 0.02

This shows the change in price needed to reduce demand by 1 unit.

(b) **Now estimate the value of a**

If a $0.02 change in price causes a change in demand of 1 unit then the first price at which demand falls to 0 from its maximum level of 110,000 can be estimated as (110,000 × $0.02) = $2,200

The demand equation can now be determined as P = a − bx

∴ P = 2,200 − 0.02x

(c) **Use the equation**

We use this to calculate the price needed to achieve the required level of sales.

P = 2,200 − 0.02 × 42,000 = $1,360

Activity 6: Optimal pricing

The correct answer is:

$11.70

Step 1

$$b = \frac{\$1}{2,500} = 0.0004$$

Estimating a:

$12 = a - (0.0004 \times 16{,}000)$

$a = 18.4$

$P = 18.4 - 0.0004X$

Step 2

MC = MR

$5 = 18.4 - 0.0008X$

Therefore, X = 16,750 units

Step 3

$P = 18.4 - (0.0004 \times 16{,}750) = \$11.70$ per unit

Test your learning

1   The price elasticity of demand for a particular good at the current price is 1.2.

    Required
    Which of the following is true?

    A   Demand is price-elastic and if the price is reduced sales revenue will rise

    B   Demand is price-inelastic and if the price is reduced sales revenue will rise

    C   Demand is price-elastic and if the price is reduced sales revenue will fall

    D   Demand is price-inelastic and if the price is reduced sales revenue will fall

2   **Required**
    What are the four stages of the product life cycle?

    A   Appearance, growth, maturity, saturation

    B   Birth, growth, adolescence, old age

    C   Introduction, expansion, maturity, death

    D   Introduction, growth, maturity, decline

3   A company knows that demand for its new product will be highly elastic.

    Required
    Is the following statement true or false?

    The most appropriate pricing strategy for the new product will be market skimming pricing.

    A   True

    B   False

4   **Required**
    Which of the following statement(s) about cost-plus pricing is, or are, true?

    A   A problem with cost-plus pricing is that it fails to appreciate the circular relationship between price, demand and cost.

    B   The size of the profit margin can be varied to ensure that a company utilises any spare capacity it has.

5   A theatre offers a special deal whereby two show tickets and pre-theatre dinner can be purchased as a package for a reduced price.

    Required
    Which of the following terms is normally used to describe this pricing strategy?

    A   Loss-leader pricing

    B   Optional extras

    C   Product bundling

    D   Price discrimination

6   **Required**
    Which of the following pricing strategies should be used if an organisation wishes to discourage new entrants into a market?

    A   Market skimming

    B   Market penetration

8

Decision making in responsibility centres

Syllabus learning outcomes

Having studied this chapter, you will be able to work through the following syllabus outcomes:

Syllabus area C: Managing and controlling the performance of organisational units	
1	Responsibility centres reporting
a	Cost centres, revenue centres, profit centres and investment centres
b	Reports for decision-making

Exam context

In the exam, you will be expected to demonstrate competence in the following representative task statements:

- Analyse responsibility centres and responsibility accounting and the relationship to an organisation's strategy (eg cost, revenue, profit, and investment centres)
- Analyse how controllable and uncontrollable costs and revenues impact a manager's performance related to responsibility centres
- Analyse appropriate costs and measures of performance for responsibility centres
- Use data analytics and visualisations to analyse responsibility centres to enhance management performance and accountability
- Prepare the reports used for each type of responsibility centre to assist management in assessing performance.

Chapter overview

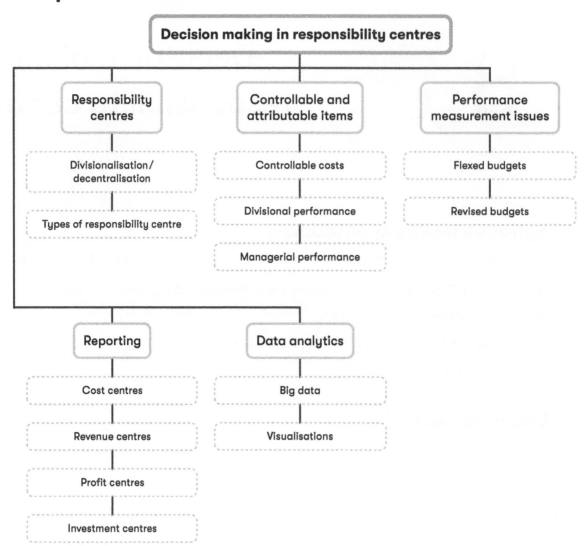

1 Introduction

An essential concept in management accounting, especially in decentralised companies, is that a manager should be held responsible and accountable only for the costs and revenues that they are in a position to control.

This chapter will also cover the use of data analytics and visualisation to enhance the performance management and accountability of responsibility centres.

2 Divisionalisation/decentralisation

As a company grows it will normally need to adapt its organisation structure so that not all decisions are taken by central, head office, management. If this does not happen, there is a risk that central management will be overwhelmed by the number of decisions they need to make. This is why it is normal for an organisation to **decentralise by creating a divisional structure.**

2.1 Advantages of divisionalisation

Quality of decisions	Divisional managers know local conditions and are able to make **more informed judgements.**
Speed of decisions	**Decisions should be taken more quickly** because information does not have to pass along the chain of command to and from top management. This allows quick and effective responses to changes in local conditions.
Motivation	If divisional managers are empowered to create their own plans to improve performance, this can also be **motivational.** In addition, divisional managers are often incentivised to improve the division's performance.
Role of head office	**Central management** are freed from detailed involvement in day-to-day operations and can devote more time to strategic planning.
Training	Divisions provide **valuable training for future members of top management** by giving them experience of management in a less complex environment than that faced by top management.

2.2 Disadvantages of divisionalisation

A danger with divisionalisation is that each division acts to achieve its own goals even if, in doing so, it damages the organisation as a whole. To prevent dysfunctional decision making, head office must reserve some power and authority for itself to control the activities of divisional managers to ensure that divisions are all working in the interests of the organisation as a whole; in other words, encouraging **goal congruence** among the organisation's separate divisions.

KEY TERM

> **Goal congruence:** 'The state which leads individuals or groups to take actions which are in their self-interest and also in the best interest of the entity' (*CIMA Official Terminology*).

Other disadvantages of divisionalisation can include:

Higher costs	It may be cheaper for **activities that are common** to all divisions, such as running the accounting department, to be centralised.
Loss of control	**Top management**, by delegating decision making to divisional managers, may **lose control**, since they may not be aware of what divisions are doing.

2.3 Types of responsibility centre

If **responsibility** for decision making is delegated to decentralised units, it will be important for head office to maintain **control** by setting targets for areas that are controlled by local managers.

KEY
TERM

> **Responsibility accounting:** Responsibility accounting is a system of accounting that segregates revenues and costs into areas of management responsibility in order to control performance.
>
> **Responsibility centre:** A **responsibility centre** is any part of an organisation which is headed by a manager who has direct responsibility for its performance and is accountable for it.

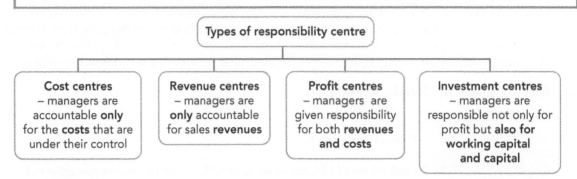

Types of responsibility centre

Cost centres – managers are accountable **only** for the **costs** that are under their control

Revenue centres – managers are **only** accountable for sales **revenues**

Profit centres – managers are given responsibility for both **revenues and costs**

Investment centres – managers are responsible not only for profit but **also for working capital and capital**

2.3.1 Cost centres

The **key point** about cost centres is that managers will focus on managing their cost base.

However, cost centres can be set up with the objective of either one of the below:

- **Minimising financial inputs** (ie costs): for a specified level of non-financial output

  For example, an accounting department producing financial accounts.

- **Maximising non-financial outputs**: from a fixed allocation of financial inputs

  For example, a call centre servicing customer queries.

Non-financial performance measures will be important in cost centres to ensure that cost control is not creating **quality** issues.

2.3.2 Revenue centres

Revenue centres have no control over most financial inputs (ie costs) but can be held accountable for some costs if these relate to sales (eg salesforce costs).

2.3.3 Profit centres

Profit centre managers have **greater autonomy** because they have responsibility for both financial inputs (costs) and financial outputs (revenue).

If internal departments (eg IT) are set up as profit centres the revenue of the department will partly be determined by the organisation's transfer pricing policy.

It is often the case for profit centres that external suppliers are permitted to compete with internal service departments, and that internal departments are allowed to search for revenue streams from outside the organisation.

For these reasons it can be argued that a profit centre, compared to a cost centre, can create an **entrepreneurial culture** which can improve performance, although it may also expose an organisation to **higher risk**.

2.3.4 Investment centres

Investment centre managers have the **highest autonomy** because they have responsibility for costs, revenue and management of the asset base.

2.3.5 Hierarchy of responsibility centres

Within an organisation, there is likely to be a **hierarchy** of responsibility centres. An example of this, for a divisionalised company producing a single product, is illustrated in the following diagram.

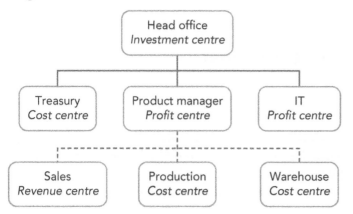

In a more decentralised company, responsibility for the investment decision may be delegated so that the product manager in the above example would then be an investment centre.

 Activity 1: Responsibility centres

Required

Which one of the following statements is true?

A   Converting a cost centre to a profit centre will encourage higher levels of quality.

B   If a responsibility centre has control over financial outputs but not financial inputs then it is more appropriate for it to be designated as a cost centre than as a profit centre.

C   A cost centre has no responsibility for non-financial performance.

D   An investment centre approach is not appropriate if investment decisions need to be approved by head office.

Solution

Exam focus

The terms introduced in this section are fundamental to performance measurement and need to be carefully learned. You may need to identify suitable performance indicators for different types of responsibility centre.

3 Controllable and attributable cost

3.1 Controllable costs

Managers should be held responsible only for the costs and revenues they are able to **control**.

KEY
TERM

Controllable and uncontrollable costs: A **controllable cost** is a cost which can be influenced by management within a given time period.

Uncontrollable costs are costs which cannot be changed by management within a given time period.

Any type of responsibility centre should have performance targets which **reflect the areas that are under the control** of local management.

The design of **managerial performance reports** should also be based on **controllable items**.

3.1.1 Controllable variable costs

Variable costs are **often assumed to be controllable** because **an organisation** has control over the amount, and type, of a product or service that it chooses to produce. However, this is **not always the case within a specific responsibility centre and** within a given **time period**.

Examples of variable costs that are partly or wholly uncontrollable	
Material	In a production division, if prices from suppliers are directly arranged at head office, then only material **usage** (not material cost) is controllable.
Labour	In a retail outlet, if staff contracts (wage rates/working hours) and staffing levels are directly arranged at head office, then labour costs may **not be controllable**.
Variable overhead	If energy supply is managed by head office, then this aspect of variable overheads may **not be controllable**.

3.1.2 Controllable fixed costs

Some fixed costs **are uncontrollable** because they are **allocated** costs (eg head office costs) or because they are **committed** costs (eg long-term leases). However, it is **not always the case that fixed costs are uncontrollable.**

Examples of fixed costs that are partly or wholly uncontrollable	
Discretionary costs	Costs such as advertising and research and development (R&D) are fixed costs but are controllable by the responsibility centre that has authority for this spending.
Avoidable costs	Costs such as short-term rental or leasing costs are fixed costs but can be avoided in future if the operation closed down.
Activity-based costs	If a responsibility centre can control the activity triggering the overhead (ie the cost driver activity), it can control its fixed overhead costs.

3.2 Divisional performance

Divisional performance should be evaluated on all the items which are directly **attributable or traceable** to the division. Divisional results may need to be **adjusted** for items that are not traceable in order to reflect **divisional performance.**

For example, **allocated** head office costs that **do not directly reflect the activity of the division** should be excluded when calculating divisional performance.

3.3 Managerial performance

Managerial performance should only be based on items that are under **managerial control.** This means that there may be a **difference** between the reporting of **divisional performance** and the reporting of **managerial performance.**

This means that **to assess managerial performance**, divisional results first have to be adjusted to reflect **traceable items** and then may need to be **further adjusted** to reflect areas that are **controllable** by divisional management by **stripping out** items over which divisional managers have **no control.**

For example, a division's results may need to be adjusted for the purpose of assessing **managerial performance,** by stripping out the effects of environmental changes that impact divisional performance (which are traceable but **not controlled** by divisional managers).

> ### Exam focus
>
> You may be expected to adjust a division's results to reflect the issues of **traceability and controllability** in the exam, so that they can be used to assess managerial performance.

Activity 2: Controllability

Beta division's latest financial results for the latest month (June 20X5) are shown below:

	$m
Revenue	78.0
Variable costs	56.0
Contribution	22.0
Fixed cost	10.0
Profit	12.0

30% of Beta division's variable costs are material costs. Due to head office selecting a new supplier from 1 June, material costs have risen by 5% per unit.

$2 million of fixed costs are for long-term lease payments, $1 million for short-term property rentals and the remainder for allocated head office costs.

Required
Calculate which measure of profit is suitable for assessing managerial performance, and which is appropriate for measuring divisional performance. (Give your answer in $m to one decimal place.)

Managerial performance: $m [   ]

Divisional performance: $m [   ]

Solution

Real life example

Nationwide (a UK financial institution) may run individual high street stores as revenue centres or profit centres. Larger retail outlets, such as supermarkets and department stores, require experienced managers on-site to manage complex situations. As well as being responsible for hitting revenue targets, these store managers would expect to have discretion over costs, thus making their stores profit centres.

However, a manager of smaller retail branches with only a few staff (bookshops, fashion retailers etc) is likely to have much less autonomy. Such managers are effectively administrators who follow a bureaucratic approach from head office under the monitoring of an area manager. In such situations, the branch manager is a revenue centre manager.

4 Performance measurement issues

4.1 Flexed budgets

Some **costs** are determined by factors that are outside the control of the manager of the cost centre.

A cost budget is prepared based on budgeted levels of sales and production. If the actual level of sales, and therefore of production, varies from the budget this will affect some costs (those that are variable). The level of sales achieved is **outside the control** of the cost centre manager.

To reflect this, a budget may need to be **flexed** to reflect that actual activity levels are different from budget.

KEY
TERM

> **Flexed budget:** A **flexed budget** is a budget that has been prepared based on **actual activity levels** for budgetary control purposes.

A **flexed budget** allows an analysis of actual costs vs budget to be made on the same level of activity. A flexed budget forms the basis for standard variance analysis.

4.1.1 Flexed budgets using ABC data

Instead of flexing budgets according to the number of units produced or sold, in an ABC environment it is possible to use **more meaningful bases for flexing the budget**. The budget cost allowance for each activity can be determined according to the number of **cost drivers**.

4.1.2 Worked example

Suppose the budget for a production department for a given period is as follows.

	$
Wages	220,000
Materials	590,000
Equipment	20,000
Power, heat and light	11,000
	841,000

This budget gives little indication of the link between the level of activity in the department and the costs incurred.

Suppose the activities in the department have been identified as sawing, hammering, finishing, reworking and production reporting. The **budget might therefore be restated** as follows.

Activities	Cost driver	Budgeted cost per unit of cost driver	Budgeted activity level of drivers	Budget
		$		$
Sawing	Number of units sawed	50.00	5,000	250,000
Hammering	Number of units hammered together	10.00	35,000	350,000
Finishing	Number of sq metres finished	0.50	400,000	200,000
Reworking	Number of items reworked	12.40	2,500	31,000
Production Reporting	Number of reports	400.00	25	10,000
				841,000

Costs classified as fixed in the first budget can now be seen to be variable and hence can be **more readily controlled.**

The **implications of increases/decreases in levels of activity** are also immediately apparent.

For example, if acceptable quality levels were raised, requiring an additional 200 units per annum to be reworked, budgeted costs would increase by 200 × $12.40 = $2,480.

A **flexed budget** would be prepared on the basis of actual activity as follows.

	Actual cost driver activity	Budgeted cost per unit of cost driver	Flexed budget	Actual cost	Variance
		$	$	$	$
Sawing	6,000	50.00	300,000	297,000	3,000 (F)
Hammering	40,000	10.00	400,000	404,000	4,000 (A)
Finishing	264,400	0.50	132,200	113,200	19,000 (F)
Reworking	4,500	12.40	55,800	56,100	300 (A)
Production Reporting	30	400.00	12,000	13,700	1,700 (A)
			900,000	884,000	16,000 (F)

4.2 Revised budgets

As already noted, a budget is prepared based on assumptions that may turn out not to be true, for reasons that are outside the control of the manager; eg if the level of sales in the industry as a whole are below the level expected at the time the budget was produced.

To reflect this, a budget may need to be **revised** on the basis of more reasonable assumptions, to create a more reasonable benchmark against which managerial performance can be assessed.

However, any **revisions will need to be approved** by senior management to ensure that poor operational performance is not masked by revising the budget to make performance targets easier to achieve.

5 Reporting

If the managers of responsibility centres are to attempt to meet budgets, they must receive regular performance reports so that they can monitor their centre's operations and take any necessary control action.

Different types of responsibility centre will require different information to assess performance.

The **qualities of** good information can be applied to responsibility reporting.

Accurate

The reports based on source data that is accurate and up to date.

Complete

The reports must include all relevant information (eg including non-financial information where relevant)

Cost-beneficial

The reports must add value to the business, over and above the cost of producing them. Management accountants should survey users to determine whether the reports add value.

User-targeted

Operational managers will require detailed information, while senior managers will only want a high level overview. Senior managers may prefer to just receive exception reports (ie notification only when a significant variance is recorded).

Relevant

Managers will want to focus on their own areas so should not be swamped with background information that is not relevant to them.

Authoritative

The management accountant needs to give confidence that the reports are meaningful and trustworthy.

Timely

The reports would usually be prepared monthly, but should give managers an opportunity to review and act on the information before the next month's report is generated if required.

Easy to use

The report should be in a consistent format and, where appropriate, use graphs to demonstrate key trends and variances. A dashboard presentation is often appropriate.

5.1 Cost centres

A cost centre manager is responsible for, and has control over, the costs incurred in the cost centre. The manager has **no responsibility for earning revenues** or for **controlling the assets and liabilities of the centre**.

A performance report for a cost centre might look like this.

COST CENTRE X PERFORMANCE REPORT FOR THE PERIOD Budgeted activity (units): Actual activity (units):				
	Budgeted costs (original) $	Budgeted costs (flexed) $	Actual costs $	Variance $
Material				
Labour				
Variable overhead				
Controllable profit				
Depreciation				
Divisional profit				

Two important points to note about this report are as follows.

(a) A clear distinction should be made between **controllable costs** and **uncontrollable costs**.

(b) The actual costs are compared with a budget that has been **flexed to the actual activity level achieved**. This provides a more meaningful comparison and method of control.

A cost centre manager would normally provide a **commentary** on the figures, explaining any significant variances and highlighting any relevant non-financial factors.

5.1.1 Discretionary cost centres

The use of flexible budget information is appropriate for control comparisons in production cost centres, but the costs attributed to **discretionary cost centres** are more difficult to control. Examples of discretionary cost centres include advertising, research and development and training cost centres. Management has a **significant amount of discretion** as to the amount to be budgeted for the particular activity in question.

Moreover, with discretionary cost centres there is no optimum relationship between the inputs (as measured by the costs incurred) and the outputs achieved. **Fixed budgets** must be used for the control of discretionary costs.

5.2 Revenue centres

The manager of a revenue centre is responsible **only** for raising revenue but has no responsibility for forecasting or controlling costs.

Revenue centres are often used for control purposes in **not-for-profit organisations** such as charities. For example, a revenue centre manager may have responsibility for revenue targets within an overall fundraising exercise, but that manager does not control the costs incurred. Such responsibility would pass to a more senior manager to whom the revenue centre manager reports.

As with cost centres, it would be appropriate for the revenue centre manager to provide a commentary on the report, explaining any non-financial factors and highlighting any decisions that may impact on cost centres (eg the recruitment of additional sales staff).

5.3 Profit centres

For a profit centre organisation structure to be established, it is necessary to identify units of the organisation to which both revenues and costs can be separately attributed.

Revenues might come from sales of goods and services to **external customers,** or from goods and services **provided to other responsibility centres within the organisation**. These internal 'sales' are charged at a notional selling price or **transfer price**.

A profit centre's performance report, in the same way as that for a cost centre, would identify separately the controllable and non-controllable costs. A profit centre performance report might look like this.

PROFIT CENTRE X PERFORMANCE REPORT FOR THE PERIOD Budgeted activity (units): Actual activity (units):				
	Budgeted costs (original) $	Budgeted costs (flexed) $	Actual costs $	Variance $
Sales revenue				
Variable cost of sales				
Contribution				
Directly controllable fixed costs				
Controllable profit				
Uncontrollable costs				
Divisional profit				

Again, the budget for the sales revenue and variable cost of sales will be **flexed according to the activity level achieved**.

The variances could be analysed in further detail for the profit centre manager.

Notice that three different 'profit levels' are highlighted in the report.

(a) Contribution, which is within the control of the profit centre manager

(b) Controllable profit, which is also within the manager's control

(c) Divisional profit, which is calculated after charging certain uncontrollable costs and which is therefore not controllable by the profit centre manager

5.4 Investment centres

In an investment centre, because managers have a degree of control over both profits and the asset base, performance measures need to cover both of these areas. This can be achieved using return on investment (ROI), residual income (RI) or economic value added (EVA™); these techniques are covered in the next chapter.

Activity 3: Type of responsibility centre

Required

Determine the appropriate responsibility centre for each manager:

Manager A is responsible for the performance of a sales team which sells double-glazing over the phone. He has authority over staffing levels, including recruitment and training.

Manager B runs the office canteen which is fully subsidised by the employer.

Manager C has been tasked with a project to secure funding for a new project. She works on her own and is responsible for identifying appropriate government grants and completing successful applications. [▼]

Picklist:

Cost centre

Revenue centre

Profit centre

Investment centre

Solution

6 Data analytics and visualisations

6.1 Big data

The reports described above are designed to measure performance and inform decision making. With that in mind, the more effective the information is, the more sophisticated and advanced the subsequent decision making can be.

De Mauro, Greco and Grimaldi (2016) explain that advances in technology have revolutionised the volume, variety and velocity of data available:

Volume

Businesses can use technology to capture and store unprecedented volumes of detailed data about their operations and customers.

Variety

Whereas traditional analysis relied on structured data, modern algorithms can also analyse unstructured data (eg pictures, videos, audio clips, opinions).

Velocity

The speed with which this analysis takes place has changed data analytics from a backward-looking review (ie what has happened) to a forward-looking prediction (ie what is likely to happen based on historic information).

These **three Vs** are characteristics of what is known collectively as **big data** and are often seen as an increasing source of competitive advantage for organisations.

Over time, the definition of **big data** has been expanded to include **veracity** and **value**.

Veracity

Is the data trustworthy and accurate? If not, the old IT proverb, 'garbage in = garbage out' applies.

Value

Big data creates a unique opportunity to create new value for an organisation.

Real life example

In 1995, the supermarket chain Tesco launched a Clubcard loyalty card scheme. Customers were offered a card which recorded all their purchases in return for points which could be redeemed for various benefits.

Tesco was, in effect, gathering detailed data about customer buying patterns.

In the years since its initial launch, more sophisticated algorithms have been developed which allow more complex patterns to be analysed and predictions to be made. Tesco's latest plans are to use data analytics to make more sophisticated predictions about customer buying patterns in the short term (ie what is each store going to sell in the coming week?). This information will enable it to manage stock levels more efficiently, reducing the risk of obsolete or deteriorated stock (eg fruit and vegetables going off) while still ensuring that there is sufficient inventory to meet demand (*Smale, 2014*).

6.2 Visualisations

With an increased volume of data available, the presentation of meaningful information becomes more important. Particular attention therefore needs to be paid to the **format**, **colour** and **size** of graphics, charts and visualisations used to communicate information, and to ensure that the conventions used are **consistent** across each responsibility centre.

Format: Is it easy to see how values relate and compare?

Colour: Does colour highlight key points without being overwhelming?

Size: Is the size of graphics compatible with the device being used to access the information (eg mobile phone)?

Drill-down facility: Is it possible to click on the visual image to obtain further detailed information if required?

Exam focus

The three Vs (and five Vs) associated with big data are likely to be examined so you will need to make sure that you learn these terms and can apply them to assessment questions.

Chapter summary

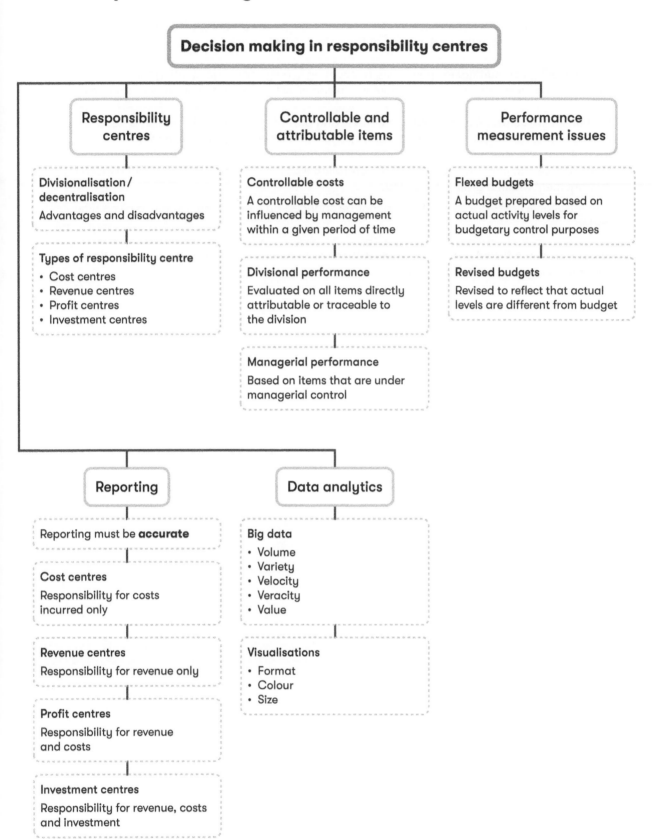

Decision making in responsibility centres

Responsibility centres

Divisionalisation / decentralisation
Advantages and disadvantages

Types of responsibility centre
- Cost centres
- Revenue centres
- Profit centres
- Investment centres

Controllable and attributable items

Controllable costs
A controllable cost can be influenced by management within a given period of time

Divisional performance
Evaluated on all items directly attributable or traceable to the division

Managerial performance
Based on items that are under managerial control

Performance measurement issues

Flexed budgets
A budget prepared based on actual activity levels for budgetary control purposes

Revised budgets
Revised to reflect that actual levels are different from budget

Reporting

Reporting must be **accurate**

Cost centres
Responsibility for costs incurred only

Revenue centres
Responsibility for revenue only

Profit centres
Responsibility for revenue and costs

Investment centres
Responsibility for revenue, costs and investment

Data analytics

Big data
- Volume
- Variety
- Velocity
- Veracity
- Value

Visualisations
- Format
- Colour
- Size

Key terms

Goal congruence: 'The state which leads individuals or groups to take actions which are in their self-interest and also in the best interest of the entity' (*CIMA Official Terminology*).

Responsibility accounting: Responsibility accounting is a system of accounting that segregates revenues and costs into areas of management responsibility in order to control performance.

Responsibility centre: A **responsibility centre** is any part of an organisation which is headed by a manager who has direct responsibility for its performance and is accountable for it.

Controllable and uncontrollable costs: A **controllable cost** is a cost which can be influenced by management within a given time period.

Uncontrollable costs are costs which cannot be changed by management within a given time period.

Flexed budget: A **flexed budget** is a budget that has been prepared based on **actual activity levels** for budgetary control purposes.

Activity answers

Activity 1: Responsibility centres

The correct answer is:

Converting a cost centre to a profit centre will encourage higher levels of quality.

A profit centre is less likely to compromise on quality since poor quality may impact revenues.

Notes on incorrect answers:

- If a responsibility centre has control over financial outputs but not financial inputs then it is more appropriate for it to be designated as a cost centre than as a profit centre.
- If a cost centre has no responsibility for non-financial performance, some areas of non-financial performance impact cost and these will need to be controlled by a cost centre.
- An investment centre still has responsibility for making the investment proposal and justifying its acceptance. This will be deemed as sufficient to suggest it has 'control' over its investment base.

Activity 2: Controllability

The correct answer is:

Managerial performance: $m21.8

Divisional performance: $m19.0

Controllable profit (for assessing managerial performance) can be assessed as follows:

	$m	
Revenue	78.0	Assumed to be controllable
Variable costs	55.2	30% of variable costs are material cost ie $16.8m Before the choice of new supplier (non-controllable) this would have been $16.8m/1.05 = $16m so actual costs should be reduced by $0.8m to reflect controllable variable costs.
Contribution	22.8	
Fixed cost	1.0	$2m are not controllable because they are committed, and $7m are not controllable because they are allocated
Controllable profit	21.8	

Attributable/traceable profit (for assessing divisional performance can be assessed as follows:

	$m	
Revenue	78.0	
Variable costs	56.0	This is attributable to the division
Contribution	22.0	
Fixed cost	3.0	$7m not controllable because allocated
Attributable profit	19.0	

Activity 3: Type of responsibility centre

The correct answer is:

Manager A is responsible for the performance of a sales team which sells double-glazing over the phone. He has authority over staffing levels, including recruitment and training. **Profit centre**

Manager B runs the office canteen which is fully subsidised by the employer. **Cost centre**

Manager C has been tasked with a project to secure funding for a new project. She works on her own and is responsible for identifying appropriate government grants and completing successful applications. **Revenue centre**

Manager A has responsibility for both sales and some expenses (staff costs) and is therefore a **profit centre manager**.

Manager B is responsible for incurring costs but does not receive any revenue and is therefore a **cost centre manager**.

Manager C is responsible for generating income. Although this is not 'revenue' in the customer sense, it is closest to the **revenue centre** model and is likely to be reported on that basis.

Test your learning

1 **Required**
   In an organisation that is highly decentralised, what form of responsibility centre will its divisions be classified as?

   A Cost centre

   B Profit centre

   C Revenue centre

   D Investment centre

2 X plc wishes to encourage an entrepreneurial culture among its divisional managers but has limited funds available for investment.

   Required
   Which type of responsibility centre should be implemented?

   A Cost centre

   B Profit centre

   C Revenue centre

   D Investment centre

3 **Required**
   Which factor can most accurately be said to cause a flexed budget to vary?

   A Production

   B Activity

   C Sales

   D Purchasing

4 The following are characteristics of good information: 1) Accurate; 2) Cost-beneficial; 3) User-friendly; 4) Timely; 5) Easy to use.

   Required
   Which three characteristics are missing from this list?

   [   ]

   [   ]

   [   ]

5 **Required**
   In a manager has responsibility for sales volume but does not control the sales price, and also controls operating costs, what form of responsibility centre will this division be classified as?

   A Cost centre

   B Profit centre

   C Revenue centre

   D Investment centre

6 **Required**
   Complete the following list of the characteristics of the three Vs of big data.

   Variety

   Volume

   [   ]

BPP
LEARNING
MEDIA

9 Performance measurement

Syllabus learning outcomes

Having studied this chapter, you will be able to work through the following syllabus outcomes:

Syllabus area C: Managing and Controlling the Performance of Organisational Units	
2	Approaches to the performance and control of organisations
a	Budgets and performance review
b	Other approaches to performance review

Exam context

In the exam, you will be expected to demonstrate competence in the following representative task statements:

- Identify and calculate key KPIs for each type of responsibility centre (eg profitability, liquidity, asset turnover, return on investment, residual income, and economic value added)
- Analyse key KPIs for each type of responsibility centre
- Use internal and external benchmarking as a key input in performance evaluation
- Use non-financial measures as a key input in performance evaluation
- Use a balanced scorecard approach to measure an organisation's performance from the four key perspectives

Chapter overview

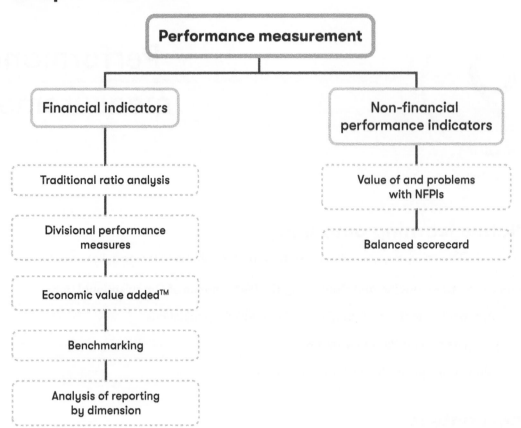

1 Introduction

Performance measurement involves the use of traditional ratio analysis that you will have encountered throughout your CIMA qualification. In addition, this chapter examines a range of performance measures for use in investment centres and also a range of other measures, such as benchmarking and the balanced scorecard, which are designed to give a fuller picture of performance.

2 Financial performance indicators

Ratios are commonly used to assess performance, either:

(a) Between one year and the next for a particular business or division; or

(b) Between one business or division and another.

2.1 Cost, revenue and profit centres

For cost, revenue and profit centres, key financial performance indicators will depend on the type of responsible centre being considered. Non-financial performance indicators will also be important and are discussed in Section 4.1.

Type of responsibility centre	Possible financial indicators
Cost centre	• Assessment of **cost per unit of input purchased** (eg cost per kg of material, cost per labour hour) compared to budget • Assessment of **usage of inputs** (eg materials, labour or machine hours) compared to budget (valued at standard cost)
Revenue centre	• Assessment of **price per unit** of sales units compared to budget • Assessment of **units sold** compared to budget (valued at standard profit or contribution)
Profit centre	• Analyses for cost **and** revenue centres would be relevant here; in addition, analysis of profit margin (see later) would be relevant

2.2 Investment centres

Investment centres control their profits **and their asset base**.

Financial performance measures for investment centres will focus on the ability of an investment centre to manage the asset base effectively to maintain liquidity and to generate profits.

2.2.1 Liquidity ratios

Liquidity: Liquidity is the amount of cash a company can obtain quickly to settle its debts (and possibly to meet other unforeseen demands for cash payments too).

Liquid funds include current assets such as cash, short-term investments, inventories and trade receivables.

The **current ratio** is the standard test of liquidity.

Formula to learn

$$\text{Current ratio} = \frac{\text{Current assets}}{\text{Current liabilities}}$$

An investment centre will often aim to have enough current assets that give a promise of 'cash to come' to comfortably meet its commitments to pay its current liabilities; ie to maintain a current ratio well in **excess of 1.**

Formula to learn

$$Quick\ ratio = \frac{Current\ assets\ less\ inventory}{Current\ liabilities}$$

Companies may not be able to convert all their current assets into cash very quickly – in particular, raw material inventories which must be used in production to create finished goods. Even finished goods might be warehoused for a long time, or sold on lengthy credit. Therefore in some businesses, inventories are not very liquid assets.

For this reason, the **quick ratio** (or acid test ratio) excludes inventory from current assets.

The quick ratio should ideally be **at least 1** for companies with a **slow inventory turnover**. For companies with a **fast inventory turnover**, a quick ratio can be **less than 1** without indicating that the company is in cash flow difficulties.

Activity 1: Liquidity ratios

The latest financial results for Division Beta are as follows:

	20X8
	$m
Turnover	2,065.0
Cost of sales	1,478.6
Gross profit	586.4
Current assets	
Inventories	119.0
Receivables	400.9
Short-term investments	4.2
Cash at bank and in hand	48.2
	572.3
Payables: amounts falling due within one year	
Loans and overdrafts	49.1
Corporation taxes	62.0
Dividend	19.2
Payables	370.7
	501.0

Required
Calculate the current ratio and the quick ratio for Division Beta. (Give your answer to two decimal places.)

Current ratio: ☐

Quick ratio: ☐

Solution

Do not forget that the current ratio and the quick ratio can also be **too high**.

A company with large volumes of inventories and receivables might be **overinvesting** in working capital, and so tying up more funds in the business than it needs to.

2.2.2 Profitability ratios

The profitability measure is return on capital employed (ROCE), also known as return on investment (ROI). This is covered in further detail in Section 3, but is introduced here.

ROCE states profit as a percentage of capital employed, and shows how well the investment centre utilises the funds invested in it.

> **Formula to learn**
>
> $$ROCE = \frac{\text{Profit before interest and tax}}{\text{Capital employed}}\%$$

To understand the reasons for capital employed changing it can be helpful to analyse whether the change is due to changes in operating profit margin (PBIT ÷ Revenue) or asset turnover (Revenue ÷ Capital employed).

$$ROCE = Profit\,margin \times Asset\,turnover$$

Operating profit margin is a useful indicator for measuring how effectively management is controlling the costs in a business. A high profit margin indicates that either sales prices are high or total costs are being kept well under control. A low profit margin could suggest problems in controlling input costs.

Asset turnover shows the revenue that is generated from each $1 worth of assets employed. A rise in asset turnover may either indicate that the asset base is being efficiently managed, or that the business is failing to invest adequately in its asset base which may cause problems over the longer term but in the short term helps to improve its ROCE.

Capital employed can be calculated as total assets less current liabilities **or** as long-term debt plus shareholders' funds.

Activity 2: Profitability ratios

Two divisions of a company produce very similar products and the company's directors wish to compare their performance. Details for the two divisions for the year ended 20X8 are as follows.

	Division A	Division B
	$'000	$'000
Revenue	2,400	1,485
Cost of sales:		
Variable production costs	600	600
Fixed production costs (including depreciation, see below)	1,200	585
Gross profit	600	300
Administration costs (fixed)	180	120
Operating profit	420	180
Non-current assets:		
Cost	3,000	2,700
Depreciation (see below)	600	1,845
	2,400	855
Net current assets	300	225
	2,700	1,080

Notes

(a) Assume that the non-current assets of both divisions are all used in their manufacturing processes.

(b) The two divisions use different depreciation policies. Division A depreciates its non-current assets using straight-line depreciation at the rate of 20% of cost with no residual value. Division B uses the reducing balance method of depreciation at a rate of 25% per annum.

(c) Included in the fixed element of cost of sales for the year ended 31 December 20X8 is depreciation of $600,000 for Division A and $285,000 for Division B.

(d) Division A's assets are newer.

Division A's management team have argued that it is unfair to compare them with Division B because the two divisions have different depreciation policies and Division A's assets are newer.

Restating Division B's assets to make them comparable to those of Division A gives a depreciation charge for the year of $369,000 and a net book value of $1,108,500.

Required

Use the revised figures to calculate Division B's performance measures. (Give your answer to one decimal place.)

ROCE: [   ] %

Operating margin: [   ] %

Asset turnover: [   ]

Solution

3 Performance measures for investment centres

In addition to ROCE, there are a number of other financial performance measures used to evaluate the performance of investment centres.

Non-financial performance measures are also important and are covered in Section 4.

Any performance measure can be evaluated by reference to three criteria:

(a) Does it provide an incentive to the divisional manager to make decisions which are in the best interests of the overall company? Ie **goal congruence**

(b) Does it only include factors for which the manager (division) can be held **accountable** (responsibility accounting)?

(c) Does it recognise the **long-term objectives** as well as short-term objectives of the organisation?

3.1 Return on investment (ROI)

Return on investment is another term used for return on capital employed, and the basic calculation has been covered in the previous section.

When ROI is used to evaluate managerial performance, it should be based on the aspects of an investment centre's activities that are **controllable** by its management.

A question may allow you to calculate controllable profit from the information given in the question.

There may also be an aspect of the investment base that is not controllable at a divisional level, and if so then this should be excluded from the calculation of ROI. For example, if credit control is a head office function then receivables should be excluded from a division's investment base in the calculation of divisional ROI.

3.1.1 Comparator for ROI

Return on investment (ROI) will be normally be compared against an ROI target, or against last year's ROI. (Often the target will be based on historic performance.)

3.1.2 Dysfunctional behaviour

If ROI is used as the principal performance measure then it is likely that a manager will only take decisions that will increase divisional ROI, which may be at the expense of growth in corporate profits. This may occur because:

(a) New projects have an immediate impact on the division's asset base but may only increase profits over time

(b) The current ROI may be artificially high because the division has been underinvesting in recent years (as with ROCE, one of the problems of ROI is that it can encourage short-term decision making)

Exam focus

You could be asked to discuss the conflict that may arise between NPV and ROI in an investment decision.

3.2 Residual income (RI)

Residual income (RI) gives a hurdle figure for profit based on the minimum return required from a division.

Formula to learn	
	$
Controllable divisional profit	X
Less imputed interest (investment × cost of capital	(X)
RI	X

Activity 3: ROI and RI

Brace Co is an electronics company specialising in the manufacture of home audio equipment.

Brace Co is split into two divisions, A and B, each with their own cost and revenue streams. Each of the divisions is managed by a divisional manager who has the power to make all investment decisions within the division.

The cost of capital for both divisions is 12%. Historically, investment decisions have been made by calculating the return on investment (ROI) of any opportunities and, at present, the return on investment of each division is 16%.

A new manager who has recently been appointed in Division A has argued that using residual income (RI) to make investment decisions would result in 'better goal congruence' throughout the company.

Each division is currently considering the following separate investments:

	Project for Division A	Project for Division B
Capital required for investment	$82.8 million	$40.6 million
Sales generated by investment	$44.6 million	$21.8 million
Operating profit margin	28%	33%

The company is seeking to maximise shareholder wealth.

Required

Calculate both the return on investment and residual income of the new investment for each of the two divisions. (Give your answer to two decimal places.)

Also consider whether the project wold be accepted or rejected using each technique.

Division A project ROI: [＿＿＿＿＿＿] %

Division A project RI: $ [＿＿＿＿＿＿] m

Division B project ROI: [＿＿＿＿＿＿] %

Division B project RI: $ [＿＿＿＿＿＿] m

Solution

3.2.1 Dysfunctional behaviour

RI is **less likely than ROI** to encourage dysfunctional behaviour because it encourages any investments earning above the cost of capital.

However, dysfunctional behaviour may still occur if new projects have an immediate impact on the division's asset base but may only increase profits over time.

3.3 ROI vs RI

In practice, ROI is used more frequently than RI. RI is, however, technically superior.

3.3.1 Advantages of RI vs ROI

(a) There is a higher risk of dysfunctional behaviour with ROI than with RI.

(b) RI is more **flexible** since a different cost of capital can be applied to evaluate different divisions with different risk characteristics.

3.3.2 Weaknesses of RI vs ROI

(a) It **does not facilitate comparisons** between companies or divisions of different sizes because it does not relate the size of a centre's income to the size of the investment.

(b) It can be **difficult to decide on an appropriate and accurate measure of the capital employed** on which to base the imputed interest charge (especially when applied to divisions).

3.3.3 Reasons for greater popularity of ROI

In practice, ROI may be used more frequently than RI for the following reasons.

(a) ROI is **consistent with corporate assessment** (ROCE).

(b) **Ratios** are more easily understood compared with, say, costs of capital and are **more appropriate for comparing divisions of different sizes.**

(c) Calculation of cost of capital in RI is **subjective and time consuming.**

(d) A company may feel that the **dysfunctional behaviour** associated with ROI, such as underinvestment, is unlikely to occur. For example, if a company is using ROI as a part of a balanced scorecard then customer, internal business and innovation measures should all highlight the impact of underinvestment.

3.3.4 Problems common to ROI and RI

The calculation of **'profit'**:

(a) Profit may need to be adjusted to reflect **controllable and traceable items** only.

(b) Transfer prices or quantities may be imposed or set at non-commercial rates.

(c) Both **ignore tax.**

The calculation of **'investment'**:

(a) Historic, net book or replacement value. Using net book value (NBV) **discourages replacement**. Replacement value is complex to obtain and update.

(b) Cash may be controlled by the company's treasury department (ie not at divisional level).

(c) Intangible assets may have no accounting value or may be complex to update. **It is hard to apply to service divisions** (create more value from intangible assets).

3.4 Economic value added (EVA™)

KEY TERM

> **EVA:** EVA™ is calculated as net operating profit after tax (NOPAT) less a capital charge (where the capital charge = weighted average cost of capital × net assets at the start of the period).

The logic behind EVA™ is that if the primary objective of commercial organisations is to **maximise the wealth of their shareholders**, then performance measures should evaluate whether an organisation has added to its economic value by making an economic profit in excess of the return required from the capital that has been invested to earn that profit.

EVA™ is a variation of RI developed by the management consulting firm Stern Stewart; it differs from RI in the figures it considers as profits and assets (*Drury, 2018: pp.502–506*).

3.4.1 Net operating profit after tax (NOPAT)

There are **differences in the way that profit is calculated**, compared with the profit figure that is used for RI (and ROCE).

(a) Costs which would normally be treated as expenses in the financial statements, but which are considered within an EVA™ calculation as **investments building for the future** are added back to derive a figure for **'economic profit'**. These costs are included instead as assets in the figure for net assets employed; in other words, they are deemed to be investments for the future. Costs treated in this way include such items as **research and development expenditure, goodwill** and **advertising costs**.

(b) Investors are primarily interested in cash flows, so accounting adjustments for non-cash items – such as provisions or allowances for doubtful debts – are eliminated.

(c) The charge for accounting depreciation in the income statement should be added back to profit, and a charge for **economic depreciation** made instead. The value of non-current assets (and therefore capital employed) should also be adjusted to reflect the revised charge. Economic depreciation reflects the **true change in value of the assets** during the period. If no detail is given about economic depreciation in a question scenario, then you should assume that accounting depreciation is a reasonable approximation for it, and therefore you should not make any change to the depreciation figure.

(d) **Tax paid** (in cash terms) is **deducted** from the profit figure. (Remember, 'NOPAT' stands for net operating profit **after** tax.)

(e) **Interest (net of tax) is excluded from NOPAT** because interest costs are taken into account in the capital charge (adjust for tax by multiplying by (1 − tax rate)).

Two alternative ways of laying out your NOPAT calculations are shown in the following table.

Approach 1	Approach 2
PAT	**PBIT** less (cash) taxes paid on operating profit
Add back	**Add back**
Goodwill amortised	Goodwill amortised
R&D and advertising	R&D and advertising
Non-cash items (eg provisions)	Non-cash items (eg provisions)
Depreciation (charge economic depreciation)	Depreciation (charge economic depreciation)
Interest (net of tax)	

3.4.2 Assets

There are **differences in the way that the asset base is calculated**, compared with the approach that is used for RI (and ROCE).

(a) Assets are usually valued at their **opening year value** and at **replacement cost** (if these are given).

(b) The asset base is also increased by any costs that have been **capitalised**. Where accounting adjustments are made to NOPAT (eg to add back R&D expenditure and advertising, or non-cash items) a similar adjustment needs to be made to capital employed in the relevant year.

Activity 4: EVA and RI

B Division of Z Ltd has operating profits and assets for the year ended 31 December 20X5 as below:

	$'000
Operating profit	156.0
Less: non-cash expenses	8.0
amortisation of goodwill	5.0
interest @ 10%	15.0
Profit before tax	128.0
Tax @ 30%	38.4
Profits after tax	89.6
Total equity	350.0
Long-term debt	150.0
	500.0

Z Ltd has a target capital structure of 25% debt/75% equity. The cost of equity is estimated at 15%. The capital employed at the start of the year amounted to $470,000. Goodwill previously written off against reserves on acquisitions in previous years amounted to $40,000.

Required

Calculate EVA™ and residual income for B Division for the year ended 31 December 20X5. (Give your answer in $m to one decimal place.)

EVA: $m [   ]

RI: $m [   ]

(Consider the meaning of the results.)

Solution

3.4.3 Evaluation of EVA™

Advantages	Disadvantages
Calculates return in line with shareholder expectations, therefore **aligns to the objective of maximising shareholder wealth**	**Complex** due to adjustments required
Replaces multiple goals with **one financial measure** that can be used at all levels of decision making	**Based on historical data** (ie accounts) so may have limited use as a guide to future performance
Encourages expenditure in areas that create benefits for the long term (eg advertising and research and development)	**Absolute measure,** making interdivisional comparisons difficult (where divisions are different sizes)
Removes distortion from the impact of accounting policies (eg the impact of provisions is removed)	**Inconsistent with published financial information**
Consistent with NPV (both show the return on investments in relation to the cost of financing them)	

4 Non-financial performance indicators (NFPIs)

Although it is important for organisations to measure and monitor their financial performance, there may be **disadvantages to focusing solely on financial performance**.

(a) Performance measurement will concentrate only on variables which can be expressed in monetary terms, **ignoring other important variables which cannot be expressed in monetary terms** (eg productivity, quality, employee morale).

(b) Performance measurement will **not convey the full picture** of a company's performance in a modern business environment, such as quality and customer satisfaction. It will measure success but **not measure the factors that ensure success**; ie in relation to a business's critical success factors.

(c) Financial indicators are normally produced at 'month end', but NFPIs can often be produced in **real time** (eg per shift, daily), providing managers with a more timely indication of performance levels.

(d) Financial measures focus on the **short term** (eg annual profit), but these may not be directly linked to longer-term organisational objectives (eg innovation and new product development). NFPIs provide information about key areas such as quality, customer and employee satisfaction; these are **lead indicators** of profit.

(e) NFPIs are measures of performance based on non-financial information which may originate in and be used by operating departments to control their activities, without any accounting input. As such they are normally **easy to calculate and easier** for non-financial managers **to understand and use.**

4.1 Cost, revenue and profit centres

For cost, revenue and profit centres, the selected NFPIs will depend on the type of responsible centre being considered and on the nature of the industry. The chosen NFPIs should focus on areas that are **critical** to the success of a responsibility centre and to the organisation as a whole.

Type of responsibility centre	Possible non-financial indicators
Cost centre	• Capacity utilisation of facilities and personnel • Number of units produced per day • Average set-up time for new production run
Revenue centre	• Number of repeat customer orders received • Number of complaints • Number of new accounts gained or lost • Number of visits by representatives to customer premises • Sales growth by product or service • Size of customer base • Market share by product or service
Profit centre	• The analyses for cost **and** revenue centres would be relevant here • In addition, market share would be relevant

4.2 The balanced scorecard

The balanced scorecard (*Kaplan & Norton, 1996*) focuses on **four** different perspectives and aims to establish goals for each together with **a combination of financial and non-financial measures** which can be used to evaluate whether these goals have been achieved. This is most likely to be applied to **an investment centre**, since it assumes that the responsibility centre being evaluated has a high degree of autonomy.

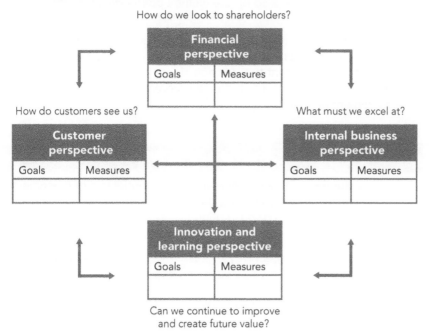

Customer measures often focus on quality, delivery time, performance and service.

Internal business measures will focus on processes that are important to meeting **customer expectations** such as quality, time and cost.

Innovation and learning measures are concerned with improving key **internal processes** and creating value for **customers.** Measures often focus on the amount of innovation and the success of innovation, and also achieving long-term targets for improving business processes

Financial measures – successful strategies should create value for **shareholders**. Measures will normally cover **survival** (cash flow), **success** (sales or profit) and **prosperity** (shareholder value).

4.2.1 Features/benefits of the balanced scorecard

- It links performance measures to key elements of a company's **strategy**.
- It requires a balanced consideration of all **four perspectives**, to prevent improvements being made in one area at the expense of another.
- It considers **financial and non-financial** measures and goals and both **internal** and **external** factors.
- It attempts to establish the needs and concerns of customers in order to identify **new products and markets.**

4.2.2 Problems with using the balanced scorecard

- It can be difficult to select which measures to include, and how many to include. There could be a danger of **information overload**. It is important to only include indicators because they add value, not because they are easy to measure.
- Having a number of different indicators (or too many indicators) can make **interpretation** of overall performance **difficult**. Worse performance in some areas leads to improved performance in other areas (eg higher material costs may cause profits to fall in the short term, but could lead to higher customer satisfaction).
- The needs of internal stakeholders (particularly **staff**) are not explicitly included. Also, the scorecard doesn't take account of **corporate social responsibility** (CSR).

4.2.3 Worked example

ZJET is an airline company that operates both domestically and internationally using a fleet of 20 aircraft. Passengers book flights using the internet or by telephone and pay for their flights at the time of booking using a debit or credit card.

The airline has also entered into profit sharing arrangements with hotels and local car hire companies that allow rooms and cars to be booked by the airline's passengers through the airline's website.

ZJET currently measures its performance using financial ratios. The new managing director has suggested that other measures are equally as important as financial measures and has suggested using the balanced scorecard to identify three non-financial performance measures (**one** from **each** of **three** different perspectives of the balanced scorecard) that ZJET could use as part of its performance measurement process.

A possible solution would be:

Perspective	Measure	Why?
Customer	Number of times customer fails to make a booking due to website crash or busy phone lines	Potential loss of customers
Internal	Number of take-offs on time	Measures efficiency of process
Innovation and learning	Number of new destinations	Attracts more customers to airline

Exam focus

You need to be prepared to identify which part of the balanced scorecard a specific NFPI relates to.

5 Benchmarking

Benchmarking: 'Benchmarking is the establishment, through data gathering, of targets and comparators, through whose use relative levels of performance (and particularly underperformance) can be identified. By the adoption of identified best practices it is hoped that performance will improve.' (*CIMA Official Terminology*)

Benchmarking can be applied to **any of the performance measures discussed** in this chapter.

There are several types of benchmarking:

(a) **Internal benchmarking**: A method of comparing one operating unit or function with another within the same organisation

(b) **External benchmarking**: This involves gathering information about other companies

    (i) **Competitor benchmarking**: This may involve reverse engineering (covered in Chapter 3)

    (ii) **Strategic benchmarking**: This involves comparing against an external database of industry average performance data

    (iii) **Functional benchmarking**: This involves comparing against non-competing businesses with similar processes

There are a number of **potential disadvantages** that businesses should consider prior to performing a benchmarking exercise.

(a) Businesses may find it difficult to **identify the 'best in class'** for each activity.

(b) It is often difficult to **persuade other organisations** to share information.

(c) Successful practices in one organisation **may not transfer** successfully to another.

(d) There is a risk of **copying** other companies and failing to create a distinctive position in the marketplace.

Exam focus

An assessment question could ask you to identify the advantages or disadvantages of a specific form of benchmarking.

Chapter summary

Performance measurement

├── **Financial indicators**

│   ├── **Traditional ratio analysis**
│   │   Profitability:
│   │   - ROCE
│   │   - Gross profit margin
│   │   - Operating profit margin
│   │
│   │   Liquidity:
│   │   - Current ratio
│   │   - Receivables period
│   │   - Payables period
│   │   - Inventory days
│   │
│   │   Asset turnover =
│   │   Sales/Capital employed
│   │
│   │   Profit =
│   │   Cash flow – Depreciation
│   │
│   ├── **Divisional performance measures**
│   │   ROI = Controllable divisional profit/Divisional investment
│   │   - Only projects which increase the existing ROI should be undertaken
│   │
│   │   RI = Divisional profit less imputed interest
│   │   (Investment × Cost of capital)
│   │   - Projects with a positive residual income should be undertaken
│   │   - Advantages vs disadvantages
│   │
│   ├── **Economic value added™**
│   │   EVA™ = Economic profit (NOPAT)
│   │   Less capital charge
│   │   (net assets × cost of capital)
│   │   Accounting profit adjusted for:
│   │   - Economic depreciation
│   │   - Advertising/development costs
│   │   Net assets are valued at replacement cost
│   │
│   ├── **Benchmarking**
│   │   - Adopting best practices
│   │   - Internal
│   │   - External competitive
│   │   - Reverse engineering
│   │   - Intra-group
│   │   - Inter-industry
│   │
│   └── **Analysis of reporting by dimension**
│   - Segment
│   - Product
│   - Channel

└── **Non-financial performance indicators**

    ├── **Value of and problems with NFPIs**
    │   - Can measure anything
    │   - Quantitative and qualitative
    │   - Gather information on key areas eg quality, customers, employees
    │   - Good indicator of future prospects
    │   - Can provide too much information
    │   - Can forget overall goal
    │
    └── **Balanced scorecard**
        Enables focus on both internal and external factors and on key elements of business strategy
        Four dimensions are:
        - Customer
        - Internal
        - Financial
        - Innovation and learning

Key terms

Liquidity: Liquidity is the amount of cash a company can obtain quickly to settle its debts (and possibly to meet other unforeseen demands for cash payments too).

EVA: EVA™ is calculated as net operating profit after tax (NOPAT) less a capital charge (where the capital charge = weighted average cost of capital × net assets at the start of the period).

Benchmarking: 'Benchmarking is the establishment, through data gathering, of targets and comparators, through whose use relative levels of performance (and particularly underperformance) can be identified. By the adoption of identified best practices it is hoped that performance will improve.' (*CIMA Official Terminology*)

Activity answers

Activity 1: Liquidity ratios

The correct answer is:

Current ratio: 1.14

Quick ratio: 0.90

Current assets − Inventory = 572.3 − 119.0 = 453.3

	20X8
Current ratio	572.3/501.0 = 1.14
Quick ratio	453.3/501.0 = 0.90

Activity 2: Profitability ratios

The correct answer is:

ROCE: 7.2%

Operating margin: 6.5%

Asset turnover: 1.1

Revised operating profit = 180,000 + 285,000 − 369,000 = $96,000

Revised capital employed = 1,080,000 − 855,000 + 1,108,500 = $1,333,500

ROCE = 96,000/1,333,500 = 7.2%

Operating profit margin = 96,000/1,485,000 = 6.5%

Asset turnover = 1,485,000/ 1,333,500 = 1.1

Activity 3: ROI and RI

The correct answer is:

Division A project ROI: 15.08%

Division A project RI: $2.55m

Division B project ROI: 17.72%

Division B project RI: $2.32m

	Operating profit	Capital employed	Return on investment	Residual income
Division A	$44.6m × 28% = $12.488m	$82.8 million	$12.88m/$82.8m = 15.08% Using ROI the project is rejected	Imputed interest charge = $82.8m × 12% = $9.936m Residual income = $12.488 − $9.936 = $2.55m Using RI the project is accepted
Division B	$21.8m × 33% = $7.194m	$40.6 million	$7.194m/$40.6m = 17.72% Using ROI the project is accepted	Imputed interest charge = $40.6m × 12% = $4.872 Residual income = $7.194 − $4.872 = $2.32m Using RI the project is accepted

Activity 4: EVA and RI

The correct answer is:

EVA: $m46.8

RI: $m78.0

PAT	$'000	$'000
Net profit		89.6
Add back:		
Non-cash expenses	8	
Amortisation of goodwill	5	
Interest (net of 30% tax) 15 × 0.7	10.5	
NOPAT		113.1

Alternative approach:

PAT	$'000	$'000
PBIT		143.0
Less tax @ 30%		(42.9)
Add back		
Non-cash expenses		5.0
Amortisation of goodwill		8.0
NOPAT		113.1

Assets		
At start of year		470
Add back amortised goodwill		40
		510

WACC		
Equity 15% × 75%		0.1125
Debt (10% × 0.7) × 25%		0.0175
WACC		0.1300

EVA™ NOPAT	113.1
Capital charge	
13% × $510	66.3
	46.8

RI	$'000
PBIT	143.0
Capital charge	
13% × $500	65.0
	78.0

The business is creating value, as its return (however calculated) is greater than the group's WACC.

Test your learning

1   **Required**
    Insert the correct phrase from the list above to complete the following sentence.

    In general, a current ratio [▼] should be expected.

    Picklist:

    in excess of 1

    of less than 1

    of approximately zero

2   **Required**
    Insert the correct word from the list to complete the following sentences.

    ROI based on profits as a % of net assets employed will [▼] as an asset gets
    older and its book value [▼] . This could therefore create a(n)
    [▼] to investment centre managers to reinvest in new or replacement assets.

    Picklist:

    increases

    disincentive

    increase

    reduces

    decrease

    incentive

3   The use of residual income in performance measurement will avoid dysfunctional decision making
    because it will always lead to the correct decision concerning capital investments.

    Required
    Is the preceding statement true or false?

    A   True

    B   False

4   An investment centre with capital employed of $570,000 is budgeted to earn a profit of $119,700
    next year. A proposed non-current asset investment of $50,000, not included in the budget at
    present, will earn a profit next year of $8,500 after depreciation. The company's cost of capital is
    15%.

    Required
    What is the budgeted ROI for next year, both with and without the investment? (Give your answer
    to one decimal place.)

    ROI without investment: [   ] %

    ROI with investment: [   ] %

5   An investment centre with capital employed of $570,000 is budgeted to earn a profit of $119,700
    next year. A proposed non-current asset investment of $50,000, not included in the budget at
    present, will earn a profit next year of $8,500 after depreciation. The company's cost of capital is
    15%.

    Required
    What is the budgeted RI for next year, both with and without the investment? (Give your answer to
    the nearest $.)

RI without investment: $ _____

RI with investment: $ _____

6   EVA™ is calculated as operating profit less a capital charge.

Required
Is the preceding statement true or false?

A   True

B   False

7   Company H has reported annual profits for 20X7 of $83.4 million. This is after charging $8.3 million for development costs of a new product that is expected to last for the current year and two more years.

The cost of capital is 12% per annum.

Non-current assets have a historical cost of $110 million and the replacement cost of these assets at the beginning of the year is $156 million. The assets have been depreciated at 10% per year and economic depreciation is expected to be 10% of replacement value. The company has working capital of $25.2 million.

Required
Ignoring the effect of taxation, what is the EVA™ of the company? (Give your answer to the nearest $m.)

$ _____

10

Transfer pricing

Syllabus learning outcomes

Having studied this chapter, you will be able to work through the following syllabus outcomes:

Syllabus area C: Managing and controlling the performance of organisational units
3   Explain the behavioural and transfer pricing issues related to the management of responsibility centres
a   Behavioural issues
b   Use and ethics of transfer pricing

Exam context

In the exam, you will be expected to demonstrate competence in the following representative task statements:

- Understand the likely behavioural consequences of performance measurement within an organisation including the behavioural consequences of performance management and control in responsibility centres and the behavioural consequences arising from divisional structures including internal competition and internal trading
- Understand the theory of transfer pricing, including perfect, imperfect, and no market for the intermediate good
- Calculate negotiated, market, cost-plus and variable cost-based transfer prices
- Determine dual transfer prices and lump sum payments as means of addressing some of the issues that arise in transfer pricing decisions
- Determine how the different methods of calculating transfer prices affect manager autonomy, motivation, goal congruence, and unit performance
- Analyse the effects of transfer pricing on divisional and group profitability

Chapter overview

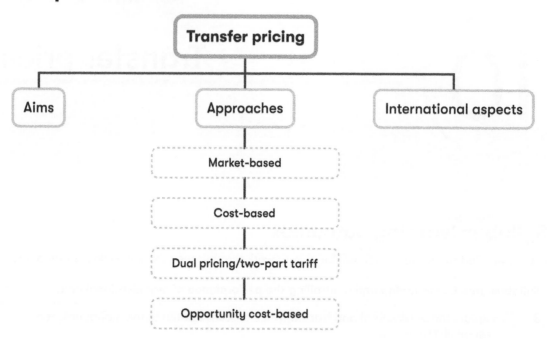

1 Introduction

In an organisation with profit centres and investment centres, it is very likely there will be interconnection between the centres, with some centres supplying goods and services to others. When this interdivisional trading happens, the centre providing the goods or services will want to earn income from the transfer. The price of the transfer is difficult to establish and agree, and this chapter will look at the issues and techniques involved.

2 Transfer pricing aims

The decision to create responsibility centres often creates the need for a transfer price to be agreed between divisions for goods and services that are provided to each other.

> **Transfer price:** A **transfer price** is the price at which goods or services are transferred from one division to another, or from one member of a group to another.

Where there are transfers of goods or services between responsibility centres, these **transfers could be made 'free' or 'as a favour'** to the division receiving the benefit.

However, attaching a transfer price to these internal trades brings a number of advantages:

- **Control**

  Transfer pricing allows a **record** of interdivisional work to be maintained.

- **Performance and motivation**

  Transfer pricing allows the responsibility centre providing the good or service to receive credit for the work done. This facilitates **fairer** performance measurement and will also **motivate** the responsibility centre to provide a good level of service (especially if they are having to compete with other internal and external providers for 'internal' revenue).

Real life example

A car dealership has two divisions: one for car repairs and servicing and the other for car sales. The servicing division is also required to service cars before they are sold and delivered to customers.

In the absence of a transfer pricing system, the servicing division could do its work for the car sales division **without making any record** of the work done.

However, unless the cost or value of service work performed for the sales division is recorded, management cannot **control** the amount of resources (like labour time) being used on servicing cars for the sales division.

In the absence of a transfer price, the service division does not receive any credit for the work it does for the sales division, so its revenue and profitability are effectively understated. Conversely, the **performance of the sales** division is overstated. Therefore, transfer prices are required to prevent the performance of the two divisions being distorted.

The absence of a transfer price may also **motivate** the repair and services division to do a poor job (as they don't get any credit for the work performed). This could **damage the interests of the company as a whole** (if the cars subsequently sold on to customers have problems which should have been fixed by the service division, but weren't).

2.1 Aims of transfer pricing

Aim	How it is achieved
Goal congruence	Decisions that managers take to improve the profit of their division will also improve the profit of the company as a whole.
	This is achieved by setting a transfer price which reflects the **true cost to the company** of products or services being transferred between divisions.

Aim	How it is achieved
Autonomy	Allowing managers to retain autonomy by not forcing internal transfers on to a division. The existence of a transfer price allows divisions to decide where they buy from or who they supply, and in what quantities.
Performance evaluation	Preventing unfair impact on performance measures of either the division supplying or receiving the internally provided good or service.

Exam focus

The three general aims of transfer pricing are likely to be regularly tested. They can be remembered as 'GAP' (G for goal congruence, A for autonomy and P for performance evaluation).

2.1.1 Internal transfers - overview

In the remainder of this chapter, reference will be made to Division S, the 'supplying' division, and Division R, the 'receiving' division. These are explained in the diagrams below.

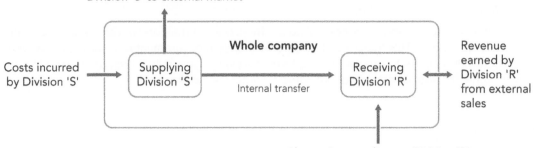

General rule

A transfer price should reflect the true cost to the company of an internal transfer taking place

2.2 General rules

2.2.1 Maximum transfer price

The **maximum transfer price** is the highest price the receiving division would be prepared to pay.

This will be influenced by the **market price** for the transferred unit (if there is one) or by **the revenue the receiving division will receive from selling the final product less any further processing costs** (net marginal revenue).

2.2.2 Minimum transfer price

The **minimum transfer price** is the sum of the supplying **division's marginal cost and opportunity cost** of the item transferred.

Opportunity cost: The **opportunity cost** of an item is the contribution forgone by the supplying division **in transferring that item internally rather than selling goods externally** (or by not using the same facilities in the producing division for their next best alternative use). Opportunity cost is sometimes referred to as **shadow price**.

If there is **no external market** for the item being transferred, and **no alternative uses for** the division's facilities, then opportunity cost = 0.

Where the supplying division is at **full capacity**, the opportunity cost will be the **lost contribution** from not selling to the external market (eg market price less variable costs).

The opportunity cost-based approach is often viewed as an ideal way of setting a transfer price. Opportunity cost-based approaches should always result in **goal congruent** behaviour, with both buyer and seller happy to transfer when it is in the group's best interest to do so.

Activity 1: Minimum transfer price

Division S produces two products, A and B. Each product has an external market, but B can also be transferred to Division R.

After incurring extra costs of $60, Division R then sells the unit for $300.

The maximum quantity that might be required for transfer is 150 units of B.

Information on the products is as follows.

	A	B
External market price per unit	$150	$200
Variable production cost per unit	$86	$95
Labour hours required per unit	4	6
Maximum external sales, in units	2,000	1,250

In the current period, labour hours in the profit centre are limited to 12,000, and this is insufficient to satisfy maximum external demand.

Therefore, using limiting factor analysis, the optimal production plan has been calculated as:

	A	B
Contribution per unit	$64	$105
Labour hours required	4	6
Contribution per hour	$16	$17.50
Ranking	2rd	1st

Optimal production plan

Product	Units	Hours/unit	Hours
B	1,250	6	7,500
A (balance)	1,125	4	4,500
			12,000

Required

Given that Division S is operating at full capacity, what is the minimum acceptable transfer price? (Consider what would happen if Division R was not willing to pay it, too.)

$ _____

Solution

3 Types of transfer pricing

In reality, a variety of approaches are used to establish a transfer price. These can be evaluated by comparing them to the general rules covered in the previous section.

3.1 Market-based approaches to transfer pricing

Where a market price exists it is often used as the basis for a transfer price.

Supplying division	Receiving division
Earns the same level of profit on internal sales as external sales	Happy to accept transfer (cannot buy cheaper elsewhere)
Happy to transfer unless at full capacity making other units that have a greater contribution	

The managers of both divisions should therefore both behave in a **goal congruent** way.

If the supplying division is at full capacity then the revenue it loses as a result of an internal transfer shows the true cost of an internal transfer.

If a division would have to incur marketing costs to sell externally then the market price can be **adjusted** to reflect the fact that an internal transfer would not incur this cost. So the transfer price becomes lower ie market price less marketing costs.

3.1.1 Perfect intermediate market

In a perfect market, the supplying division can choose to supply the component it is producing (described here as an intermediate product) to the external market at the prevailing market price only. The market is **large enough to absorb all of the supplying division's capacity**.

In this situation the market price is easy to establish.

Activity 2: Range of prices

The following data relates to the production of a component produced by Division S.

		$
Division S	Variable (marginal) costs	10.00
	Fixed overhead	2.00
		12.00

There is a large external market for this component and Division S is able to sell as much or as little of its capacity as it wishes at the market price of $17 per unit.

Division S saves costs of $2 per unit if it sells to another Division within the same company (Division R).

Required

Which of the following shows the correct minimum transfer price for Division S and maximum transfer prices for Division R?

A   Minimum $12, Maximum $17

B   Minimum $12, Maximum $15

C   Minimum $10, Maximum $15

D   Minimum $15, Maximum $17

Solution

3.1.2 Imperfect intermediate market

It is much more likely, in reality, that the supplying division can choose to supply to the external market at a range of prices (selling less at a higher price and more at a lower price).

In this situation it is **harder to apply the principle** that the revenue it loses as a result of an internal transfer shows the true cost of an internal transfer.

This is because if production is diverted to internal sales and less capacity is available to sell to the external market, a firm may be able to increase the price it sells at to the **external market** (because it has fewer units that it needs to sell).

This makes the market price approach to transfer pricing much more complicated to use.

3.2 Cost-based methods of transfer pricing

The supplying division has its costs of manufacturing refunded and may also be allowed a mark-up to encourage the transfer.

3.2.1 Actual cost or standard cost

Standard costs are preferred to actual costs. If actual costs are used then any inefficiencies can be passed by Division S to Division R, so there is no encouragement to control costs within Division S.

3.2.2 Full cost (or full cost +)

Full cost means variable costs plus fixed overheads. **Sometimes this also includes a mark-up.**

This approach may lead to an excessively high transfer price, and therefore the receiving division may look to use an external supplier instead. This may lead to the wrong decision being made, because fixed costs are not a 'relevant' cost for decision making.

3.2.3 Standard variable (marginal) cost

The selling division (S) should transfer goods to the buying division at the variable (or marginal) cost of production if:

(a) S has **spare capacity,** as the marginal costs reflect the true cost to the company of the transfer taking place

(b) S has **no external market** so could operate as a cost centre; if S is a profit centre, it will be demotivated as internal transfers will not generate any contribution towards its fixed costs

Activity 3: Spare capacity

Goods are transferred from Division S to Division R at standard full cost + 10%.

Division S		$
	Variable costs	20.00
	Fixed overhead	8.00
		28.00
	Standard profit @ 10%	2.80
	Transfer price	30.80

Currently Division S has **spare capacity.**

Division R, the receiving division, has been approached by an external supplier offering to provide equivalent goods at $26 per unit.

Required

Which TWO of the following are a likely outcome of setting the transfer price at $30.80?

A   Division R will not want to buy goods from Division S.

B   Division R will not behave in the best interests of the company as a whole (goal congruence).

C   Division S will receive an unfair share of total profit.

D   Division R will receive an unfair share of total profit.

Solution

3.2.4 Dual pricing and two-part tariffs

The need for the supplying division to receive some contribution towards their fixed costs can be considered in a **marginal cost-based transfer pricing system** in the following ways:

(a) Dual pricing

Where an external market exists, credit the selling division with the market price of the transfers made but debit the buying division with the variable cost.

(b) Two-part tariff

Transfer prices are set at variable cost and once a year there is a **transfer of a fixed fee to the supplying division** representing an allowance for its fixed costs. This should allow the supplying division to cover its fixed costs and make a profit.

Activity 4: Two-part tariff

TY comprises two divisions, both of which are profit centres. Division Y is a production division, and Division T is a sales division. Division Y manufactures a single component which it sells to Division T.

The following statement shows the performance of each division for the year ended 31 August:

Division	Y	T
Units sold	200,000	200,000
	$	$
Sales	1,440,000	1,840,000
Variable cost	720,000	1,440,000
Contribution	720,000	400,000
Fixed costs	500,000	230,000
Operating profit	220,000	170,000

During the year to 31 August Division Y operated at 80% capacity and produced 200,000 units, all of which were sold to Division T and sold on by Division T to external customers.

The manager of Division T has identified another customer which it can sell another 20,000 units to at a price of $7.10 per unit.

The manager of Division T is proposing that a more suitable transfer pricing system, to be applied to all units transferred, is a variable cost plus a lump sum of $750,000.

Required

Calculate the impact (in $'000) on the profit of each division and the company as a whole of the proposed new transfer pricing arrangement. (Give your answer to the nearest $'000.)

Note. Also consider the impact on the motivation of each division.

Division Y ⬚

Division T ⬚

Total ⬚

Solution

Exam focus

The impact of a change in transfer pricing on performance appraisal is a likely area to feature in assessment questions.

3.3 Negotiated transfer prices

A transfer price based on opportunity cost is often difficult to identify, due to lack of suitable information about costs and revenues in individual divisions.

In this case it is likely that transfer prices will be set by means of **negotiation**. The agreed price may be finalised from a mixture of accounting, arithmetic, politics and compromise.

For example, a negotiated price might be based on market value, but with some reductions to allow for the internal nature of the transaction, which saves external selling and distribution costs.

3.3.1 Behavioural implications

Even so, interdepartmental **disputes** about transfer prices are likely to arise and these may need the **intervention or mediation of head office** to settle the problem. Head office management may then **impose a price** which maximises the profit of the company as a whole.

On the other hand, head office management might restrict their intervention to the **task of keeping negotiations in progress** until a transfer price is eventually settled.

The **more head office has to impose** its own decisions on profit centres, the less **decentralisation of authority** (autonomy) there will be and the **less effective the profit centre system** of accounting will be for **motivating** divisional managers.

Exam focus

The discussion areas that have been covered need to be carefully reviewed. Behavioural factors are clearly highlighted in the P2 syllabus as being a key area, so don't just focus on the numbers.

4 International issues

Factor	Explanation
Taxation in different countries	If tax on profits is 20% in Country A and 50% of profits in Country B, a company may try to 'manipulate' profits by changing transfer pricing so that profits are maximised for a subsidiary in Country A, by reducing profits for a subsidiary in Country B. Artificial attempts to reduce tax liabilities could be considered unethical; it may upset a country's tax officials if they discover it and may lead to a penalty. Many tax authorities have the power to modify transfer prices in computing tariffs or taxes on profit, although a genuine **arm's length market price** should be accepted. There are **three methods** the tax authorities can use to determine an arm's length price. (a) The **comparable price method (also known as comparable uncontrolled price, or CUs)** involves setting the arm's length price based on the price of similar products (usually the market price). This is the preferred method where possible. (b) The **resale price method** involves setting the arm's length price based on the price paid for a final product by an independent party and a suitable mark-up (to allow for the seller's expenses and profit) is deducted. This method is often used for the transfer of goods to distributors where goods are sold on with little further processing. (c) The **cost-plus method** involves obtaining an arm's length gross margin and applying it to the seller's manufacturing costs. Many countries have **double taxation agreements** that mean that a company will pay tax on a transaction in only one country. If a tax authority determines that a company has set an unrealistic transfer price and has paid less tax than is due, the company would then pay tax in both countries, plus any applicable penalties. A mitigation against this is an **advanced pricing agreement**, entered into with both of the tax authorities involved.
Import tariffs/ customs duties	Country A imposes an import tariff of 20% on the value of goods imported. A multinational company has a subsidiary in Country A which imports goods from a subsidiary in Country B. The company could minimise costs by keeping the transfer price to a minimum.
Exchange controls	If a country imposes restrictions on the transfer of profits from domestic subsidiaries to foreign multinationals, the restrictions on the transfer can be overcome if head office provides some goods or services to the subsidiary and charges exorbitantly high prices, disguising the 'profits' as sales revenue, and transferring them from one country to the other. The ethics of such an approach should, of course, be questioned.
Anti-dumping legislation	Governments may take action to protect home industries by preventing companies from transferring goods cheaply into their countries. They may do this by, for example, insisting on the use of a fair market value for the transfer price.
Competitive pressures	Transfer pricing can be used to enable profit centres to match or (sometimes unfairly) undercut local competitors.

BPP LEARNING MEDIA

Chapter summary

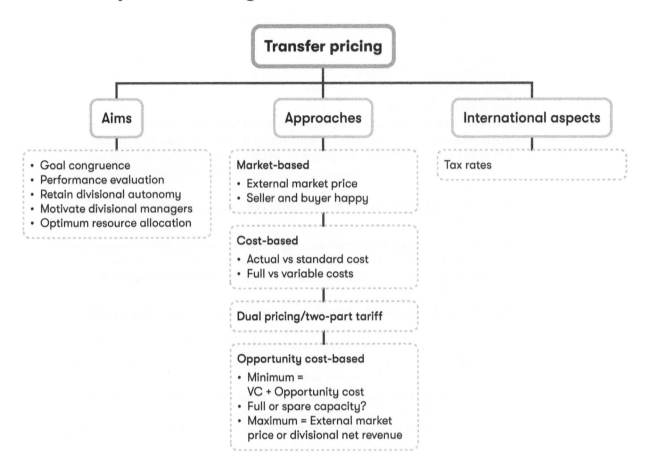

Transfer pricing

Aims
- Goal congruence
- Performance evaluation
- Retain divisional autonomy
- Motivate divisional managers
- Optimum resource allocation

Approaches

Market-based
- External market price
- Seller and buyer happy

Cost-based
- Actual vs standard cost
- Full vs variable costs

Dual pricing/two-part tariff

Opportunity cost-based
- Minimum =
  VC + Opportunity cost
- Full or spare capacity?
- Maximum = External market
  price or divisional net revenue

International aspects

Tax rates

Key terms

Transfer price: A **transfer price** is the price at which goods or services are transferred from one division to another, or from one member of a group to another.

Opportunity cost: The **opportunity cost** of an item is the contribution forgone by the supplying division **in transferring that item internally rather than selling goods externally** (or by not using the same facilities in the producing division for their next best alternative use). Opportunity cost is sometimes referred to as **shadow price**.

Activity answers

Activity 1: Minimum transfer price

The correct answer is:

$191

If labour is diverted for the transfer, hours will come from product A which is earning contribution of $16 per hour.

Minimum transfer price:

	$
	$
Variable unit cost	95
Opportunity cost 6 hrs × $16	96
	191

Division R would be willing to pay this because it is below the market price ($200) and because their net marginal revenue is $300 – $60 = $240. If they were not willing to pay the price of $191 it would either be because the market price or net marginal revenue was below $191; if either of these outcomes were true, then it would be goal congruent for Division R not to use Division S.

Activity 2: Range of prices

The correct answer is:

Minimum $15, Maximum $17

Division S will need to cover its marginal cost ($10) plus lost revenue from selling to the external market ($17 – $10 marginal cost – $2 selling cost = $5). This gives a minimum price of $10 + $5 = $15.

Division R will be prepared to pay as a maximum the market price of $17.

A transfer price can therefore be negotiated between the range $15 and $17.

Activity 3: Spare capacity

The correct answers are:

- Division R will not want to buy goods from Division S.
- Division R will not behave in the best interests of the company as a whole (goal congruence).

The transfer will not take place, but from the point of view of the company as a whole the internal transfer is preferable because the true cost to the company of an internal transfer is really the variable cost of Division S of $20 which is cheaper than the price being paid to the external supplier.

Activity 4: Two-part tariff

The correct answer is:

Division Y	30
Division T	40
Total	70

The current transfer price is $1,440,000/200,000 = $7.20.

At this price, the extra business with another customer will not be in the interests of Division T and therefore will not happen.

The variable cost of Division Y is $720,000/200,000 = $3.60. At this price the extra business with another customer WILL be in the interests of Division T.

	Y	T	Total
Units sold (10% increase)	220,000	220,000	
	$'000	$'000	$'000
Sales value		1,982	
	792	($1,840,000 + 220,000 units × $7.10)	
	(220,000 units × $3.60)		
Variable cost (10% increase)	792	792	
Contribution	0	1,190	1,190
Change in contribution	(720)	790	70
Lump sum	750	(750)	
Change in profit	30	40	70

The proposal will **improve** contribution for the company as a whole and therefore is **recommended**.

The performance of Division Y will **improve**.

The performance of Division T will **improve**.

This happens because the revenue from the new customer of $7.10 creates contribution for the company of $3.50 per unit ($7.10 – variable cost of $3.60) and this is worth $3.50 × 20,000 = $70,000.

The previous transfer price was excessive. Division Y has capacity to produce 200,000/0.80 = 250,000.

Given its excess capacity the opportunity cost of accepting more internal work is 0 and the transfer price should be set at marginal cost to reflect this. The effect of the lump sum is to allow Division Y to show an improvement in performance which reflects the improvement in the profits of the company as a whole.

This is therefore encouraging goal congruence and is fair in terms of performance evaluation; this makes it a sensible proposal.

BPP
LEARNING
MEDIA

Test your learning

1 **Required**

Which of the following does transfer pricing aim to achieve?

Select all that apply

A   Should encourage dysfunctional decision making

B   Should encourage output at an organisation-wide profit-maximising level

C   Should encourage divisions to act in their own self-interest

D   Should encourage divisions to make entirely autonomous decisions

2 **Required**

Insert the words from the list to complete the following statement.

A word may be used more than once.

When transfer prices are based on opportunity costs, opportunity costs are either the

[▼] foregone by the supplying division in transferring [▼]

rather than selling [▼] , or the [▼] forgone by not using the

relevant facilities for their [▼] alternative use.

Picklist:

next best

profit

cheapest

internally

externally

contribution

3 Division P transfers its output to Division Q at variable cost. Once a year P charges a fixed fee to Q, representing an allowance for P's fixed costs.

Required

This type of transfer pricing system is commonly known as:

A   Dual pricing

B   Negotiated

C   Opportunity cost

D   Two-part tariff

4 **Required**

Which of the following does transfer pricing aim to achieve?

Select all that apply

A   Should enable the measurement of profit centre performance

B   Should reward the transferring division

C   Should be a reasonable cost for receiving division

D   Should discourage goal congruence

5 Taxation on profits in country C is charged at a higher rate than in country D. When goods are transferred from a subsidiary in country C to a subsidiary in country D it would be beneficial, from the point of view of the whole organisation, to charge a higher transfer price so that the total taxation cost for the organisation is lower.

Required

Is the above statement true or false?

A   True

B   False

6   **Required**

Insert one of the words from the list to complete the following statement.

Each word can be used more than once.

The more head office has to impose its own decisions on profit centres, the ▢▼

decentralisation of authority there will be and the ▢▼ effective the profit centre

system of accounting will be for motivating divisional managers.

Picklist:

more

less

11

Risk and uncertainty

Syllabus learning outcomes

Having studied this chapter, you will be able to work through the following syllabus outcomes:

Syllabus area D: Risk and control	
1	Analyse risk and uncertainty associated with medium-term decision making
a	Sensitivity analysis
b	Analysis of risk

Exam context

In the exam, you will be expected to demonstrate competence in the following representative task statements:

- Use sensitivity analysis, expected values, standard deviations and probability tables to quantify and analyse risk
- Use probabilistic models and interpretations of distribution of project outcomes for risk quantification
- Use the results of digital analyses to test the impact of varying inputs on project viability
- Use decision trees for multi-stage medium-term decision problems
- Understand decision making in conditions of uncertainty

Chapter overview

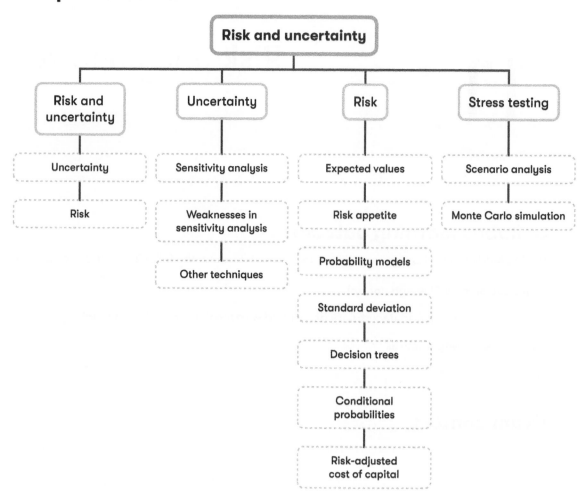

1 Introduction

Decisions such as investment and pricing decisions, are based on predictions on what will happen in the future and therefore decision making in these areas will involve a high element of unpredictability.

This chapter considers a number of different attitudes that organisations may have to risk, and distinguishes between risk and uncertainty.

The main focus of this chapter is on the variety of numerical decision-making techniques that are available for assessing risk and uncertainty.

2 Risk and uncertainty

Many decisions are based on predictions on what will happen in the future and therefore involve an element of unpredictability. This unpredictability can be described as **risk** or **uncertainty**. There is an important technical distinction between these two concepts.

2.1 Uncertainty

> **Uncertainty**: Uncertainty exists when the future is unknown and the decision maker has no past experience on which to base predictions of change. There are therefore a number of possible outcomes but **the probability of each outcome is not known**.

Uncertainty can be **described** to managers to assist in decision making (see Section 3).

2.2 Risk

> **Risk**: Risk exists where a decision maker has knowledge that several different future outcomes are possible, the probabilities of which are known, or can be estimated, usually due to past experience.

Risk can be analysed to **quantify** the appropriate decision for a company given its risk-appetite profile (see Section 4).

3 Uncertainty

An important technique for managing **uncertainty** is sensitivity analysis.

3.1 Sensitivity analysis

3.1.1 What-if analysis

Sensitivity analysis can be used to describe the impact on a decision of changing **one variable** (eg what the impact on a project's NPV would be if its project life were 10% shorter); this is often referred to as 'what-if' analysis.

3.1.2 Percentage change needed to change a decision

Alternatively, sensitivity analysis can be used to assess the required change in **one variable** before a project would fail to achieve its objectives; eg the percentage change necessary to reach an NPV of zero.

Formula to learn

$$\text{Sensitivity \%} = \frac{\text{NPV of project}}{\text{NPV of variable}} \times 100$$

The smaller the percentage change required, the more sensitive the project is to this variable, and the greater the uncertainty surrounding the project; such variables need to be **carefully managed** if a project is implemented.

Activity 1: NPV & sensitivity

A company is evaluating a three-year project, the NPV has been assessed as follows:

	t_0	t_1	t_2	t_3
	$'000	$'000	$'000	$'000
Sales		4,200	4,900	5,300
Variable costs		(2,850)	(3,100)	(4,150)
Pre-tax cash flow		1,350	1,800	1,150
Tax @ 21%		(284)	(378)	(242)
Investment	(2,000)			
Net cash flow	(2,000)	1,066	1,422	908
DF @ 7%	1	0.935	0.873	0.816
PV	(2,000)	997	1,241	741

NPV = $979,000

Required

Calculate the sensitivity of the NPV to the changes in sales volume, and to changes in the selling price. (Give your answer to one decimal place.)

Volume: ⬚ %

Selling price: ⬚ %

Solution

3.2 Weaknesses in sensitivity analysis

(a) The method requires changes in each key variable to be **examined one at a time**, but management is more interested in the combination of the effects of changes in two or more key variables. Looking at factors in isolation is unrealistic since they are often interdependent.

(b) Sensitivity analysis does not examine the **probability** that any particular variation in costs or revenues might occur.

3.3 Other techniques for managing uncertainty

Setting a minimum payback period for projects	Cash flows become **more uncertain over time**, so reducing reliance on project's with later cash flows reduces uncertainty (covered in Chapter 5).
Scenario analysis	**Describing** a variety of possible scenarios (changing more than one variable at a time) to assess the range of possible outcomes.

Exam focus

Exam questions will test your understanding of the advantages and disadvantages of sensitivity analysis compared to other techniques, as well as testing your ability to perform calculations.

4 Risk

Where there is **risk**, a range of possible future outcomes can be **quantified** (eg best, worst and most likely) and probabilities assigned to them and an expected value or weighted average of these outcomes can be calculated.

Exam focus

Exam questions will expect you to understand the difference between risk and uncertainty.

4.1 Expected values (EV)

In the absence of any information about a particular risk attitude (see Section 4.2) it can be assumed that a decision maker, when faced with a number of alternative decisions, will select the one with the **best expected value** (EV).

An expected value is a weighted average that is calculated using probabilities. It is likely that you have used this technique before.

Formula provided

$$E(X) = \sum(\text{probability} \times \text{payoff})$$

Activity 2: ENPV

Harry Co is choosing between two mutually exclusive projects. The NPV of these projects in $m depends on the rate of growth of the economy over the next five years. Forecast NPV is shown under scenarios of low, average and high growth are shown below:

Probability	Forecast	Project A	Project B
[ ]	Low growth	1.00	−8.00
[ ]	Medium growth	2.50	4.00
[ ]	High growth	4.00	16.00
[ ]	Expected value	[ ]	[ ]

Low growth and high growth are equally likely, and medium growth is twice as likely as these two scenarios.

Required
Complete the table (working to two decimal places) to calculate each project's expected NPV (and consider which project would be chosen).

Solution

4.1.1 Value of perfect information (VOPI)

Information may be available about uncertain variables, eg from market research. If the information is guaranteed to predict the future with certainty, it is defined as 'perfect information'. Perfect information **removes risk**.

> **VOPI:** VOPI is calculated as the expected value with perfect information minus the expected profit without this information.

Illustration 1: VOPI

Continuing the previous activity

Required
Identify the expected NPV if perfect information was available about the future state of the economy and use this to calculate the value of perfect information.

$m $\boxed{}$

Solution

The correct answer is:

$m2.25

Expected values with perfect information can be calculated as follows.

	Probability	Project A	Project B
Low growth	0.25	+1.0 Project A chosen if the information forecasts the economy will grow at this rate	
Medium growth	0.50		+4.0 Project B chosen if the information forecasts the economy will grow at this rate
High growth	0.25		+16.0 Project B chosen if the information forecasts the economy will grow at this rate
Expected value			(1 × 0.25) + (4 × 0.50) + (16 × 0.25) = **6.25**

Value of perfect information = $6.25m (EV with perfect information) – $4m (EV without perfect information) = **$2.25m**

4.1.2 Limitations of EV

(a) Ignores attitudes to risk (see next section)

(b) Heavily dependent on probability estimates which may not be reliable

(c) It is a long run average and may not be appropriate if a decision is a one-off (an EV may not correspond to any of the possible outcomes)

4.2 Risk appetite

Risk appetite or attitude is the amount of risk (or uncertainty) an organisation is willing to take on, or is prepared to accept, in pursuing its strategic objectives. Organisations may be **risk seekers, risk neutral** or **risk averse**.

KEY
TERM

> **Risk appetite:** A **risk seeker** is a decision maker who is interested in trying to secure the best outcomes, no matter how small the chance that they may occur.
>
> A decision maker is **risk neutral** if they are concerned with what will be the most likely outcome.
>
> A **risk-averse** decision maker acts on the assumption that the worst outcome might occur.

4.2.1 Maximax, maximin and minimax regret

Risk attitude will influence the method used to evaluate decisions.

> **KEY TERM**
>
> **Maximax, maximin and minimax regret**: Maximax looks at the best possible results from each decision option and selects the option that gives the best possible result.
>
> Maximin suggests that a decision maker should select the alternative that offers the least unattractive worst outcome.
>
> Minimax regret aims to minimise the regret from making the wrong decision.

Risk attitude	Decision-making technique
Risk seeker	For this risk appetite **maximax** may be appropriate. This involves making decisions that are based on making the maximum possible return (regardless of the probability of this).
Risk averse	For this risk appetite **maximin** may be appropriate. This involves selecting decisions that minimise downside risk by selecting the option that gives the best of the worst outcomes (regardless of the probability of the worst outcomes occurring). **Minimax regret** may also be appropriate here; this is where a decision is chosen that minimises the impact of it turning out to be the wrong decision.
Risk neutral	Only a risk-neutral decision maker will be concerned with the most likely outcome, using **expected values** (EVs).

A risk-averse attitude may result from a business being under cash flow pressure, so that it cannot afford an unexpected drop in cash flow (ie it has a low **risk capacity**). One reason for this may be that the business has high financial gearing and has interest payments that need to be made.

A risk-seeking attitude may reflect the values of the decision maker and may also be affected by any incentives that are based on ambitious performance targets being hit. Venture capitalists often encourage a risk-seeking attitude because they are often highly ambitious in their growth targets.

Activity 3: Decision making and risk appetite

Continuing from the previous illustration.

NPV $m	Project A	Project B
Low growth	+1.0	−8.0
Medium growth	+2.5	+4.0
High growth	+4.0	+16.0

1 Required

Identify the key outcome for a risk seeker (and consider which project would be chosen).

$m [   ]

2 Required

Identify the key outcome using maximin (and consider which project would be chosen).

$m [   ]

3 Required

Identify the outcome that results in minimax regret (and consider which project would be chosen).

$m [   ]

Solution

1

2

3

4.3 Probability models

As well as being used to calculate expected values, probabilities are also useful in determining the probability of a specific outcome (eg of a project delivering a negative NPV) and also the most likely outcome.

Here, the concept of joint probability is useful.

KEY TERM

Joint probability: Joint probability is the probability of two risky outcomes occurring at the same time and is calculated as the probability of one outcome multiplied by the probability of the other.

Activity 4: Joint probabilities

An investment in a new product is being planned. The product has an expected life of two years. An analysis of similar projects has resulted in the following annual cash flow projections:

	Year 1		Year 2	
Cash flow projection 1 (high)	$56m p.a.	60% chance	$44m p.a.	30% chance
Cash flow projection 2 (low)	$44m p.a.	40% chance	$36m p.a.	70% chance

The outcome in Year 2 is not dependent on the outcome in Year 1.

Set-up costs of $77m are payable immediately. The cost of capital is 10%. You are the management accountant and you are worried about the risk of the project.

The possible outcomes have been further analysed as follows:

Year 1 $44m (low)	Year 2 $36m (low)	NPV = $–7,268m
Year 1 $44m (low)	Year 2 $44m (high)	NPV = $–660m
Year 1 $56m (high)	Year 2 $36m (low)	NPV = $+3,640m
Year 1 $56m (high)	Year 2 $44m (high)	NPV = $+10,248m

Ignore the impact of taxation.

1 **Required**

Identify the mean (expected) NPV of the project. (Give your answer to the nearest $'000.)

$'000 [   ]

2   Required

Identify the probability of the project having a negative NPV. (Give your answer as a percentage to one decimal place.)

☐ %

3   Required

Identify the NPV of the most likely outcome. (Give your answer to the nearest $'000.)

$'000 ☐

Solution

1

2

3

4.4 Standard deviation

One way of measuring risk is to estimate the **variability of returns,** or the range of possible outcomes, resulting from a decision. This can be measured as **standard deviation.**

> **Standard deviation:** Standard deviation (SD) measures the difference between the (expected) outcomes of a decision and the average (expected) outcome.

 Formula provided

$$SD = \sqrt{\frac{\Sigma(X-\bar{X})^2}{n}} \quad \text{or}$$

$$SD = \sqrt{\frac{\Sigma f X^2}{\Sigma f} - \bar{X}^2}$$

In the preceding formulae, f represents the frequency (or probability) of each possible outcome. If probabilities are being used, then the denominator will equal 1 and can be ignored.

Standard deviation can also simply be calculated as the square root of the variance (if this is provided in a question).

4.4.1 Worked example

This example uses the information from the preceding activities.

Project A	Probability	Project A	Probability × outcome squared
Expected value ($\bar{X}$) = \$2.5m			
Low growth	0.25	+1.0	$0.25(1)^2$= 0.25
Medium growth	0.50	+2.5	$0.5(2.5)^2$= 3.125
High growth	0.25	+4.0	$0.25(4)^2$= 4.0

Project A	Probability	Project A	Probability × outcome squared
Expected value ($\overline{X}$) = $2.5m			
$\dfrac{\Sigma fX^2}{\Sigma f}$			0.25 + 3.125 + 4.0 = 7.375
$\sqrt{\dfrac{\Sigma fX^2}{\Sigma f} - \overline{X}^2}$			7.375 - 2.5² = 1.125
$\sqrt{\dfrac{\Sigma fX^2}{\Sigma f} - \overline{X}^2}$			$\sqrt{1.125} = 1.1$

Project B	Probability	Project A	Probability × outcome squared
Expected value ($\overline{X}$) = $4m			
Low growth	0.25	-8.0	0.25(-8)² = 16.0
Medium growth	0.50	+4.0	0.5(4)² = 8.0
High growth	0.25	+16.0	0.25(16)² = 64.0
$\dfrac{\Sigma fX^2}{\Sigma f}$			16 + 8 + 64 = 88
$\sqrt{\dfrac{\Sigma fX^2}{\Sigma f} - \overline{X}^2}$			88.0 - 4² = 72
$\sqrt{\dfrac{\Sigma fX^2}{\Sigma f} - \overline{X}^2}$			$\sqrt{72} = 8.5$

Project A has a **lower average (expected) NPV** than project B but its outcomes are less widely dispersed about the mean – it therefore has a smaller **standard deviation** (compared to project B), and is therefore **less risky**.

Although project A is **less risky** than project B, it also has a lower expected return, so it is not clear which is a more attractive project.

Which project is preferred depends on the decision maker's **risk appetite**.

4.4.2 Co-efficient of variation

Standard deviation is affected by the absolute value of the numbers being analysed. So a project might have a lower standard deviation simply because the expected value of the project is lower.

For this reason it is more meaningful to analyse standard deviation in comparison to the expected value. This measure is called a **co-efficient of variation**.

KEY
TERM

> **Co-efficient of variation: Co-efficient of variation** is calculated as standard deviation ÷ expected value.

4.4.3 Worked example

Continuing the previous example.

	Project A	Project B
Standard deviation	1.1	8.5
Expected value	2.5	4.0
Co-efficient of variation	1.1/2.5 = 0.44	8.5/4 = 2.13

This clearly demonstrates that project B carries a far higher degree of risk than project A.

4.4.4 Normal distribution tables

Standard deviation can also be interpreted using the concept of a normal distribution. Some of the properties of a normal distribution are shown in the following illustration (σ = standard deviation):

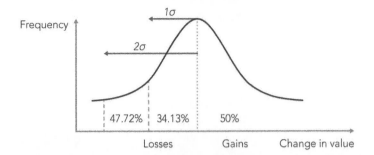

Frequency

1σ

2σ

47.72% | 34.13% | 50%

Losses | Gains | Change in value

This shows that the chance of an outcome **being between its expected value and one standard deviation below** the expected value is **34.13%.** The chance of the outcome being **no worse than one standard deviation below the expected outcome** is therefore 34.13% + 50% (50% being the chance of the outcome being **above** the expected value) which equals 84.13%.

Similarly, the chance of an outcome **being between its expected value and two standard deviations below** the expected value is **47.72%.** The chance of the outcome being **no worse than two standard deviations below the expected outcome** is therefore 47.72% + 50% = 97.72%

Normal distribution tables can also be used to calculate the **maximum loss that could be expected with a given level of confidence**; this is often referred to as value at risk. For example, if the standard deviation is $1m then the value at risk, with 97.72% confidence, is $1m × 2 (see previous paragraph) = $2m.

Confidence levels are normally set at 95% or 99%.

In the exam **you are provided with a normal distribution table** (this table is available at the back of the course book), to show the probabilities associated with outcomes that are expressed in terms of the number of standard deviations (or Z values). The following illustration shows how to use normal distribution tables either to assess probabilities or to calculate value at risk at a 95% or 99% confidence level.

KEY
TERM

> **Value at risk**: The maximum loss that could be expected with a given level of confidence.

 Illustration 2: Normal distribution

A company is considering a project which is expected to deliver a profit of $1.645m and has an estimated standard deviation of $1m.

Required
Calculate the probability of this project making a loss (showing your answer to the nearest %).

 %

Solution

The correct answer is:

5%

If a commercial decision is expected to deliver a profit of $1.645m and standard deviation has been calculated as $1m then the number of standard deviations required for profit to fall to zero is 1.645.

Using the extract from the normal distribution table shown here (the full table is given in the exam and is available at the back of the course book), 1.645 standard deviations is assessed as having a probability of 0.45.

$Z=\frac{(x-\mu)}{\sigma}$	0.00	0.01	0.02	0.03	0.04	0.05	0.06	0.07	0.08	0.09
0.0	.0000	.0040	.0080	.0120	.0160	.0199	.0239	.0279	.0319	.0359
0.1	.0398	.0438	.0478	.0517	.0557	.0596	.0636	.0675	.0714	.0753
0.2	.0793	.0832	.0871	.0910	.0948	.0987	.1026	.1064	.1103	.1141
0.3	.1179	.1217	.1255	.1293	.1331	.1368	.1406	.1443	.1480	.1517
0.4	.1554	.1591	.1628	.1664	.1700	.1736	.1772	.1808	.1844	.1879
0.5	.1915	.1950	.1985	.2019	.2054	.2088	.2123	.2157	.2190	.2224
0.6	.2257	.2291	.2324	.2357	.2389	.2422	.2454	.2486	.2517	.2549
0.7	.2580	.2611	.2642	.2673	.2704	.2734	.2764	.2794	.2823	.2852
0.8	.2881	.2910	.2939	.2967	.2995	.3023	.3051	.3078	.3106	.3133
0.9	.3159	.3186	.3212	.3238	.3264	.3289	.3315	.3340	.3365	.3389
1.0	.3413	.3438	.3461	.3485	.3508	.3531	.3554	.3577	.3599	.3621
1.1	.3643	.3665	.3686	.3708	.3729	.3749	.3770	.3790	.3810	.3830
1.2	.3849	.3869	.3888	.3907	.3925	.3944	.3962	.3980	.3997	.4015
1.3	.4032	.4049	.4066	.4082	.4099	.4115	.4131	.4147	.4162	.4177
1.4	.4192	.4207	.4222	.4236	.4251	.4265	.4279	.4292	.4306	.4319
1.5	.4332	.4345	.4357	.4370	.4382	.4394	.4406	.4418	.4429	.4441
1.6	.4452	.4463	.4474	.4484	.4495	.4505	.4515	.4525	.4535	.4545

The Z value of 1.645 is half way between 1.64 and 1.65, so we can say that half way between 0.4495 and 0.4505 ie 0.45 is the correct answer.

So, the chance of the outcome being **no worse than 1.645 standard deviations below the expected outcome** is therefore 45% + 50% (the chance of the outcome being better than expected, as shown in the following diagram) which gives 95%.

This means that the chance of the outcome being worse than this, and therefore of a loss being made is 100% - 95% = 5%.

This can be illustrated as follows:

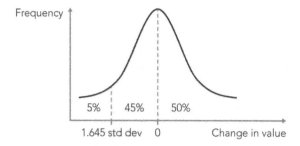

If the question had asked for **the value at risk at 95% confidence to be calculated**, then the normal distribution table is inspected to identify the figure of 45% or 0.45. We know that this is 1.645 standard deviations. The value at risk is then 1.645 × standard deviation of $1m = $1.645m. We can be 95% confident that this is the maximum loss because there is only a 5% chance of it being exceeded.

If the question had asked for value at risk with 99% confidence, then the normal distribution table is inspected to identify the figure of 49% or 0.49 and the same procedure is followed to calculate value at risk.

Activity 5: Confidence level

Company B is planning a cost saving project which it anticipates will create savings of $2m.

The standard deviation of the project has been estimated as $0.2m.

Company B's management need to report to Head Office the predicted cost saving from the project but want to be 95% sure that the figure they report is achievable.

Required

Calculate the minimum savings that can be expected with 95% confidence. (Give your answer in $'s to three decimal places)

$ [   ] m

Solution

4.5 Decision trees

A decision tree is a pictorial method of showing a sequence of interrelated decisions and their expected outcomes. Decision trees are most useful when there are several decisions and ranges of outcome.

Decision trees will often involve the use of **joint probabilities.**

4.5.1 Three-step approach

The steps involved are:

(a) **Draw the decision tree from left to right.**

    (i)   Illustrate decision points with a square shape.

(b) **Evaluate the tree from right to left (sometimes called 'rollback analysis').**

    (i)   Calculate expected values at outcome points (denoted by a circle).

    (ii)   Take highest benefit at decision points.

(c) **Recommend a course of action.**

 Illustration 3: Decision tree

Beethoven Co has a new wonder product, the Vylin, of which it expects great things.

The company has two courses of action open to it, to test market the product or abandon it.

If the company test markets it, the cost will be $100,000 and the market response could be positive or negative with probabilities of 0.60 and 0.40 respectively.

If the response is positive, the company could either abandon the product or market it full scale.

If it markets the Vylin full scale, the outcome might be low, medium or high demand, and the respective net gains/(losses) would be (200), 200 or 1,000 in units of $1,000. These outcomes have probabilities of 0.20, 0.50 and 0.30 respectively.

If the result of the test marketing is negative and the company goes ahead and markets the product, estimated losses would be $600,000.

If, at any point, the company abandons the product, there would be a net gain of $50,000 from the sale of scrap. All the financial values are in present value terms.

Required

Use a decision tree to evaluate the expected outcome from the recommended course of action for Beethoven Co. (Give your answer to the nearest $'000.)

$'000s [   ]

Solution

The correct answer is:

$'000s 136

Step 1

We start on the **left** and **work** towards the right left-hand side showing the appropriate decisions and outcomes. The starting point for the tree is to **establish what decision has to be made now; ie** to test market or abandon. Depending on the outcome of the test marketing, another decision will then be made, to abandon the product or to go ahead.

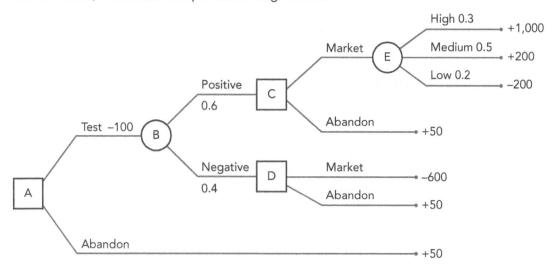

Step 2

Next we start on the **right-hand side** of the tree and **work back** towards the left-hand side and the current decision under review (sometimes known as 'rollback' technique or 'rollback analysis'). Working from **right to left**, we calculate the **EV of revenue, cost, contribution or profit** at each outcome point on the tree.

In the example above, the right-hand-most outcome point is point E, and the EV is as follows.

	Profit x	Probability p	px
	$'000		$'000
High	1,000	0.3	300
Medium	200	0.5	100
Low	(200)	0.2	(40)
EV			360

This is the EV of the decision to market the product if the test shows a positive response. It may help you to write the EV on the decision tree itself, at the appropriate outcome point (point E).

(a) **At decision point C**, the **choice** is as follows.

    (i)   Market, EV = +360 (the EV at point E)

    (ii) Abandon, value = +50

The choice would be to market the product, and so the EV at decision point C is +360.

(b) **At decision point D**, the **choice** is as follows.

    (i)   Market, value = −600

    (ii) Abandon, value = +50

The choice would be to abandon, and so the EV at decision point D is +50.

The second-stage decisions have therefore been made. If the original decision is to test market, the company will market the product if the test shows a positive customer response, and will abandon the product if the test results are negative.

The evaluation of the decision tree is completed as follows.

(c) **Calculate the EV at outcome point B.**

       0.6 × 360   (EV at C)

+   0.4 ×   50   (EV at D)

=   216 + 20 = 236.

Step 3

Finally, compare the options at point A, which are as follows.

(a) Test: EV = EV at B minus test marketing cost = 236 − 100 = 136

(b) Abandon: Value = 50

The choice would be to test market the product, because it has a **higher EV of profit**.

Activity 6: Decision trees

Consider the following diagram.

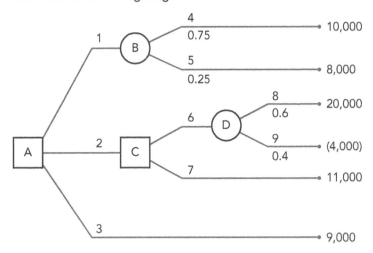

Required

If a decision maker wished to maximise the value of the outcome, which option or options should be selected?

A   Options 2 and 7

B   Option 3

C   Options 1 and 4

D   Options 2, 6 and 8

Solution

4.6 Conditional probabilities

Conditional probability is the probability of an event occurring given that another event has occurred.

One way of analysing this is to use contingency tables. These are created by tabulating and analysing the various possible outcomes.

 Illustration 4: Contingency tables

A company has two factories that are used to produce its finished product.

In factory A, which produces 25% of the company's output, it is estimated that 6% of output is defective.

In factory B, which produces the remainder of the company's output, it is estimated that 8% of output is defective.

A customer has complained that a product is defective.

Required
What is the probability that this product was produced by factory A?

Insert your answer to the nearest percentage.

Probability [   ] %

Solution

The correct answer is:

Probability   20%

This can be analysed by producing a contingency table showing the possible outcomes for a given level of output eg 1,000 units, which would mean that factory A produces 250 units and factory B produces 750 units.

	Factory A	Factory B	Total
Defective output	15 (6% of 250)	60 (8% of 750)	75

	Factory A	Factory B	Total
Non-defective	235	690	925
Total	250	750	1,000

Therefore, there is a 15/75 (=0.20) chance of the defective unit coming from factory A. This is a probability of 20%.

Activity 7: Conditional probability

A manager of a car sales business wants to know the probability that buyers of a Model X car took a test drive in the car before buying. Records are kept of 'prospects', people visiting the showroom who are potential buyers of particular models of cars.

Based on data collected, the probability that a potential Model X car buyer takes a test drive is 0.4. Of those who take a test drive, 30% buy a Model X. 1 in 10 prospects who do not take a test drive buy a Model X.

Required
What is the probability that a customer took a test drive given that they bought a Model X car?

Insert your answer to the nearest percentage.

Probability: ☐ %

Solution

4.7 Risk-adjusted cost of capital

Finally, risk can be incorporated into project appraisal by increasing the discount rate used to appraise a project. This recognises that investors will require a higher return if risk is high.

5 Stress testing

> **Stress testing: Stress testing is the process of assessing** hypothetical scenarios in order to analyse the **vulnerability of a decision to specific situations.** Stress testing often involves highly complex, computer-generated simulation models.

Common examples of stress testing include scenario analysis and simulation.

5.1 Scenario analysis

Scenario analysis was introduced earlier. By identifying the worst case scenario across a range of variables, management can identify a worst-case scenario.

This can help to show the downside risk associated with a decision which can help to inform decision making.

It can also facilitate contingency planning to identify how this scenario could be managed.

5.2 Monte Carlo simulation

Monte Carlo simulation is an extension of scenario analysis. This works by assigning random numbers to each possible value for each uncertain variable in a way that reflects their probabilities.

A computer would calculate the NPV many times over using the values established in this way with more random numbers, and the results would be analysed to provide an **expected NPV** for the project and a **statistical distribution** pattern for the possible variation in the NPV above or below this average

The decision on whether to go ahead with the project would then be made on the basis of **expected return** and **risk**. Again this can help to show the downside risk associated with a decision which can help to inform decision-making and to facilitate contingency planning.

5.2.1 Worked example

The following probability estimates have been prepared for a proposed project.

	Year	Probability	$
Cost of equipment	0	1.00	(40,000)
Revenue each year	1–5	0.15	40,000
		0.40	50,000
		0.30	55,000
		0.15	60,000
Running costs each year	1–5	0.10	25,000
		0.25	30,000
		0.35	35,000
		0.30	40,000

The cost of capital is 12%.

A simulation model assigns random number digits to each possible value for each of the uncertain variables. The random numbers match their respective probabilities.

Revenue				Running costs		
$	Probability	Random numbers		$	Probability	Random numbers
40,000	0.15	00–14	*	25,000	0.10	00–09
50,000	0.40	15–54	**	30,000	0.25	10–34
55,000	0.30	55–84	***	40,000	0.35	35–69
60,000	0.15	85–99		40,000	0.30	70–99

*   Probability is 0.15 (15%). Random numbers are 15% of range 00–99.

**   Probability is 0.40 (40%). Random numbers are 40% of range 00–99 but starting at 15.

***   Probability is 0.30 (30%). Random numbers are 30% of range 00–99 but starting at 55.

Numbers have been assigned to cash flows so that when numbers are selected at random, the cash flows have exactly the same probability of being selected as is indicated in their respective probability distribution above. Random numbers would then be generated by a computer programme and these would be used to assign values to each of the uncertain variables.

For example, if the random numbers 37, 84, and 20, 01 were generated, the values assigned to the variables would be as follows (these would then be used to build a picture of possible project NPVs).

Calculation	Random number	Revenue Value $	Random number	Costs Value $
1	37	50,000	84	40,000
2	20	50,000	01	25,000

Chapter summary

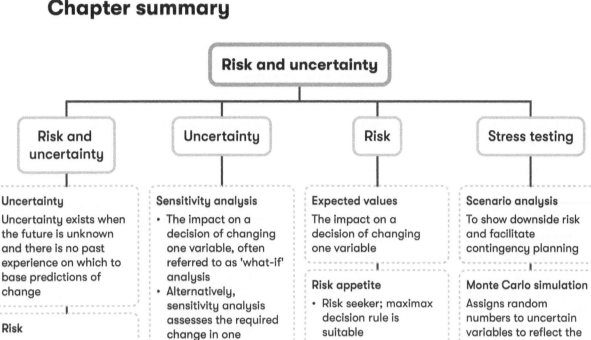

Risk and uncertainty

Risk and uncertainty

Uncertainty
Uncertainty exists when the future is unknown and there is no past experience on which to base predictions of change

Risk
A decision maker has knowledge that several different future outcomes are possible, the probabilities of which are known, or can be estimated

Uncertainty

Sensitivity analysis
- The impact on a decision of changing one variable, often referred to as 'what-if' analysis
- Alternatively, sensitivity analysis assesses the required change in one variable before a decision will fail to achieve its objectives

Weaknesses in sensitivity analysis
- Ignores interdependencies between variables
- Ignores probabilities

Other techniques
- Payback period
- Scenario analysis

Risk

Expected values
The impact on a decision of changing one variable

Risk appetite
- Risk seeker; maximax decision rule is suitable
- Risk averse; maximin decision rule is suitable
- Risk neutral; expected values are suitable

Probability models
Joint probabilities help to assess most likely outcome, and probability of worst case scenarios

Standard deviation
- Estimate of variability of returns around an average
- Sometimes expressed as a percent of the average (coefficient of variation)

Decision trees
- Draw from left to right
- Evaluate from right to left
- Uses joint probabilities

Conditional probabilities
Contingency tables

Risk-adjusted cost of capital
Increased cost of capital if risk is higher

Stress testing

Scenario analysis
To show downside risk and facilitate contingency planning

Monte Carlo simulation
Assigns random numbers to uncertain variables to reflect the probability of a range of values

Key terms

Uncertainty: Uncertainty exists when the future is unknown and the decision maker has no past experience on which to base predictions of change. There are therefore a number of possible outcomes but **the probability of each outcome is not known**.

Risk: Risk exists where a decision maker has knowledge that several different future outcomes are possible, the probabilities of which are known, or can be estimated, usually due to past experience.

VOPI: VOPI is calculated as the expected value with perfect information minus the expected profit without this information.

Risk appetite: A **risk seeker** is a decision maker who is interested in trying to secure the best outcomes, no matter how small the chance that they may occur.

A decision maker is **risk neutral** if they are concerned with what will be the most likely outcome.

A **risk-averse** decision maker acts on the assumption that the worst outcome might occur.

Maximax, maximin and minimax regret: Maximax looks at the best possible results from each decision option and selects the option that gives the best possible result.

Maximin suggests that a decision maker should select the alternative that offers the least unattractive worst outcome.

Minimax regret aims to minimise the regret from making the wrong decision.

Joint probability: **Joint probability** is the probability of two risky outcomes occurring at the same time and is calculated as the probability of one outcome multiplied by the probability of the other.

Standard deviation: Standard deviation (SD) measures the difference between the (expected) outcomes of a decision and the average (expected) outcome.

Co-efficient of variation: **Co-efficient of variation** is calculated as standard deviation ÷ expected value.

Value at risk: The maximum loss that could be expected with a given level of confidence.

Stress testing: **Stress testing is the process of assessing** hypothetical scenarios in order to analyse the **vulnerability of a decision to specific situations.** Stress testing often involves highly complex, computer-generated simulation models.

Activity answers

Activity 1: NPV & sensitivity

The correct answer is:

Volume: 32.9%

Selling price: 9.9%

Volume

PV of contribution = Project NPV + Outlay = $979,000 + $2,000 = $2,979,000

Sensitivity = $979,000/$2,979,000 × 100% = 32.9%

A fall of 32.9% in sales volume is required for the project NPV to fall to zero. This will probably be considered to be unlikely which means that the uncertainty associated with this project looks low with regard to sales volume.

Selling price

PV of sales (including the impact on taxable profit)

	t_1	t_2	t_3
	$'000	$'000	$'000
Sales	4,200	4,900	5,300
Tax @ 21%	(882)	(1,029)	(1,113)
Net cash flow	3,318	3,871	4,187
DF @ 7%	0.935	0.873	0.816
PV	3,102	3,379	3,417

Total PV of sales = $9,898,000

Sensitivity = $979,000/$9,898,000 × 100% = 9.9%

A fall of 9.9% in sales price is required for the project NPV to fall to zero. This will probably be considered to be unlikely which means that the uncertainty associated with this project also looks low with regard to sales price.

Activity 2: ENPV

The correct answer is:

Probability	Forecast	Project A	Project B
0.25	Low growth	1.00	−8.00
0.50	Medium growth	2.50	4.00
0.25	High growth	4.00	16.00
1.00	Expected value	2.50	4.00

If X = probability of low and high growth then the probability of medium growth = 2X and X + X + 2X = 1.0

So 4X = 1.0 so X =0.25

Expected values can now be calculated as follows.

	Probability	Project A	Project B
Low growth	X = 0.25	+1.0	−8.0
Medium growth	2X = 0.50	+2.5	+4.0
High growth	X = 0.25	+4.0	+16.0

	Probability	Project A	Project B
Expected value	1.0	(1 × 0.25) + (2.5 × 0.50) + (4 × 0.25) = **2.5**	(−8 × 0.25) + (4 × 0.50) + (16 × 0.25) = **4.0**

Project B has a higher expected value and would therefore be chosen.

Activity 3: Decision making and risk appetite

1 **The correct answer is:**

$m 16.0

Maximax is the appropriate technique for a risk seeker, so project B is chosen because project B has the highest best outcome.

2 **The correct answer is:**

$m 1.0

Project A is chosen because project A has the highest worst outcome.

3 **The correct answer is:**

$m 9.0

NPV $m	Project A	Project B	Regret if project A chosen	Regret if project B chosen
Low growth	+1.0	−8.0	0 If low growth happens and project A had been chosen the decision is correct so there is no regret	9.0 If low growth happens and project B had been chosen the decision is $9m worse than if project A had been chosen
Medium growth	+2.5	+4.0	1.5 If medium growth happens and project A had been chosen the decision is $1.5m worse than if project B had been chosen	0.0 Correct decision so 0 regret.
High growth	+4.0	+16.0	12.0 If high growth happens and project A had been chosen the decision is $12m worse than if project B had been chosen	0.0 Correct decision so 0 regret.

The maximum regret from project A is $12m and from project B is $9m, so the project that minimises maximum regret is project B.

Activity 4: Joint probabilities

1 The correct answer is:

$'000 1,259

Possible outcome	Probability Year 1	Probability Year 2	Joint probability
Year 1 low & Year 2 low	0.4	0.7	0.4 × 0.7 = 0.28
Year 1 low & Year 2 high	0.4	0.3	0.4 × 0.3 = 0.12
Year 1 high & Year 2 low	0.6	0.7	0.6 × 0.7 = 0.42
Year 1 high & Year 2 high	0.6	0.3	0.6 × 0.3 = 0.18
			<u>1.0</u>

Expected NPV = (−7,268 × 0.28) + (−660 × 0.12) + (3,640 × 0.42) + (10,248 × 0.18) = **+1,259**

Alternative calculation of expected NPV

Time	0	1	2
		(56,000 × 0.6) + (44,000 × 0.4) =	(44,000 × 0.3) + (36,000 × 0.7) =
Cash flow ($'000)	−77,000	51,200	38,400
DF @ 10%	<u>1</u>	<u>0.909</u>	<u>0.826</u>
PV	−77,000	46,541	31,718
NPV	**+1,259**		

2 The correct answer is:

40.0%

Cash flows are low in Years 1 and 2, which has a probability of 0.28 or 28%.

Cash flows are low in Year 1 and high in Year 2, which has a probability of 0.12 or 12%.

Total probability = 0.28 + 0.12 = 0.40 or 40%

3 The correct answer is:

$'000 3,640

The most likely outcome in terms of the highest joint probability is that the cash flow in Year 1 is high and Year 2 is low. So, the most likely outcome is +3,640 ($'000).

Activity 5: Confidence level

The correct answer is:

$1.671m

95% confidence means that we are looking for a figure of 0.45 in the normal distribution table since 45% + 50% (the chance of the outcome being better than expected, as shown in the following diagram) gives 95%.

Reading a probability value of 0.45 from the normal distribution tables delivers a Z value of 1.645 (half way between 1.64 with a value of 0.4495 and 1.65 with a value of 0.4505).

1.645 standard deviations gives a value of 1.645 × 0.2 = $0.329m.

The minimum cost savings with 95% confidence is therefore $2m - $0.329m = $1.671m.

Activity 6: Decision trees

The correct answer is:

BPP
LEARNING
MEDIA

Options 2 and 7

The various outcomes must be evaluated using expected values.

EV at point B: (0.75 × 10,000) + (0.25 × 8,000) = 9,500

EV at point D: (0.6 × 20,000) + (0.4 × (4,000)) = 10,400

EV at point C: Choice between 10,400 and 11,000

EV at point A: Choice between B (9,500), C (10,400 or 11,000) and choice 3 (9,000).

If we are trying to maximise the figure, option 2 and then option 7 would be chosen, to give 11,000.

Activity 7: Conditional probability

The correct answer is:

Probability: 67%

This can be analysed by producing a contingency table showing the possible outcomes for a given level of prospects eg 1,000, which would mean that 400 took a test drive and 600 did not.

	Test drive	No test drive	Total
Purchases	120 (30% of 400)	60 (10% of 600)	180
Non-purchases	280	540	820
Total	400	600	1,000

Therefore, there is a 120/180 (=0.67) chance of the defective unit coming from factory A. This is a probability of 67%.

Test your learning

1 Sensitivity analysis allows for uncertainty in project appraisal by assessing the probability of changes in the decision variables.

Required
Is this true or false?

A   True

B   False

2 A probability can be expressed as any value from –1 to +1.

Required
Is this true or false?

A   True

B   False

3 A manager is trying to decide which of three mutually exclusive projects to undertake. Each of the projects could lead to varying net costs which the manager calls outcomes I, II and III. The following payexpected table or matrix has been constructed.

			Outcomes (Net profit)	
Project		I (Worst)	II (Most likely)	III (Best)
A		60	70	120
B		85	75	140
C		100	120	135

Required
Using the minimax regret decision rule, decide which project should be undertaken.

A   A

B   B

C   C

4 **Required**
If the decision maker is trying to maximise the figure, what figure would the decision maker choose at point B in the diagram below?

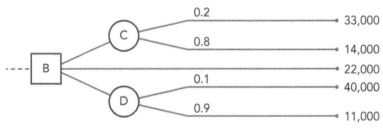

A   40,000

B   11,800

C   13,900

D   22,000

5 AB can choose from five mutually exclusive projects. The projects will each last for one year only and their net cash inflows will be determined by the prevailing market conditions. The forecast net cash inflows and their associated probabilities are shown below.

Market conditions	Poor	Good	Excellent
Probability	0.20	0.40	0.40
	$'000	$'000	$'000
Project L	550	480	580
Project M	450	500	570
Project N	420	450	480
Project O	370	410	430
Project P	590	580	430

Required

Based on the expected value of the net cash inflows, which project should be undertaken?

Project [   ]

6   AB can choose from five mutually exclusive projects. The projects will each last for one year only and their net cash inflows will be determined by the prevailing market conditions. The forecast net cash inflows and their associated probabilities are shown below.

Market conditions	Poor	Good	Excellent
Probability	0.20	0.40	0.40
	$'000	$'000	$'000
Project L	550	480	580
Project M	450	500	570
Project N	420	450	480
Project O	370	410	430
Project P	590	580	430

Required

Calculate the value of perfect information about the state of the market. (Give your answer to the nearest $'000.)

$'000 [   ]

12

Analysis and management of risk

Syllabus learning outcomes

Having studied this chapter, you will be able to work through the following syllabus outcomes:

Syllabus area D: Risk and Control	
2	Types of risk in the medium term
a	Types of risk
b	Managing risk

Exam context

In the exam, you will be expected to demonstrate competence in the following representative task statements:

- Determine upside and downside risks
- Use the TARA framework – transfer, avoid, reduce, and accept
- Determine business risks and the ethical implications and risk to the public interest
- Determine the costs and benefits associated with investing in information systems and big data

Chapter overview

BPP
LEARNING
MEDIA

1 Introduction

This chapter continues to look at risk, this time focusing on the types of risk faced by a business, as well as how risk can be managed at an organisational level and by the use of information systems.

2 Types of risk

2.1 Upside and downside risk

Risk can be thought of as the possibility that an actual outcome will be **different from what is expected.**

2.1.1 Downside risk

If an outcome is worse than expected, then this is **downside** risk. Some issues, like the risk of fire or theft, only involve downside (or pure) risk.

2.1.2 Two-way risk

However, an outcome may also be better than expected. This is upside risk.

Many business decisions (eg investment decisions) involve both upside and downside risk. It is necessary to invest to remain competitive and to generate higher returns to shareholders; this means that a degree of **risk is essential** if an organisation is to survive and prosper.

Decisions that have both an upside and downside potential are sometimes referred to as two-way risk.

KEY TERM

> **Directions of risk: Downside (or pure) risk** is a risk involving the possibility of loss (only).
>
> **Two-way risk** involves both upside and downside risk.

2.2 Business and non-business risk

KEY TERM

> **Business risk:** The risk faced due to a business's operations or products.

Business risk arises from the **type of business** the organisation is involved in and relates to uncertainty about the future and the organisation's **business prospects**.

Examples of **business risk** include:

Strategic risk	Due to failings in long-term planning
Product risk	Risk of low demand for new or existing products
Operational risk	Failings in procedures or systems; can cause damage to an organisation's reputation (**reputational risk**)
Commodity price risk	Risk due to changes in commodity prices (eg oil)

> ### Exam focus
> The main focus in the P2 exam is on business risk; however, it is important that you can classify a given risk appropriately.

2.2.1 Non-business risk

Non-business risks include event risk and financial risk.

Event risks are due to a single **adverse event** such as an accident, natural disaster or cyber attack.

Financial risk includes the risk of short-term cash flow problems (eg due to exchange rate movements) and also longer-term risks arising from the use of debt finance (high debt levels will make profits more volatile).

3 Risk management

> **Risk management**: 'The process of understanding and managing the risks that an organisation is inevitably subject to in attempting to achieve its corporate objectives' (*CIMA*).

Risk management aims to control downside risk and to maximise upside risk.

3.1 Risk mapping

A starting point for risk management is to consider which risks are the most significant. This can be assessed by considering the **probability** of the risk occurring and the severity of its potential **impact.** This analysis is often presented as a **risk map**.

Each quadrant (numbered 1–4 below) will be managed in a different way.

		Severity	
		Low	High
Probability	Low	2	1
	High	3	4

The **policy options** in each quadrant can be generalised as follows:

Quadrant 1 **Transfer**: Insure against risk or implement contingency plans

Contingency planning involves identifying the **responsibilities** in the event of a crisis and realistic **rehearsals** of implementing the contingency plan.

Risk can also be shared eg via a **joint venture.**

Quadrant 2 **Accept:** Risks are not significant

This approach is also used where if the **cost of avoiding** the risk is considered to be too great, it is set against the potential loss that could be incurred.

In addition, risks may be deliberately accepted if they are an inevitable consequence of a commercial decision which could lead to higher returns.

Quadrant 3 **Reduce/control:** Improve controls to reduce probability of occurrence

Often risks can be controlled or reduced, but not avoided altogether. This is true of many business risks, where the risks of launching new products can be reduced by market research, advertising and so on.

Many businesses undertake **hazardous activities** where there is a risk of injury or loss of life (eg an oil rig). These risks cannot be avoided completely. However, they have to be **reduced to an acceptable level** by incurring the costs associated with improving controls (risk mitigation).

Methods of controlling risk over the whole organisation include **diversification** (eg producing a range of different products) and **hedging** risks (eg fixed price contracts for supply of oil).

Quadrant 4 **Abandon/avoid:** Abandon activities (withdraw from market or outsource activity)

A company may deal with risk by **abandoning** operations; for example, abandoning operations in politically volatile countries where the risks of loss (including loss of life) are considered to be too great or the costs of security are considered to be too high.

Exam focus

Risk mapping is an important area. It is important that you can determine appropriately responses to risk. The policy options can be remembered as TARA.

- Risk **T**ransfer
- Risk **A**voidance
- **R**eduction
- Risk **A**cceptance

Activity 1: TARA

Flitish Airways is a well-known international airline with a strong reputation for customer service. However, it has recently installed a new automated baggage-handling system which has demotivated staff and dramatically increased the number of bags delayed in transit, although almost all lost bags are tracked down and re-united with their owners within 12 hours.

Required

Determine an appropriate strategy for responding to each risk.

Passenger luggage being lost   [▼]

In-flight entertainment system breaks down   [▼]

Unsafe food on flights   [▼]

Industrial action by airline staff   [▼]

Picklist:

Transfer

Avoid

Reduce

Accept

Solution

4 Ethical implications

4.1 Ethics

> **Ethics:** Ethics are the moral principles or standards of behaviour by which people act or do business.

Blanchard and Peale (*Blanchard & Peale, 1988*) offer three questions when considering whether an action is ethical:

(a) Is it legal?

(b) Is it fair to the parties involved?

(c) How would you feel if others knew you had taken this decision?

A business may choose to operate on principles which are:

*   Ethical and legal
*   Unethical but legal
*   Ethical but illegal
*   Unethical and illegal

Real life example

Ethical and legal

*   Organisations that pride themselves on their ethical credentials such as Fairtrade or The Body Shop

Unethical but legal

*   Organisations providing products and services which are at odds with social norms (eg a military arms manufacturer selling its weapons to repressive regimes)

Ethical but illegal

*   Organisations that breach legislation in order to address a social wrong; this might include publishing stolen documents that expose a government scandal

Unethical and illegal

*   Employing child labour or selling illegal drugs would be included in this category

4.1.1 Ethical frameworks

There are two methods of encouraging organisations to comply with ethical standards.

*   A **compliance-based approach** seeks to establish a clear set of legal rules which must be adhered to.
*   An **integrity-based approach** seeks to offer principles for individuals to apply when faced with an ethical dilemma.

	Compliance	Integrity
Ethos	Comply with external standards	Choose ethical standards
Objective	Keep to the law	Enable legal and responsible conduct
Originators	Lawyers	Management with lawyers, HR specialists etc

	Compliance	Integrity
Methods (both include education, audits, controls, penalties)	Reduced employee discretion	Leadership, organisation systems
Behavioural assumptions	People are solitary, self-interested beings	People are social beings with values
Standards	The law	Company values, aspirations (including law)
Staffing	Lawyers	Managers and lawyers
Education	The law, compliance system	Values, the law, compliance systems
Activities	Develop standards, train and communicate, handle reports of misconduct, investigate, enforce, oversee compliance	Integrate values into company systems, provide guidance and consultation, identify and resolve problems, oversee compliance

4.1.2 CIMA's Code of Ethics

CIMA's Code of Ethics is an integrity-based approach founded on the International Federation of Accountants (IFAC) Code of Ethics:

Professional competence and due care

A professional accountant has an ongoing duty to maintain professional knowledge and skill, and act diligently in accordance with relevant technical standards.

Integrity

A professional accountant should be straightforward and honest in all professional and business relationships.

Professional behaviour

A professional accountant should comply with relevant laws and regulations and avoid any actions that discredit the profession.

Confidentiality

A professional accountant should respect the confidentiality of information acquired as a result of professional and business relationships.

Objectivity

A professional accountant should not allow bias, conflict of interest or undue influence of others to override professional or business judgements.

4.1.3 Threats to ethical guidelines

The following situations could be a threat to the ethical guidelines:

Advocacy threats occur when an accountant promotes an opinion to the point that subsequent objectivity may be compromised.

Self-interest threats occur as a result of the financial or other interests of an accountant or an immediate or close family member.

Intimidation threats occur when an accountant is deterred from acting objectively by real or perceived threats.

Familiarity threats occur when, because of a close relationship, an accountant becomes too sympathetic to the interests of others.

Self-review threats occur when an accountant is expected to objectively re-assess a decision they were previously responsible for.

Activity 2: Threats

A management accountant has been asked to advise the board of Brookfield Ltd on the financial viability of a major capital investment project. The accountant has a close personal relationship with the finance director, who is a passionate advocate of the project.

Required

Which threat to ethical guidelines has arisen and which ethical principle is at risk of being compromised?

Threat to ethical guidelines: [▼]

Ethical principle: [▼]

Choose from the following words:

A   Advocacy

B   Familiarity

C   Intimidation

D   Self-interest

E   Self-review

F   Confidentiality

G   Integrity

H   Objectivity

I   Professional behaviour

J   Professional competence

Solution

Exam focus

The relationship creates the threat of familiarity. The principle at stake is objectivity. As you would expect, it is important to be able to apply CIMA's Code and understand the threats to these ethical principles.

4.1.4 Encouraging ethical behaviour

Ways in which organisations can encourage ethical behaviour include:

- Adopting a company code of ethics or practice
- Ensuring that senior managers are seen to exemplify ethical standards
- Training staff in the importance of ethics and making judgements
- Developing a recruitment policy that rejects dishonest people
- Enforcing disciplinary action for employees behaving unethically
- Providing whistleblowing channels that allow staff to report ethical concerns
- Ensuring segregation of duties and other internal controls

4.2 Corporate social responsibility

> **Social responsibility**: Social responsibility comprises those values and actions which the organisation is not obliged to adopt for business reasons, which it adopts for the good and wellbeing of stakeholders within and outside the organisation.

An organisation's policy on corporate social responsibility (CSR) considers the **public interest** and will impact many aspects of its business:

- An organisation's CSR policy is often considered by customers before making a purchase.
- Organisations with a good CSR policy will find it easier to attract and retain high-quality employees.
- Any organisation is part of a wider social system and therefore needs to consider the impact it has on other parts of the community. This is particularly the case with regard to environmental factors (eg pollution and waste).
- Organisations are regulated by legislation and codes of practice.

Businesses will need to balance their CSR position with the objective to maximise shareholder wealth.

Real life example

IKEA's vision is 'to create a better everyday life for the many people'. In commercial terms, this is achieved through 'a wide range of well-designed, functional home furnishing products at prices so low that as many people as possible will be able to afford them' (Ikea.com, 2019).

The IKEA Foundation (www.ikeafoundation.org) was established by Ingvar Kamprad, founder of IKEA, to extend IKEA's vision to those living in extreme poverty. He said: 'We all share basic needs: a secure home, good health, a regular income, a desire to keep our children safe, to see them get a good education and succeed in life. That's why the IKEA Foundation has decided to focus our funding on these key necessities.'

5 Information systems

5.1 Information systems strategy

An **information system** (IS) is a platform or function that manages or processes information.

Information technology (IT) refers to the technology that is used to operate an information system.

For example, an organisation may have an information system that stores customer information. This system operates as a manual card file index or it might use information technology (eg a spreadsheet or database).

Earl (1989) identified nine reasons why IS/IT is a high risk area which needs to be treated as a strategic issue and managed at board level:

Critical to the success of a business

High cost (especially capital investment)

Effective management required due to the highly technical nature

Source of competitive advantage for most organisations

Structural changes may be achieved as a result of IS/IT

Stakeholders are affected, so the impact on them needs to be considered

Technical issues arise both inside and outside the IT department

All staff have the potential to be impacted by IS/IT developments

Revolutionary changes are possible

5.2 Cost–benefit analysis

Cost–benefit analysis can be used to evaluate investments in information systems.

Costs	Benefits
Capital items	Improvements in productivity
Installation costs	Improvements in performance
Development costs	Improvements in the quality of operational and control information
Changes in operational costs	Improved responsiveness and flexibility
Switching costs	Better customer service

While a financial cost–benefit analysis can be conducted using relevant cash flows, there are other non-financial factors that need to be considered when investing in information systems.

- **Switching costs**: Reduced efficiency arising from a new, unfamiliar system
- **Locking in costs**: Having to commit to a supplier (eg software provider) for the duration of a licence
- **Opportunity cost**: Funds used for IS/IT cannot be used elsewhere

The technical complexity of IT systems creates additional risks which need to be considered when planning an IS/IT project, for example:

- Risk of hardware theft or damage
- Risk of unauthorised access to the system by hackers potentially leading to a loss of commercially important data or to litigation relating to data protection legislation.
- Lack of compatibility with existing systems
- Technical faults, especially if the level of support provided by the systems vendor is poor.

5.2.1 Opportunities

IS/IT solutions can be used to **manage risk** in the following ways;

- Using Big Data to generate meaningful information that supports strategic decision making (eg capital investment)
- Developing cybersecurity solutions to protect an organisation's IS/IT infrastructure and data
- Preparing business continuity planning and back-ups in the event of a major incident

> **Exam focus**
>
> Given that the benefits of investments in IS/IT are not easily quantifiable, what-if analysis may be required to justify investment; for example, what increase in sales would be needed to justify the investment.

Chapter summary

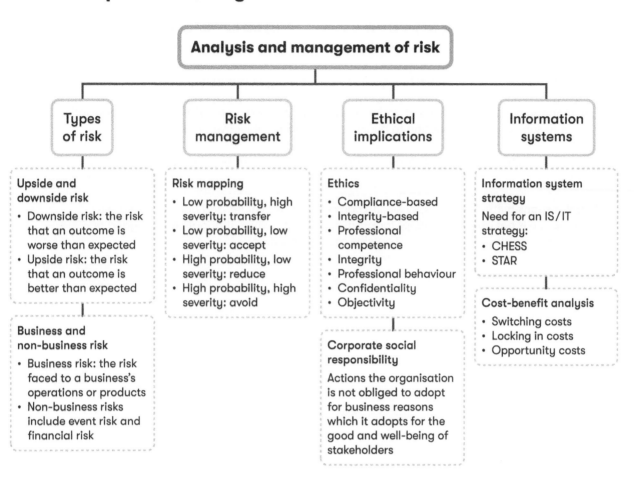

Analysis and management of risk

Types of risk

Upside and downside risk
- Downside risk: the risk that an outcome is worse than expected
- Upside risk: the risk that an outcome is better than expected

Business and non-business risk
- Business risk: the risk faced to a business's operations or products
- Non-business risks include event risk and financial risk

Risk management

Risk mapping
- Low probability, high severity: transfer
- Low probability, low severity: accept
- High probability, low severity: reduce
- High probability, high severity: avoid

Ethical implications

Ethics
- Compliance-based
- Integrity-based
- Professional competence
- Integrity
- Professional behaviour
- Confidentiality
- Objectivity

Corporate social responsibility

Actions the organisation is not obliged to adopt for business reasons which it adopts for the good and well-being of stakeholders

Information systems

Information system strategy

Need for an IS/IT strategy:
- CHESS
- STAR

Cost-benefit analysis
- Switching costs
- Locking in costs
- Opportunity costs

Key terms

Directions of risk: Downside (or pure) risk is a risk involving the possibility of loss (only).
Two-way risk involves both upside and downside risk.

Business risk: The risk faced due to a business's operations or products.

Risk management: 'The process of understanding and managing the risks that an organisation is inevitably subject to in attempting to achieve its corporate objectives' (*CIMA*).

Ethics: Ethics are the moral principles or standards of behaviour by which people act or do business.

Social responsibility: Social responsibility comprises those values and actions which the organisation is not obliged to adopt for business reasons, which it adopts for the good and wellbeing of stakeholders within and outside the organisation.

Activity answers

Activity 1: TARA

The correct answer is:

Passenger luggage being lost	**Reduce**
In-flight entertainment system breaks down	**Accept**
Unsafe food on flights	**Transfer**
Industrial action by airline staff	**Avoid**

Flitish Airway's strong reputation means that problems with unsafe food or a breakdown of the in-flight entertainment system are a low probability. While unsafe food would be a severe incident, the loss of in-flight entertainment would not be.

The new baggage-handling system has increased the probability of industrial action and lost luggage. While the industrial action could have a severe effect, the fact that luggage is recovered within 12 hours means that the outcome is less severe.

Activity 2: Threats

The correct answer is:

Threat to ethical guidelines: **Familiarity**

Ethical principle: **Objectivity**

Note. While the scenario instinctively raises ethical questions, it is important to specify the precise nature of the threat and the ethical principle at stake.

Test your learning

1 **Required**
   Using the TARA framework, how should a low probability/high severity risk be managed?

2 **Required**
   Using the TARA framework, how should a low probability/low severity risk be managed?

3 **Required**
   Using the TARA framework, how should a high probability/high severity risk be managed?

4 **Required**
   Using the TARA framework, how should a high probability/low severity risk be managed?

5 **Required**
   Complete the words to identify the five IFAC ethical principles.

   P   Professional competence and due care

   I   [   ]

   P   Professional behaviour

   C   [   ]

   O   [   ]

6 **Required**
   Which ethical framework does CIMA adopt?

   A   Integrity-based

   B   Compliance-based

Test your learning answers

Chapter 1

1   The correct answer is:

True

The use of cost drivers links resource consumption over the long term to activity levels.

2   The correct answer is:

Level 1: Unit

Level 2: Batch

Level 3: Product sustaining

Level 4: Facility sustaining

Factual knowledge, important for your final exam.

3   The correct answer is:

This is where a high percentage of profits come from a small percentage of customers.

4   The correct answer is:

Unprofitable customers identified by CPA should be persuaded to **alter their buying behaviour** so they become profitable customers.

CPA analysis should also indicate where **cost reduction efforts should be focused.**

5   The correct answer is:

Soup	$0.10
Bleach	$0.04
Toilet rolls	$1.11

The space costs would be allocated as follows.

Soup: $1.00 × 0.02 × 5 = $0.10 per pack

Bleach: $1.00 × 0.01 × 4 = $0.04 per pack

Packs of toilet rolls: $1.00 × 0.37 × 3 = $1.11 per pack

Chapter 2

1   The correct answer is:

- Cost of non-conformance = Cost of internal failure + Cost of external failure
- Cost of conformance = Cost of appraisal + Cost of prevention

These are definitions.

2   The correct answer is:

Internal failure

Quality control should **prevent** defects occurring.

Product liability and lower selling prices means the customer has received a defective product ie **external failure.**

Testing is another word for **appraisal.**

3   The correct answer is:

JIT purchasing requires **small, frequent** deliveries **as near as possible to** the time the raw materials and parts are needed.

In a JIT environment, the responsibility for the quality of goods lies with the **supplier.**

Local suppliers and frequent deliveries of small amounts are essential for a zero-inventory system to function. Responsibility for quality lies with the supplier.

4   The correct answer is:

The theory of constraints is an approach to production management which aims to maximise sales revenue less **material costs.** It focuses on internal processes that are **bottlenecks** which act as **constraints.**

Local suppliers and frequent deliveries of small amounts are essential for a zero-inventory system to function. Responsibility for quality lies with the supplier.

5   The correct answer is:

TA ratio = **Throughput contribution** per factory hour divided by **Total factory cost** per factory hour.

This is a definition.

6   The correct answers are:

- Costs are reduced by implementing continuous improvement.
- The aim is to achieve cost reduction targets.

Kaizen is about improving performance – not maintaining it. This requires the co-operation of employees.

Chapter 3

1   The correct answer is:

(1) Cost

(2) Profit

(3) Selling price

Price results from the application of a mark-up to forecast product cost.

2   The correct answer is:

(1) Selling price

(2) Profit

(3) Cost

Target cost results from the deduction of a mark-up from the forecast selling price.

3   The correct answer is:

Value engineering is cost avoidance or cost prevention before production whereas **Kaizen costing** is cost reduction during production.

These are definitions

4   The correct answer is:

The prestige the customer attaches to the product is **esteem value**

The market value of the product is **exchange value**

What the product does is **use value**

The cost of producing and selling the product is **cost value**

These are definitions.

5   The correct answer is:

False

Value chain analysis can also involve studying linkages to the value chain of suppliers or customers, and also the linkages between different primary activities (and between different support activities).

Chapter 4

1   The correct answer is:

True

Both are crucial before moving on to a financial appraisal.

2   The correct answer is:

The relevant cash flow is $200

Is this a cost or a saving? Saving

The relevant cash flow arising is a saving of $200 because the project will result in 200 kg of material X having to be disposed of. The historic cost is not relevant.

3   The correct answer is:

Yes

This cost has not yet been incurred so is relevant and should not be excluded from the calculation.

4   The correct answer is:

No

This is a non-cash flow item so should be excluded from the calculation.

5   The correct answer is:

No

Finance costs are covered by the cost of capital so should be excluded from the calculation.

6   The correct answer is:

No

This is a relevant cost so should not be excluded from the calculation.

Chapter 5

1   The correct answer is:

Accounting rate of return (ARR)

ARR is based on accounting profits, which includes depreciation as a charge.

IRR is based on cash flows, and depreciation is not a cash flow.

2   The correct answer is:

$9,700

$3,000 × 3.605 = present value at time 1 of $10,815

Discounting this back to a present value gives $10,815 × 0.893 = $9,658 or $9,700 to the nearest $100.

Alternatively, $3,000 × (4.111 (time 1–6 cumulative df) − 0.893) = $9,654 or $9,700 to the nearest $100.

3   The correct answer is:

17.2%

15% + {(3,670/[3,670 + 1,390]) × 3%} = 17.2%

4   The correct answer is:

The disposal value of equipment at the end of its life

Non-cash items, sunk costs and financing items (which are in the cost of capital) are not included.

5   The correct answer is:

5.7%

1.11 ÷ 1.05 = 1.057

1.057-1= 0.057 or 5.7%

6   The correct answer is:

11.24%

1.08 × 1.03 = 1.1124

Chapter 6

1   The correct answer is:

False

This describes **soft** capital rationing.

2   The correct answer is:

Divisible

This is because PI is used to ascertain the return per $ spent on a project, and this is only relevant if a project is divisible (so there really is a decision on how to spend each $).

3   The correct answer is:

To follow on

Redeploying is an aspect of the abandonment option.

4   The correct answer is:

$320

	NPV per $ invested	Ranking
K	3.0	3
L	4.0	1
M	3.3	2
N	2.0	4

After funding K, L and M, $90,000 has been spent, leaving $10,000 to finance 10/60 = 16.67% of N.

So the total NPV will be 100% of projects K, L and M = 90 + 60 + 150 = 300

Also 16.67% of project N = 0.1667 × 120 = 20

This gives a total of $320,000.

5   The correct answer is:

$300

Affordable combinations	Total NPV	Ranking
K + L + M	90 + 60 + 150 = **300**	1
K + N	90 + 120 = 210	2

Chapter 7

1   The correct answer is:

Demand is price-elastic and if the price is reduced sales revenue will rise

This value means that for a given fall in price, quantity demanded will rise by 20% more than the price change. This will mean that demand is elastic, and that revenue will rise.

2   The correct answer is:

Introduction, growth, maturity, decline

Factual – the stages need to be learnt.

3   The correct answer is:

False

Market penetration pricing would be more appropriate if demand is price-sensitive.

4   The correct answer is:

- A problem with cost-plus pricing is that it fails to appreciate the circular relationship between price, demand and cost.

- The size of the profit margin can be varied to ensure that a company utilises any spare capacity it has.

A high initial cost is likely if volumes are low; this can then lead to prices being high which in turn can mean that volumes remain low – this is a classic problem of cost-plus pricing.

The mark-up does not have to be fixed, so if there is spare capacity the mark-up can be cut to allow prices to fall and sales to rise.

5   The correct answer is:

Product bundling

Product bundling involves selling a number of products or services as a package at a price lower than the aggregate of their individual prices.

6   The correct answer is:

Market penetration

Market penetration keeps prices low, and thereby reduces the incentive and/or ability of new entrants to enter the market.

Chapter 8

1   The correct answer is:

Investment centre

An investment centre manager controls revenue, cost and the investment base and therefore has a high level of autonomy that will be a characteristic of highly decentralised organisations.

2   The correct answer is:

Profit centre

Profit centres will encourage an entrepreneurial culture while still allowing head office to retain control over investments.

3   The correct answer is:

Activity

Flexed budgets are revised in the light of actual activity levels (which may be production, sales etc).

4   The correct answer is:

Complete

Relevant

Authoritative

This is a definition.

5   The correct answer is:

Profit centre

There is an element of control over revenue and cost (but not over capital expenditure), so this will be a profit centre.

6   The correct answer is:

Velocity

This is a definition.

Chapter 9

1   The correct answer is:

In general, a current ratio **in excess of 1** should be expected.

However, this will depend on the industry.

2   The correct answer is:

ROI based on profits as a % of net assets employed will **increase** as an asset gets older and its book value **increase**. This could therefore create a(n) **disincentive** to investment centre managers to reinvest in new or replacement assets.

This is a problem with ROI unless other controls exist to prevent this type of behaviour from occurring.

3   The correct answer is:

False

An attractive project (ie positive NPV) can still cause RI to fall in its early years and therefore may be rejected by divisional managers. RI may reduce the risk of dysfunctional behaviour but does not eliminate it.

4   The correct answer is:

ROI without investment: 21.0%

ROI with investment: 20.7%

Without investment

Profit	$119,700	Capital employed	$570,000
ROI	$119,700/$570,000= 21.0%		

With investment

Profit	$128,200	Capital employed	$620,000
ROI	$128,200/$620,000= 20.7%		

This is likely to mean that the investment is rejected.

The problem is that the investment earns a return of $8,500/$50,000 = 17.0%, which, despite being attractive relative to the cost of capital of 15%, is less than the existing return of 21.0%.

5   The correct answer is:

RI without investment: $34,200

RI with investment: $35,200

Without investment

Profit	$119,700	Capital employed	$570,000
RI	$119,700 – (0.15 × $570,000) = $34,200		

With investment

Profit	$128,200	Capital employed	$620,000
RI	$128,200 – (0.15 × $620,000) = $35,200		

This is likely to mean that the investment is accepted.

This is because the investment earns a residual income of $8,500 – (0.15 × $50,000) = $1,000, which means it is attractive relative to the cost of capital of 15%.

6   The correct answer is:

False

EVA™ = NOPAT less a capital charge

7   The correct answer is:

$64

	$m
Profit	83.40
Add	
Current depreciation (110 × 10%)	11.00
Development costs (8.3 × 2/3)	5.53
Less	
Replacement depreciation (156 × 10%)	(15.60)
	84.33
Less cost of capital (W)	(20.54)
EVA™	63.79

Working: Cost of capital charge

	$
Fixed assets (156 – 15.6)	140.40

Working capital	25.20	
Development costs	5.53	
	171.13	´ 12% = 20.54

Chapter 10

1 The correct answer is:

Should encourage output at an organisation-wide profit-maximising level

A transfer pricing decision should **discourage** dysfunctional decision making, and encourage the organisation's best interests to be achieved.

2 The correct answer is:

When transfer prices are based on opportunity costs, opportunity costs are either the **contribution** foregone by the supplying division in transferring **internally** rather than selling **externally**, or the **contribution** forgone by not using the relevant facilities for their **next best** alternative use.

Contribution is a more accurate measure than profit because it excludes fixed costs, which are not generally relevant for decision making.

3 The correct answer is:

Two-part tariff

This is a definition.

4 The correct answer is:

- Should enable the measurement of profit centre performance
- Should reward the transferring division
- Should be a reasonable cost for receiving division

Goal congruence (ie achieving group objectives and also divisional objectives) should be encouraged.

5 The correct answer is:

False

A lower transfer price would reduce profits in C and increase profits in D, resulting in a lower tax bill.

6 The correct answer is:

The more head office has to impose its own decisions on profit centres, the **less** decentralisation of authority there will be and the **less** effective the profit centre system of accounting will be for motivating divisional managers.

Lower control of divisional profit is likely to cause a fall in motivation in divisional managers.

Chapter 11

1 The correct answer is:

False

It does not assess the probability of changes in the decision variables.

2 The correct answer is:

False

The value should be between 0 and 1.

3 The correct answer is:

C

A table of regrets can be compiled, as follows, showing the amount of profit that might be forgone for each project, depending on whether the outcome is I, II or III.

	Outcome			Maximum
	I	II	III	
Project A	40 *	50	20	50
Project B	15 **	45	0	45
Project C	0	0	5	5

* 100–60   ** 100–85 etc

The **maximum regret** is 50 with project A, 45 with B and 5 with C. The lowest of these three maximum regrets is 5 with C, and so project C would be selected if the minimax regret rule is used.

4   The correct answer is:

22,000

Choice between ((0.2 × 33,000) + (0.8 × 14,000)) = 17,800 at C, 22,000, and ((0.1 × 40,000) + (0.9 × 11,000)) = 13,900 at D.

5   The correct answer is:

Project L

		EV $'000
Project L	(550 × 0.20 + 480 × 0.40 + 580 × 0.40)	534
Project M	(450 × 0.20 + 500 × 0.40 + 570 × 0.40)	518
Project N	(420 × 0.20 + 450 × 0.40 + 480 × 0.40)	456
Project O	(370 × 0.20 + 410 × 0.40 + 430 × 0.40)	410
Project P	(590 × 0.20 + 580 × 0.40 + 430 × 0.40)	522

Project L has the highest EV of expected cash inflows and should therefore be undertaken.

6   The correct answer is:

$'000 48

Market condition	Probability	Project chosen	Net cash inflow	EV of net cash inflow $'000
Poor	0.20	P	590	118
Good	0.40	P	580	232
Excellent	0.40	L	580	232
EV of net cash inflows with perfect information				582
EV of net cash inflows without perfect information				534
Value of perfect information				48

Chapter 12

1   The correct answer is:

The risk should be transferred (eg via insurance) or a contingency plan should be implemented.

2   The correct answer is:

The risk is not significant and so should be accepted.

3   The correct answer is:

This is a serious risk and should be avoided wherever possible – for example, by outsourcing or withdrawing from the market.

4   The correct answer is:

Controls should be introduced in order to reduce the probability of occurrence.

5 The correct answer is:

I	Integrity
C	Confidentiality
O	Objectivity

These are defined terms.

6 The correct answer is:

Integrity-based

CIMA adopts an integrity-based approach, because it seeks to offer principles for individuals to apply when faced with an ethical dilemma as opposed to a set of legal rules to follow (compliance-based approach).

Appendix 1: Mathematical tables & exam formulae

Present value table

Present value of \$1, that is $(1+r)^{-n}$ where r = interest rate; n = number of periods until payment or receipt.

Periods (n)	\multicolumn{10}{c}{Interest rates (r)}									
	1%	2%	3%	4%	5%	6%	7%	8%	9%	10%
1	0.990	0.980	0.971	0.962	0.952	0.943	0.935	0.926	0.917	0.909
2	0.980	0.961	0.943	0.925	0.907	0.890	0.873	0.857	0.842	0.826
3	0.971	0.942	0.915	0.889	0.864	0.840	0.816	0.794	0.772	0.751
4	0.961	0.924	0.888	0.855	0.823	0.792	0.763	0.735	0.708	0.683
5	0.951	0.906	0.863	0.822	0.784	0.747	0.713	0.681	0.650	0.621
6	0.942	0.888	0.837	0.790	0.746	0705	0.666	0.630	0.596	0.564
7	0.933	0.871	0.813	0.760	0.711	0.665	0.623	0.583	0.547	0.513
8	0.923	0.853	0.789	0.731	0.677	0.627	0.582	0.540	0.502	0.467
9	0.914	0.837	0.766	0.703	0.645	0.592	0.544	0.500	0.460	0.424
10	0.905	0.820	0.744	0.676	0.614	0.558	0.508	0.463	0.422	0.386
11	0.896	0.804	0.722	0.650	0.585	0.527	0.475	0.429	0.388	0.350
12	0.887	0.788	0.701	0.625	0.557	0.497	0.444	0.397	0.356	0.319
13	0.879	0.773	0.681	0.601	0.530	0.469	0.415	0.368	0.326	0.290
14	0.870	0.758	0.661	0.577	0.505	0.442	0.388	0.340	0.299	0.263
15	0.861	0.743	0.642	0.555	0.481	0.417	0.362	0.315	0.275	0.239
16	0.853	0.728	0.623	0.534	0.458	0.394	0.339	0.292	0.252	0.218
17	0.844	0.714	0.605	0.513	0.436	0.371	0.317	0.270	0.231	0.198
18	0.836	0.700	0.587	0.494	0.416	0.350	0.296	0.250	0.212	0.180
19	0.828	0.686	0.570	0.475	0.396	0.331	0.277	0.232	0.194	0.164
20	0.820	0.673	0.554	0.456	0.377	0.312	0.258	0.215	0.178	0.149

Periods (n)	\multicolumn{10}{c}{Interest rates (r)}									
	11%	12%	13%	14%	15%	16%	17%	18%	19%	20%
1	0.901	0.893	0.885	0.877	0.870	0.862	0.855	0.847	0.840	0.833
2	0.812	0.797	0.783	0.769	0.756	0.743	0.731	0.718	0.706	0.694
3	0.731	0.712	0.693	0.675	0.658	0.641	0.624	0.609	0.593	0.579
4	0.659	0.636	0.613	0.592	0.572	0.552	0.534	0.516	0.499	0.482
5	0.593	0.567	0.543	0.519	0.497	0.476	0.456	0.437	0.419	0.402
6	0.535	0.507	0.480	0.456	0.432	0.410	0.390	0.370	0.352	0.335
7	0.482	0.452	0.425	0.400	0.376	0.354	0.333	0.314	0.296	0.279
8	0.434	0.404	0.376	0.351	0.327	0.305	0.285	0.266	0.249	0.233
9	0.391	0.361	0.333	0.308	0.284	0.263	0.243	0.225	0.209	0.194
10	0.352	0.322	0.295	0.270	0.247	0.227	0.208	0.191	0.176	0.162
11	0.317	0.287	0.261	0.237	0.215	0.195	0.178	0.162	0.148	0.135
12	0.286	0.257	0.231	0.208	0.187	0.168	0.152	0.137	0.124	0.112
13	0.258	0.229	0.204	0.182	0.163	0.145	0.130	0.116	0.104	0.093
14	0.232	0.205	0.181	0.160	0.141	0.125	0.111	0.099	0.088	0.078
15	0.209	0.183	0.160	0.140	0.123	0.108	0.095	0.084	0.079	0.065
16	0.188	0.163	0.141	0.123	0.107	0.093	0.081	0.071	0.062	0.054
17	0.170	0.146	0.125	0.108	0.093	0.080	0.069	0.060	0.052	0.045
18	0.153	0.130	0.111	0.095	0.081	0.069	0.059	0.051	0.044	0.038
19	0.138	0.116	0.098	0.083	0.070	0.060	0.051	0.043	0.037	0.031
20	0.124	0.104	0.087	0.073	0.061	0.051	0.043	0.037	0.031	0.026

Cumulative present value table

Cumulative present value of $1 per annum, Receivable or Payable at the end of each year for n years $\dfrac{1-(1+r)^{-n}}{r}$

Periods (n)	Interest rates (r)									
	1%	2%	3%	4%	5%	6%	7%	8%	9%	10%
1	0.990	0.980	0.971	0.962	0.952	0.943	0.935	0.926	0.917	0.909
2	1.970	1.942	1.913	1.886	1.859	1.833	1.808	1.783	1.759	1.736
3	2.941	2.884	2.829	2.775	2.723	2.673	2.624	2.577	2.531	2.487
4	3.902	3.808	3.717	3.630	3.546	3.465	3.387	3.312	3.240	3.170
5	4.853	4.713	4.580	4.452	4.329	4.212	4.100	3.993	3.890	3.791
6	5.795	5.601	5.417	5.242	5.076	4.917	4.767	4.623	4.486	4.355
7	6.728	6.472	6.230	6.002	5.786	5.582	5.389	5.206	5.033	4.868
8	7.652	7.325	7.020	6.733	6.463	6.210	5.971	5.747	5.535	5.335
9	8.566	8.162	7.786	7.435	7.108	6.802	6.515	6.247	5.995	5.759
10	9.471	8.983	8.530	8.111	7.722	7.360	7.024	6.710	6.418	6.145
11	10.368	9.787	9.253	8.760	8.306	7.887	7.499	7.139	6.805	6.495
12	11.255	10.575	9.954	9.385	8.863	8.384	7.943	7.536	7.161	6.814
13	12.134	11.348	10.635	9.986	9.394	8.853	8.358	7.904	7.487	7.103
14	13.004	12.106	11.296	10.563	9.899	9.295	8.745	8.244	7.786	7.367
15	13.865	12.849	11.938	11.118	10.380	9.712	9.108	8.559	8.061	7.606
16	14.718	13.578	12.561	11.652	10.838	10.106	9.447	8.851	8.313	7.824
17	15.562	14.292	13.166	12.166	11.274	10.477	9.763	9.122	8.544	8.022
18	16.398	14.992	13.754	12.659	11.690	10.828	10.059	9.372	8.756	8.201
19	17.226	15.679	14.324	13.134	12.085	11.158	10.336	9.604	8.950	8.365
20	18.046	16.351	14.878	13.590	12.462	11.470	10.594	9.818	9.129	8.514

Periods (n)	Interest rates (r)									
	11%	12%	13%	14%	15%	16%	17%	18%	19%	20%
1	0.901	0.893	0.885	0.877	0.870	0.862	0.855	0.847	0.840	0.833
2	1.713	1.690	1.668	1.647	1.626	1.605	1.585	1.566	1.547	1.528
3	2.444	2.402	2.361	2.322	2.283	2.246	2.210	2.174	2.140	2.106
4	3.102	3.037	2.974	2.914	2.855	2.798	2.743	2.690	2.639	2.589
5	3.696	3.605	3.517	3.433	3.352	3.274	3.199	3.127	3.058	2.991
6	4.231	4.111	3.998	3.889	3.784	3.685	3.589	3.498	3.410	3.326
7	4.712	4.564	4.423	4.288	4.160	4.039	3.922	3.812	3.706	3.605
8	5.146	4.968	4.799	4.639	4.487	4.344	4.207	4.078	3.954	3.837
9	5.537	5.328	5.132	4.946	4.772	4.607	4.451	4.303	4.163	4.031
10	5.889	5.650	5.426	5.216	5.019	4.833	4.659	4.494	4.339	4.192
11	6.207	5.938	5.687	5.453	5.234	5.029	4.836	4.656	4.486	4.327
12	6.492	6.194	5.918	5.660	5.421	5.197	4.988	4.793	4.611	4.439
13	6.750	6.424	6.122	5.842	5.583	5.342	5.118	4.910	4.715	4.533
14	6.982	6.628	6.302	6.002	5.724	5.468	5.229	5.008	4.802	4.611
15	7.191	6.811	6.462	6.142	5.847	5.575	5.324	5.092	4.876	4.675
16	7.379	6.974	6.604	6.265	5.954	5.668	5.405	5.162	4.938	4.730
17	7.549	7.120	6.729	6.373	6.047	5.749	5.475	5.222	4.990	4.775
18	7.702	7.250	6.840	6.467	6.128	5.818	5.534	5.273	5.033	4.812
19	7.839	7.366	6.938	6.550	6.198	5.877	5.584	5.316	5.070	4.843
20	7.963	7.469	7.025	6.623	6.259	5.929	5.628	5.353	5.101	4.870

Area under the normal curve

This table gives the area under the normal curve between the mean and a point Z standard deviations above the mean. The corresponding area for deviations below the mean can be found by symmetry.

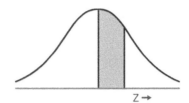

$Z=\frac{(x-\mu)}{\sigma}$	0.00	0.01	0.02	0.03	0.04	0.05	0.06	0.07	0.08	0.09
0.0	.0000	.0040	.0080	.0120	.0159	.0199	.0239	.0279	.0319	.0359
0.1	.0398	.0438	.0478	.0517	.0557	.0596	.0636	.0675	.0714	.0753
0.2	.0793	.0832	.0871	.0910	.0948	.0987	.1026	.1064	.1103	.1141
0.3	.1179	.1217	.1255	.1293	.1331	.1368	.1406	.1443	.1480	.1517
0.4	.1554	.1591	.1628	.1664	.1700	.1736	.1772	.1808	.1844	.1879
0.5	.1915	.1950	.1985	.2019	.2054	.2088	.2123	.2157	.2190	.2224
0.6	.2257	.2291	.2324	.2357	.2389	.2422	.2454	.2486	.2518	.2549
0.7	.2580	.2611	.2642	.2673	.2704	.2734	.2764	.2794	.2823	.2852
0.8	.2881	.2910	.2939	.2967	.2995	.3023	.3051	.3078	.3106	.3133
0.9	.3159	.3186	.3212	.3238	.3264	.3289	.3315	.3340	.3365	.3389
1.0	.3413	.3438	.3461	.3485	.3508	.3531	.3554	.3577	.3599	.3621
1.1	.3643	.3665	.3686	.3708	.3729	.3749	.3770	.3790	.3810	.3830
1.2	.3849	.3869	.3888	.3907	.3925	.3944	.3962	.3980	.3997	.4015
1.3	.4032	.4049	.4066	.4082	.4099	.4115	.4131	.4147	.4162	.4177
1.4	.4192	.4207	.4222	.4236	.4251	.4265	.4279	.4292	.4306	.4319
1.5	.4332	.4345	.4357	.4370	.4382	.4394	.4406	.4418	.4430	.4441
1.6	.4452	.4463	.4474	.4485	.4495	.4505	.4515	.4525	.4535	.4545
1.7	.4554	.4564	.4573	.4582	.4591	.4599	.4608	.4616	.4625	.4633
1.8	.4641	.4649	.4656	.4664	.4671	.4678	.4686	.4693	.4699	.4706
1.9	.4713	.4719	.4726	.4732	.4738	.4744	.4750	.4756	.4762	.4767
2.0	.4772	.4778	.4783	.4788	.4793	.4798	.4803	.4808	.4812	.4817
2.1	.4821	.4826	.4830	.4834	.4838	.4842	.4846	.4850	.4854	.4857
2.2	.4861	.4865	.4868	.4871	.4875	.4878	.4881	.4884	.4887	.4890
2.3	.4893	.4896	.4898	.4901	.4904	.4906	.4909	.4911	.4913	.4916
2.4	.4918	.4920	.4922	.4925	.4927	.4929	.4931	.4932	.4934	.4936
2.5	.4938	.4940	.4941	.4943	.4945	.4946	.4948	.4949	.4951	.4952
2.6	.4953	.4955	.4956	.4957	.4959	.4960	.4961	.4962	.4963	.4964
2.7	.4965	.4966	.4967	.4968	.4969	.4970	.4971	.4972	.4973	.4974
2.8	.4974	.4975	.4976	.4977	.4977	.4978	.4979	.4980	.4980	.4981
2.9	.4981	.4982	.4983	.4983	.4984	.4984	.4985	.4985	.4986	.4986
3.0	.4987	.4987	.4987	.4988	.4988	.4989	.4989	.4989	.4990	.4990
3.1	.4990	.4991	.4991	.4991	.4992	.4992	.4992	.4992	.4993	.4993
3.2	.4993	.4993	.4994	.4994	.4994	.4994	.4994	.4995	.4995	.4995
3.3	.4995	.4995	.4995	.4996	.4996	.4996	.4996	.4996	.4996	.4997
3.4	.4997	.4997	.4997	.4997	.4997	.4997	.4997	.4997	.4997	.4998

Formulae

A. Probability

$A \cup B = A$ or B. $A \cap B = A$ and B (overlap).

$P(B/A) = probability\ of\ B\ given\ A.$

Rules of Addition

If A and B are mutually exclusive:

$P(A \cup B) = P(A) + P(B)$

If A and B are not mutually exclusive:

$P(A \cup B) = P(A) + P(B) - P(A \cap B)$

Rules of Multiplication

If A and B are independent:

$P(A \cap B) = P(A) * P(B)$

If A and B are **not** independent:

$P(A \cap B) = P(A) * P(B/A)$

$E(X) = \sum(probability * payoff)$

Quadratic equations

If $aX^2 + bX + c = 0$ is the general quadratic equation, the two solutions (roots) are given by:

$$X = \frac{-b \pm \sqrt{b^2 - 4ac}}{2a}$$

B. Descriptive statistics

Arithmetic mean

$$\bar{X} = \frac{\sum X}{n} \quad \bar{X} = \frac{\sum fX}{n} \quad (frequency\ distribution)$$

Standard deviation

$$SD = \sqrt{\frac{\sum(X - \bar{X})^2}{n}}$$

$$SD = \sqrt{\frac{\sum fX^2}{\sum f} - \bar{X}^2} \quad (frequency\ distribution)$$

C. Index numbers

Price relative $= 100 * P_1/P_0$
Quantity relative $= 100 * Q_1/Q_0$

$$Price: \frac{\sum w * (\frac{P_1}{P_0})}{\sum w} \times 100$$

$$Quantity: \frac{\sum w * (\frac{Q_1}{Q_0})}{\sum w} \times 100$$

D. Time series

Additive Model   Series = Trend + Seasonal + Random

Multiplicative Model   Series = Trend * Seasonal * Random

E. Linear regression

The linear regression of y on x is given by:

$$Y = a + bX \quad or \quad Y - \bar{Y} = b(X - \bar{X})$$

Where

$$b = \frac{Covariance(XY)}{Variance(X)} = \frac{n\sum XY - (\sum X)(\sum Y)}{n\sum X^2 - (\sum X)^2}$$

And

$$a = \bar{Y} - b\bar{X}$$

Coefficient of correlation

$$r = \frac{Covariance(XY)}{\sqrt{Var(X).Var)(Y)}} = \frac{n\sum XY - (\sum X)(\sum Y)}{\sqrt{\{n\sum X^2 - (\sum X)^2\}\{n\sum Y^2 - (\sum Y)^2\}}}$$

$$R(rank) = 1 - \frac{6\sum d^2}{n(n^2 - 1)}$$

F. Financial mathematics

Compound interest (values and sums)

Future Value S, of a sum of X, invested for n periods, compounded at r% interest

$$S = X(1 + r)^n$$

Annuity

Present value of an annuity of $1 per annum receivable or payable for n years, commencing in one year, discounted at r% per annum:

$$PV = \frac{1}{r}[1 - \frac{1}{(1 + r)^n}]$$

Perpetuity

Present value of $1 per annum, payable or receivable in perpetuity, commencing in one year, discounted at r% per annum:

$$PV = \frac{1}{r}$$

Index

A

Absorption costing, 3
Accounting rate of return, 74
Activity-based cost hierarchy, 6
Activity-based costing, 3
Activity-based management, 9
Annuities, 77
Asset turnover, 169

B

Balanced scorecard, 177
Benchmarking, 179
Big data, 157
Business intelligence systems, 65
Business process reengineering, 32
Business risk, 237

C

Capital rationing, 109
CIMA's Code of Ethics, 241
Co-efficient of variation, 217
Conditional probabilities, 223
Conformance costs, 26
Contingency tables, 223
Controllable costs, 150
Corporate social responsibility, 243
Cost centres, 148
Cost of quality, 25
Cost transformation, 3
Cost-based methods of transfer pricing, 193
Cost-based pricing, 125
Cost–benefit analysis, 244
Customer profitability analysis, 9

D

Data analytics, 157
Data collection, 63
Data lake, 65
Decentralisation, 147
Decision trees, 220
Decision-making process, 59
Direct product profitability, 13
Discounted payback period, 74
Distribution channel profitability, 12
Divisionalisation, 147

Downside risk, 237
Dual pricing, 195

E

Economic value added, 174
Equivalent annual annuities, 106
Equivalent annual benefit, 108
Equivalent annual costs, 106
Ethical frameworks, 240
Ethics, 240
Expected values, 209
Experience curve, 50

F

Flexed budgets, 152
Functional analysis, 44

G

Goal congruence, 147, 189
Good information, 154

H

Hard capital rationing, 109

I

Inflation, 91
Information systems, 243
Information systems strategy, 243
Internal rate of return, 84
Investment centres, 148

J

Joint probability, 214
Just-in-time, 28

K

Kaizen, 24

L

Learning curve, 49
Life cycle costing, 48
Liquidity ratios, 167
Loss-leader pricing, 132

M

Market skimming, 129
Market-based pricing, 128
Maximax, 212
Maximin, 212

Minimax regret, 212
Modified internal rate of return, 103
Monte Carlo simulation, 225

N
Negotiated transfer prices, 196
Net present value (NPV), 76
Non-business risk, 237
Non-conformance costs, 26
Non-conventional cash flows, 86
Non-financial performance indicators, 176

O
Operating profit margin, 169
Opportunity cost, 190
Own-label pricing, 131

P
Pareto effect, 9
Payback, 73, 209
Perpetuities, 78
Premium pricing, 131
Price discrimination, 130
Price elasticity of demand, 123
Primary data, 63
Product bundling, 131
Product differentiation, 131
Product life cycle, 48
Profit centres, 148
Profitability index, 109
Profitability ratios, 169

Q
Qualitative analysis, 60
Qualities of good information, 64

R
Real options, 112
Relevant cash flows, 61
Replacement cycles, 107
Reporting, 154
Residual income, 172
Responsibility accounting, 148
Responsibility centre, 148
Return on investment, 171
Revenue centres, 148
Reverse engineering, 44

Revised budgets, 153
Risk, 207, 209
Risk appetite, 211
Risk mapping, 238
Risk-adjusted cost of capital, 224

S
Scenario analysis, 209, 225
Secondary data, 63
Sensitivity analysis, 207
Soft capital rationing, 109
Standard deviation, 216
Stress testing, 225

T
Target costing, 43
Taxation, 88
Theory of constraints, 30
Threats to ethical guidelines, 241
Throughput, 30
Time value of money, 75
Total quality management, 23
Traditional quality management, 23
Transfer pricing aims, 189
Two-part tariff, 195
Two-way risk, 237
Types of transfer pricing, 192

U
Uncertainty, 207
Upside risk, 237

V
Value at risk, 218
Value chain, 46
Value engineering, 44
Value of perfect information, 210
Visualisations, 158

W
Working capital, 89

Bibliography

Blanchard, K. and Peale, N. (1988) *The Power of Ethical Management.* New York, William Morrow & Co.

CGMA. Cost transformation tool [Online]. Available at: https://www.cgma.org/resources/tools/cost-transformation-model.html#cost-tranformation-model [Accessed 3 June 2019].

CIMA (2019) *Exam blueprints.* [Online]. Available from www.cimaglobal.com/examblueprints. [Accessed May 2019].

CIMA (2005). *CIMA Official Terminology.* Oxford, CIMA.

Cooper, R. and Kaplan, R.S. (1991) *Profit priorities from Activity-Based Costing HBR May-June 1991 issue* [Online]. Available at: https://hbr.org/1991/05/profit-priorities-from-activity-based-costing [Accessed 4 March 2019].

Cooper, R. and Kaplan, R. S. (1998) *Cost and Effect: Using Integrated Cost Systems to Drive Profitability and Performance.* Cambridge, MA, Harvard Business School Press.

De Mauro, A., Greco, M., Grimaldi, M., (2016). *A formal definition of Big Data based on its essential features.* Library Review, Vol. 65 Issue 3, pp.122-135.

Drury, C. (2018) *Management and Cost Accounting.* 10th edition. Andover, Cengage Learning.

Earl, M. (1989) *Management Strategies for IT.* 1st edition. Prentice Hall.

IKEA foundation, www.ikeafoundation.org [Accessed 04 Mar 2019].

Ikea.com, https://www.ikea.com/gb/en/this-is-ikea/about-the-ikea-group/vision-and-business-idea/ [Accessed 16 April 2019].

Kaplan, R. S. and Cooper, R. (1998). *Cost and Effect: Using Integrated Cost Systems to Drive Profitability and Performance.* Boston, MA: Harvard Business School Press.

Kaplan, R. S. and Norton, D. P. (1996) *The Balanced Scorecard: Translating Strategy into Action.* Boston, Harvard Business School Press.

Marr, B. (2015) *Big Data In Big Oil: How Shell Uses Analytics To Drive Business Success.* [Online]. Available at: www.forbes.com [Accessed 26 May 2015].

Porter, M. (1985) *Competitive Advantage.* New York, Free Press.

Review form - CIMA P2 Advanced Management Accounting

How have you used this Course Book?

(Tick one box only)

☐ Self study

☐ On a course _____

☐ Other _____

Why did you decide to purchase this Course Book?

(Tick one box only)

☐ Have used BPP materials in the past

☐ Recommendation by friend/colleague

☐ Recommendation by a college lecturer

☐ Saw advertising

☐ Other _____

During the past six months do you recall seeing/ receiving either of the following?

(Tick as many boxes as are relevant)

☐ Our advertisement in Financial Management

☐ Our Publishing Catalogue

Which (if any) aspects of our advertising do you think are useful?

(Tick as many boxes as are relevant)

☐ Prices and publication dates of new editions

☐ Information on Course Book content

☐ Details of our free online offering

☐ None of the above

Your ratings, comments and suggestions would be appreciated on the following areas of this Course Book.

	Very useful	Useful	Not useful
Chapter overviews	☐	☐	☐
Introductory section	☐	☐	☐
Quality of explanations	☐	☐	☐
Illustrations	☐	☐	☐
Chapter activities	☐	☐	☐
Test your learning	☐	☐	☐
Keywords	☐	☐	☐

	Excellent	Good	Adequate	Poor
Overall opinion of this Course Book	☐	☐	☐	☐

	Yes	No
Do you intend to continue using BPP Products?	☐	☐

The BPP author of this edition can be e-mailed at: lmfeedback@bpp.com

Review form (continued)

Tell us what you think – please note any further comments and suggestions/errors below.